PENGUIN BOOKS

Jenny Quinn's Rise to Fame

'*Jenny Quinn's Rise to Fame* is an absolute delight. A lovely novel full of warmth, courage and heart, Jenny Quinn is a heroine you'll cheer for every step of the way' AJ Pearce, *Sunday Times* bestselling author of *Dear Mrs Bird*

'The humour in *Jenny Quinn's Rise to Fame* is razor sharp and the sadness incredibly poignant . . . a fabulous, ultimately joyful read' Jennie Godfrey, *Sunday Times* bestselling author of *The List of Suspicious Things*

'A charming, heartfelt and uplifting novel . . . I loved every minute of it!' Libby Page, *Sunday Times* bestselling author of *The Lido*

'This novel is perfectly baked, utterly delicious and completely moreish' Clare Pooley, *New York Times* bestselling author of *The Authenticity Project*

'An intensely rich love letter to family, friends and new beginnings' Eva Rice, bestselling author of *The Lost Art of Keeping Secrets*

'Like a great dessert, you'll wish you could come back for more' J. Ryan Stradal, *New York Times* bestselling author of *Kitchens of the Great Midwest*

'The ultimate comfort read' Margarita Montimore, *USA Today* bestselling author of *Oona Out of Order*

'A delicious feast of warm, witty and wise' Joanna Nell, bestselling author of *The Single Ladies of Jacaranda Retirement Village*

'A gentle read that pulls at the heartstrings . . . read with a slice of cake' *Woma*

'Deliciously layered'

T0322255

'It's the love stories at the centre of this novel that so beauti-fully rise' Laurie Frankel, *New York Times* bestselling author of *This Is How It Always Is*

'A warm-hearted book' Phaedra Patrick, bestselling author of *The Curious Charms of Arthur Pepper*

'Fans of cooking competitions will find this feel-good story delectable' *Publishers Weekly*

'A delightful story full of warmth, kindness and cake' Freya Sampson, bestselling author of *The Lost Ticket*

'Comforting, moreish and as delicious as the cakes it describes' Susan Fletcher, bestselling author of *Eve Green*

'One of those books you just want to hug to your chest' Jasmine Guillory, *New York Times* bestselling author of *The Proposal*

'A tribute to kindness' *Shelf Awareness*

'As cosy as a cup of tea and cake' *People Magazine*

'Charming, uplifting and triumphant' Cathy Bramley, *Sunday Times* Top Ten best selling author of *The Lemon Tree Café*

'Transports you back to that cosy, something's-in-the-oven world' *New York Times Book Review*

'A deliciously engaging debut' *WI Life*

ABOUT THE AUTHOR

Olivia Ford has spent the last ten years in entertainment TV, most recently as a story producer. Olivia is a graduate of the Faber Academy where she wrote the beginnings of *Mrs Quinn's Rise to Fame*, which was longlisted for the 2021 Women's Prize Trust's Discoveries Prize. Raised in Lincolnshire, Olivia now lives in London.

Jenny Quinn's Rise to Fame

OLIVIA FORD

PENGUIN BOOKS

PENGUIN BOOKS

UK | USA | Canada | Ireland | Australia
India | New Zealand | South Africa

Penguin Books is part of the Penguin Random House group of companies
whose addresses can be found at global.penguinrandomhouse.com

Penguin Random House UK,
One Embassy Gardens, 8 Viaduct Gardens, London SW11 7BW

penguin.co.uk

Penguin
Random House
UK

Originally published as *Mrs Quinn's Rise to Fame* by Penguin Michael Joseph 2024
Published in Penguin Books 2025

001

Copyright © Olivia Ford, 2024

The moral right of the author has been asserted

Penguin Random House values and supports copyright.
Copyright fuels creativity, encourages diverse voices, promotes freedom
of expression and supports a vibrant culture. Thank you for purchasing
an authorized edition of this book and for respecting intellectual property
laws by not reproducing, scanning or distributing any part of it by any
means without permission. You are supporting authors and enabling
Penguin Random House to continue to publish books for everyone.
No part of this book may be used or reproduced in any manner for the
purpose of training artificial intelligence technologies or systems. In accordance
with Article 4(3) of the DSM Directive 2019/790, Penguin Random House
expressly reserves this work from the text and data mining exception

page vii: Delia Smith, *How to Fail* podcast with Elizabeth Day

Typeset by Jouve (UK), Milton Keynes
Printed and bound in Great Britain by Clays Ltd, Elcograf S.p.A.

The authorized representative in the EEA is Penguin Random House Ireland,
Morrison Chambers, 32 Nassau Street, Dublin D02 YH68

A CIP catalogue record for this book is available from the British Library

ISBN: 978-1-405-95644-4

Penguin Random House is committed to a sustainable future
for our business, our readers and our planet. This book is made from
Forest Stewardship Council® certified paper.

For Granny and Grandpa, whose love inspired this novel.
And for Noll, for everything.

Whilst bodies age, souls don't.

Delia Smith

Prologue

It was a December night, the sort which usually makes being inside feel wonderfully cosy, but tonight it didn't. The trees outside looked brittle and lifeless, their unfamiliar contortions a reminder that she was a long way from home. Reaching for her new recipe book, she stroked the cool of the cassock-blue cover, pressing it open so that the spine resisted. Hovering her pencil above the fan of pristine pages, she savoured the musk of fresh paper.

Recipe one. It had to be her favourite birthday cake — she had quite a reputation for it in the family. She wrote the heading, Jenny's Black Forest Gateau, *twisting her best handwriting into loops and flicks as she divided the page into* Ingredients *and* Method. *She could feel the wet cloth of the cream-filled piping bag, the magic of neat rosettes spiralling from its nozzle. She thought of the bitter smell of cocoa powder which clung to the back of your throat if you made the mistake of pouring it too enthusiastically, and how it complemented the tender cherry pie filling.*

She turned the page: recipe number two. This had to be something a little more everyday; the rainy day which became exciting when the mixing bowl appeared. Her mind raced through her favourite family recipes, slowing as she got to Grandma Audrey's Chocolate Crispy Cakes, *passed down through the generations to her. The cornflakes, cocoa and golden syrup melted together to make chewy nests of joy. She remembered how it felt being a small child and the Lyle's tin coming out of the cupboard, its ornate swirls in green and gold and the way her father would lever off the lid like a tin of paint, welded shut by threads of sheer, unadulterated sweetness. The inside, when observed up close, took you down an amber well, and licking the spoon had to be the purest form of pleasure on this earth.*

The final recipe would be for Christmas, but what to choose? She thought of punctuating the mince pie lids with a fork and weighing out rich mounds of dried fruit for the Christmas cake. It didn't matter that everything happened exactly the same each year like a well-rehearsed play, because it felt newly magical every time. Except this year it was different. Everything she usually looked forward to conflicted with the weight of her heart. She hoped that her strained smile would one day feel natural again.

As she rolled the pencil between her palms, she remembered her father's tiffin. The satisfaction of crushing the rich tea biscuits with a rolling pin, smashing them into tiny crumbs to form something completely new; a dense, buttery mixture of mixed peel, cocoa, syrup and raisins.

She envisioned a child of her own waking up on Christmas morning to the thrill of finding a stocking misshapen by the stuffing of gifts. Would she pull the other end of their Christmas cracker so that they won? Or see the delight in their face as they opened the gift they so dearly wanted? And, most precious of all, would she witness them sinking their teeth into her father's tiffin, just as she had done?

Tea Loaf

Sixty years later

Jennifer Quinn had no idea that at the age of seventy-seven she would become a household name.

It was a grey winter afternoon and she had decided to fill it with the small but satisfying accomplishment of baking a tea loaf, using a recipe that she suspected was even older than herself. It had found a safe home inside the faded cover of Delia Smith's *Complete Cookery Course* and was written in her grandmother's handwriting on a yellowed piece of paper that had sat beneath many cups of tea, judging by the golden rings of various sizes stained across it. *Use marjarine if no butter,* her grandmother had noted in brackets, a reminder of her lifelong struggle with spelling. It's strange, she thought, how recipes outlive the people that wrote them and yet they almost bring a part of that person back to life, as if a tiny piece of their soul lives in those instructions.

She poured the raisins into the brass bowl of her

cast-iron kitchen scales, the weights rising until they reached a delicate balance. She frowned to herself as she thought about the digital alternative that Bernard regularly suggested she purchase. Why, she wondered, did society feel a constant need to fix things that weren't broken?

Next she tore open the packet of sultanas, overwhelmed by their rich, treacly scent which reminded her of helping to make the Christmas cake as a child. She remembered stirring the brandy-soaked fruit into the thick, lumpen mixture, sneaking tiny mouthfuls when her aunt wasn't looking.

'Yoo-hoo!' called Bernard as the front door closed behind him.

She peered into the teapot. The Earl Grey had stewed to the point of bitterness, a delicate skin on its surface.

'Hello, darling,' said Bernard, 'has something fallen in there?'

'No,' she said, replacing the lid as she poured it generously over the fruit, steam dampening her cheeks, 'I'm making a tea loaf. How did you get on?'

He placed a paper bag on the worktop between the trails of sugar and flour.

'It turns out I've developed asthma in my old age,' he said, opening a small cupboard above her head and adding a box to the huddle of pharmaceutical jars. 'They've prescribed me an inhaler.'

She turned, her eyes a little wider. 'Asthma?'

'Well, it's either that or chronic obstructive pulmonary disease – I've got to keep an eye on it.'

'That's quite serious, isn't it?' she said, noticing the weight of his breath, the fragile curve of his back beneath his wool jumper.

'I mean, it wouldn't be great if it turned out to be COPD, but I'm hopeful that the inhaler will do the trick.'

'What makes them think it could be?'

'It can happen as you get older; they think it might be linked to all the years I spent doing carpentry, the dust damaging my lungs. Anyway, I've been told to take it easy which I said wouldn't be a problem – it's not as if we're about to embark on any grand adventures, is it?' He closed the cupboard door, the beginnings of a chuckle catching in the back of his throat. 'I said we're more than happy with the newspaper and slippers nowadays.'

She pressed her lips together, nodding in cautious agreement.

'I'll never take for granted the privilege of growing old together,' he said, planting a kiss on her head.

'Never,' she agreed, placing the soaking bowl of fruit on the windowsill in the hope that it would swell to the texture of fingertips after too long in the bath. Usually she would leave it overnight, but today a few hours would have to suffice.

'Now if you don't mind, I'm going to go for an afternoon nap.'

'Not at all,' she said, setting her timer with a sharp twist of the dial, each frantic *tick* amplified by the silence.

'Your programme's about to start!' called Bernard from the living room, the television briefly distracting him from his newspaper.

'Coming!' she replied as she searched through the drawer next to the oven. It contained a mixture of the most and least useful objects in the house, depending on who was looking, crammed full of things they had acquired over a lifetime together: a set of tiny screwdrivers from a Christmas cracker in 1995, a shell with bobbly eyes made by their great-niece, Poppy, and, most importantly, the grease-proof paper she was looking for. Lining the tin at lightning speed, she filled it with the mixture and slid it into the hot oven, before joining him in the living room.

Bernard's unruly eyebrows were just visible over the top of the newspaper as he tapped his well-worn slippers to the theme tune of *Britain Bakes*. He claimed to be indifferent to it and remained behind his newspaper, yet she often watched his face appear from above it as his attention was drawn into the drama of a meringue collapsing in the middle.

This week on the *Britain Bakes Christmas Special*, a cast of former contestants had been set the challenge of making a celebration cake. She twisted her fine, silver hair into a clip, feeling a sudden wave of discomfort at watching contestant Graham, a warm and likeable lorry driver, have his 'Santa in the Chimney' cake described as dry. It seemed to her that he had tried too hard to do something different with too many components. It was usually the people that did a well-executed twist on the familiar that won. As it turned out, a history teacher called Laura was awarded the golden whisk, with a chocolate, cherry and almond re-imagining of a classic Christmas cake. According to the judges, the flavours were phenomenal, but in truth, she was sure she would prefer the classic. She looked to Bernard for his reaction but it seemed he agreed since his newspaper now covered his face and was rising and falling in time with his contented snore.

As the credits rolled she contemplated the approach of her seventy-seventh Christmas, as yet another year drew to a close. She watched Bernard sleep, his breathing now developing its own strange whistle, the soprano to the tenor of his snore. She let her mind wander to a solemn thought: how many more Christmases might they have left to share together? The prospect of him sitting alone in his chair, no one to wake him up and tell him it was bedtime, was unthinkable. She contemplated the other scenario, the one where she was left alone staring at his empty chair, the dark velvet moulded to the shape of his form, an imprint of someone no longer on this earth. Her heart flooded with the urgency of their dwindling existence. She felt the painful truth of her age, of having reached a point where there was far more of life behind her than ahead of her.

She picked up the remote from beside his chair and pointed it at the television as if it might also silence her thoughts, but it was just as she was about to turn it off that the credits were interrupted by an announcement.

'Are you a keen baker? Do you have what it takes to be on next year's show? Apply now by clicking the link on the *Britain Bakes* website.'

She felt her senses sharpen, her fear turned to fantasy as she wrote local newspaper headlines in her mind:

77-YEAR-OLD FROM KITTLESHAM WINS BRITAIN'S BEST BAKER AND JUDGES MARVEL AT JENNY QUINN'S TEA LOAF

'Has it finished?' said Bernard, awakening with a jolt.

'Yes, it has – time for bed!' she said, quickly tidying her thoughts away to a hidden corner of her mind, as if she had been caught reading someone else's diary.

The following morning Jenny woke as she always did, early, to Bernard whistling downstairs in the kitchen whilst making them each a cup of tea. It was a sound so etched in her mind, she wondered if she would always hear it, even if it wasn't there.

She heard the rattle of jars as he took his various tablets, followed by great wheezing puffs as he used his new inhaler. Then came the rumble of the kettle as it reached boiling point, the suction of the fridge door as he retrieved the milk and the thud of the newspaper as it landed on the doormat. Like clockwork, he emerged with two cups of Earl Grey and a newspaper tucked under his arm, his white hair ruffled in endearing tufts that spoke of a good night's sleep.

'Morning, darling,' he said, parting the curtains and showering the quilt in cold winter light. Outside the trees were quickly becoming silhouettes as the remaining leaves were stripped from their branches, the birds plump with cold.

'I've had an idea,' he said, and it sparkled in his eyes. 'I'm going to make Poppy a doll's house for Christmas, one of those traditional Victorian ones. I know I haven't got long, but I think I could just about do it.'

'How lovely,' she said, taking a sip of hot tea, 'but are you sure you should be doing that? It sounds like a lot of dust.'

'I don't think it will make much of a difference to me now,' he said.

'I'm sure she'll love it,' she replied. Not for the first time, she thought what a wonderful father he would have made.

As Bernard headed downstairs to embark upon a busy morning in the shed, she recalled what he had said about their adventures being over, about being happy to lead smaller lives, and in quiet protest she made her way into the study. It was a boxy room and home to all manner of anti-climactic post; the sort that arrived with a transparent window and a printed address. The centrepiece was a computer and printer which made her heart thump a little faster as she sat herself in front of it, sure that it was judging her on how well she could use it.

As she moved the mouse, the engine sprang to life as if it were powered by a multitude of whirring fans that made it sound like very hard work being a computer. On the printer were some abandoned pages titled *DIY Doll's House* and she smiled as she imagined Bernard enthusiastically researching his latest project. Using just her index fingers she typed *Britain Bakes* into the search engine, clicking *Apply Now*.

Her eyes scanned the application form. There were an overwhelming number of questions and it required photographs of both herself and her best bakes. Her eyes settled on *Why do you bake and who do you bake for?* She considered this for a moment. It was a question she had never given much thought to. When life felt overwhelming, baking was as simple as eggs, sugar, butter and flour. It was the strongest connection to the past and the recipes were at the heart of some of her most cherished memories. She thought about Bernard's mother's Quinn's Crunch, each dense

Rice Krispies square as unpretentious and practical as she was. Baking immortalized some of the people she loved the most.

The box below read *What is your most impressive bake?* She remembered the birthday cakes she had made for Bernard over the years, themed to reflect his latest interests. One particular hit had been the gingerbread sports car she had constructed in the absence of being able to afford the real thing. Their wedding cake! Surely that was her proudest bake. She had made it almost sixty years ago and remembered the excitement she had felt as she piped the border in white icing, repeating her new name over and over in her head. *Mrs Jennifer Quinn.* All Saints Church had been situated on top of a hill, surrounded by fields and smelling of candle wax, frankincense and oak. Her father had walked her down the aisle towards her Bernie, a tall figure with his hands clasped nervously behind his back, his brown eyes absorbing her in that moment. His usually unruly dark hair had been combed neatly to one side, accentuating his prominent ears, a feature which caused him great humiliation but for which she had grown a great fondness.

Her attention snapped to a section of the form asking her to rate her skill level in biscuits, tarts, pies, desserts, cakes and . . . bread. She had never made a loaf of bread that she was proud of. In fact, her last attempt had ended up being so salty that even the birds had refused it, and yet here she was considering herself a contender for Britain's best baker. Sobered by her own ridiculousness, it struck her just how deluded she was to think that she was anything other than an old lady who enjoyed baking, along with millions of others.

As she scrolled down the page, she felt herself slowly deflate. At the grand age of seventy-seven she should be happy with her lot, and yet she couldn't help but wonder what she had really achieved in all that time. Without Bernard, what did she have? Guilt crept through her like smoke as she imagined that he could hear her thoughts, recoiling at her own ungratefulness.

She went to close the form when her chest grew tight. At the very bottom of the page read the deadline: **11th January**, underlined and in bold as if it were taunting her. Three weeks. She closed the website, turned off the computer and swept out of the room. Was it a sign, or just a painful coincidence?

Farmhouse Loaf

It had always been the Quinns' dream to retire to Kittle-sham, having stumbled across the village whilst holidaying on the coast one particularly hot summer in the early years of their marriage. The weather would have been the defining memory if it weren't for Bernard's brief foray into flared trousers. Nestled in the valley of the River Huckmere, it felt as if they had discovered it, like they had stepped into the secret garden or through the back of a wardrobe, and they had both agreed that it would be the perfect spot to spend their final chapter. It was a quintessential village of delightfully uneven houses and medieval pubs with doors so small that Bernard had to stoop to enter – a little less with each passing year. Even the village store felt more like somebody's pantry, and whilst the customers evolved with the decades the shop remained unchanged.

It was a crisp morning and they were walking up the high street towards the church, the frost making it look as if someone had coated it in icing sugar.

'Don't slip,' she said, gripping Bernard a little tighter as she felt the collective warmth of her hand enveloped in his, two hands that had together grown swollen at the knuckles and pigmented by the freckles of age, yet remained the perfect fit.

'Is that Ann and Fred with a pram?' said Bernard, plumes of warm breath dissipating into the icy air.

She could see a muddle of coats and hats which grew animated as they moved closer.

'I think it is,' she replied.

Ann was a neat terrier of a woman with piercing eyes as cold as her demeanour. She was one of those unfortunate people whose first impression made them unpopular, yet Jenny had grown fond of her over the years, loving her all the more for it. She was fiercely loyal, and you always knew exactly where you stood with her. Her husband, Fred, made no decisions of his own and appeared entirely happy with this dynamic.

'Hello!' called Ann, as she pushed the pram towards them with great purpose so that it juddered violently over the cobbles, Fred and their two grandchildren in tow. It was as if it were a shopping trolley and they were items on her shopping list.

'Toby, Isabelle, these are our friends Jenny and Bernard,' she said.

Isabelle promptly hid behind Fred's leg whilst Toby looked up at them, his nose pinched with cold.

'Nice to meet you,' said Jenny, watching as Bernard peered into the pram.

'That's my sister Ellie,' announced Toby, his chest puffed with pride, 'she's new.'

'Congratulations,' said Bernard. 'Isn't she wonderful?'

'We've got our hands full this weekend as you can see – grandparent duties!' said Ann.

'Lovely,' said Jenny. 'What have you been up to?'

'Pick and mix,' said Fred's leg, which almost entirely eclipsed Isabelle.

Ann rolled her eyes as she fastened the top button of Toby's coat so that it looked as if it were wearing him. 'Fred took them for pick and mix, so of course the trip to the museum has been completely forgotten.'

'How are you both?' said Fred, a little louder than necessary as a result of his poor hearing.

'We're well, thank you,' said Jenny. 'Bernard's spent all week in the shed making a doll's house for Poppy, and I'm keeping busy with the Christmas baking.'

'The luxury of endless free time,' said Ann, pulling a tissue from her sleeve and wiping Isabelle's nose in one skilled movement. 'Five grandchildren is a full-time job, isn't it, Fred?'

Fred smiled vacantly, a one-size-fits-all response that he had developed over the years.

'We'd better let you go then,' said Jenny, looking at the toe of Bernard's shoe in an attempt to avoid Ann's gaze.

'We'll see you soon,' said Ann, manoeuvring the pram in sharp jerks. 'Come on, Isabelle!'

As they continued to walk the cold grew teeth.

'What lovely children,' said Bernard, his ears turning an unhealthy shade of pink, 'and they all have that red hair, even the baby.'

'Let's pop in here,' she said, as she steered him towards the shop. 'I need some bread flour and yeast.'

*

The kitchen had remained unchanged since the day they moved in and whilst it was small and unfashionable, it was beautifully familiar. Everything in it had a place, so much so that she operated it as if it were a car which only she knew how to drive. The cupboards, once stylish and new, were now heavy on their hinges so that they didn't align, and she knew exactly how to open and close the drawers so that they stayed on their runners.

She had decided to follow one of her mother's recipes because it was entitled *Simple Farmhouse Loaf*, and she traced her handwriting with her finger. It was scrawled as if in a hurry, reminding her of her mother's constant race against the minute hand, simultaneously her most endearing and frustrating quality. She remembered being pulled down the road as a small child, feet barely touching the ground as her mother delivered her to the school gates ten seconds after the bell. Then there were the countless church services which she had slipped into the back of, tempering her breath so as not to alert anyone to the fact that she had sprinted there and was still five minutes late. Perhaps as a result of her mother's tardiness, she prided herself on her time management.

She knocked the air out of the dough with her fists, the ache in her joints a reminder of her age as she pressed her knuckles into the elastic flesh. It expanded before her eyes, as if it were alive.

'Once I've pressed the air out, this will need a second rise,' she said, smiling into the window as if it were the white-toothed TV judges on *Britain Bakes*.

'After one hour it should be ready to go into the –'

'Darling, are you all right?'

Bernard looked around the door, a figure of concern,

causing her to launch the dough over her shoulder and on to the cold kitchen tiles with a humbling slap.

'Good God!' she said as she gathered herself, scooping the soft ball from the floor in an attempt to save it. 'I was just reading the recipe aloud – sometimes it helps me to remember it.'

'I thought you were talking to someone through the window,' he said, peering out to see if anyone was there whilst she shaped the dough into a loaf tin.

'You're still going to bake it even though it landed on the floor?' he said, growing increasingly bemused by the situation.

'Bernard, is this one hundred questions?' She fanned herself with a threadbare oven glove. 'I'm just seeing if it rises. I fancied a challenge; we don't have to eat it.'

He nodded, retreating back to the shed.

It was a further two hours before her loaf was complete, making it a five-hour activity which, unlike with a cake, didn't even allow you the joy of scraping the bowl to get every last mouthful. As she cut into it, the slices fell on to their sides with a thud. It was dense and dry, and after taking a bite she knew for certain that she didn't want to take another.

'*Simple* farmhouse loaf?' she scoffed, heading out into the garden with it under her arm before tearing it apart for the birds in careless chunks.

Jenny scrubbed the mixing bowl, hot water lapping at her wrists as she watched the sun sink below the trees, when a blackbird landed weightlessly on the bird table, picking at her bread in staccato pecks.

'Well, at least he's enjoying it,' said Bernard, twisting a tea towel into a water glass as he watched for her reaction. 'If the birds are no longer rejecting it, then that's an improvement.'

The blackbird flung the crust into the air so that it scattered, before hopping away across the lawn.

'I think you've spoken too soon,' she said, her smile doused by a tinge of guilt.

If she were to even consider entering, she reasoned, she had a lot of work to do first. She would keep it to herself for now, only telling Bernard if she were to go for it and be successful. It made sense that way. In their fifty-nine years of marriage, this would be only the second secret she had ever kept from him. The first was safely buried in the depths of her, belonging to a different lifetime, a place she would hold it for all eternity.

3

Chocolate Log

Christmas Eve was the perfect time for Jenny to practise the bakes for her application form without anyone questioning why she was churning out enough treats to feed the entire village. She was in the latter stages of creating a chocolate log, a treasured family recipe belonging to Bernard's late sister Margot. She had been a great lover of life, embracing everything and everyone with such enthusiasm that to be in her company was like walking in the sun. In fact, it had once occurred to Jenny that she had lived with the generosity of someone who always knew their time would be cut short. Jenny had continued Margot's tradition every year since she had gone, in light of its significance to Bernard, and so that she would always be a part of their Christmas.

She inserted a fork tentatively into the centre of a sheet of chocolate sponge, quietly congratulating herself when it came out clean. Setting it aside to cool, she laid a tea towel over it which was covered in self-portraits drawn by Poppy's reception class. Poppy didn't have a body but instead just a large, ecstatic face with arms and legs sprouting from it, framed by an abstract interpretation of her bob. The boy next to Poppy was called Oliver and looked like a different species entirely, unusually petite but with clover-like hands and missing no vital body parts.

It struck her just how much personality lay behind these drawings. She could tell from the detail that little Oliver was quite a considered character, deeply observant. Poppy – following firmly in the footsteps of her grandmother Margot – was a chatterbox, and her big smiling face on legs spoke of a carefree confidence.

Once the sponge had cooled, she used a spatula to layer it with glossy chocolate ganache and clouds of whipped cream, imagining it to be the most indulgent sandwich in the world. She began to roll it up inch by inch, holding her breath as she coaxed the sponge with the utmost care. A crack would be disastrous, although Margot wouldn't have minded. She would have told her it would still taste the same, and that no one would notice under the icing sugar.

'Good grief, are you sure we are going to fit all of this in the car? We have the doll's house too . . .'

Bernard had walked into the kitchen where every surface was covered in baked goods and the air was warm with chocolate sponge. Lined up on cooling racks were the old family favourites: mince pies, tiffin and the chewy Rice Krispies squares of Quinn's Crunch which always made a special appearance at Christmas. Beyond those were some new and rather extravagant additions, including a bundt wreath covered in sugar-frosted berries which looked as if it had been lifted directly from the cover of a magazine.

'They'll fit in the car, I'll sit with them on my lap,' said Jenny, revelling in the satisfaction of shaking icing sugar on to the chocolate log, second only to watching real snow fall.

'Margot's chocolate log,' he said, greeting it like an old friend.

'It's never missed a Christmas,' she said. 'Now where's Ernie?'

She opened the drawer next to the oven and rifled through it, eventually retrieving a rather dishevelled-looking robin decoration which she perched on top, his beak hanging on by a thread.

'At least someone's aged worse than me,' said Bernard, pressing the lids on to the tins.

'Wait,' she said, her tone deceptively spontaneous. 'Would you mind taking a picture of all this, just whilst it looks so nice?'

He agreed, disappearing upstairs to get the camera. When he returned she had laid out their best red gingham tablecloth and was styling her creations with sprigs of holly from the garden.

'What a feast,' he said, his glasses perched on the end of his nose as he strained to look at the digital display. 'I'll get one with you in it.'

She combed her fine strands of silver hair behind her ears and put on a fresh coat of pink lipstick, smiling unnaturally towards the lens.

'How do I look?'

'Gorgeous,' he said, catching sight of his watch. 'Right, we'd better go. It could take up to three hours to get there in this traffic.'

It was a ritual that they spent Christmas with Bernard's niece Rose, her husband Jeremy and their two children,

Poppy and Max. Poppy was now eight and Max fourteen, and the Quinns' arrival marked the start of their Christmas.

Bernard arranged and rearranged the boot of the car, wrestling down the seats as he tried to fit in the doll's house amongst their bags. Once he had been successful, he slammed the boot shut, noticeably short of breath.

'Have you packed your inhaler?' she asked, barely visible beneath the tins of baked goods.

'In my suitcase,' he replied as the engine roared into life. 'God forbid we have an accident, Jenny – they'll think the car was being driven by a family of profiteroles!'

As they drove along the motorway serenaded by carols on the radio, she looked into the neighbouring cars as the passengers headed to their various Christmases. She saw a worried-looking gentleman who she imagined had been sent out in a panic, on a hunt for the forgotten brandy butter. Little did he know it was so easy to make and far more delicious. In the back of a large family vehicle were two little boys peering up at the darkening sky, their eyes searching for an early glimpse of Father Christmas. One of the little boys turned and pointed towards their car, his nose pressed against the window. For a moment she wondered if he had mistaken her for someone, but it quickly dawned on her that it was Maurice that had caught his attention; the small, tired-looking bear propped in the corner of the dashboard.

Maurice had two beady eyes, one hanging on by a thread so that it looked in a different direction, and he was balding in patches where soft fur had once been. He had lived in all of their cars but was named after their first, a Morris Minor 1000. She remembered the day they bought it,

Bernard's twenty-fifth birthday, and his beam as he stroked the domed bonnet, the colour of a duck's egg. She had initially been cautious about the great expense, but there was no dissuading Bernard who had been saving his wages for months. *Think of the adventures she'll take us on*, he'd said, and he had been right.

She looked from Maurice to Bernard as he focused on the road, the creases at the corner of his eyes and around his mouth exposing him as a kind man, a man who laughed. She admired his unusually thick eyelashes which she had coveted for half a century and thought of the hours she had spent sitting beside him as he drove. Sometimes they chatted and other times they enjoyed the silence of each other's company. She couldn't imagine a life without him in it.

A Mince Pie, Half a Carrot
and a Drop of Sherry

Jenny stood on a stool, her mother's pinny folded around her waist to stop it trailing on the floor as she watched her slice lard and margarine into small cubes which dropped silently into the flour.

'You need to rub it together,' her mother said, as she twisted off her rings and balanced them on the windowsill, slivers of Sunlight soap trapped underneath her nails from where she had been grating it for the washing.

'Like this.' She stood behind her daughter, singing as she scooped the fat and flour between her palms. 'O come let us adore Him, O come let us adore Him . . .' she rubbed her hands together as if she were trying to keep them warm, the mixture snowing down, '. . . O come let us adore Him, Christ the Lord.'

Jenny nodded, the soft fabric of her mother's box pleat skirt brushing against the backs of her legs. She tried to emulate what she had done, her small palms significantly less effective.

'That's it,' said her mother, stroking her hair behind her ears and planting a kiss on her head. 'You just have to be patient; eventually it will look like breadcrumbs.'

The fat clung between her fingers so that she had to keep stopping and pulling it off as if it were a pair of gloves, dropping it back into the bowl and going again. There was something so satisfying about using her hands, the tickle of the flour as it fell between her fingers.

Her mother gasped.

'Two o'clock!' she said, leaning over to finish the last bit at rapid speed, before pouring in a little cold water. 'I promised Granny we'd be at hers by now – I don't know where the time's gone.'

She mixed it all together with a knife, her body shaking as her locket tapped against her chest. Shaping it into a ball with her delicate hands, she dusted the pastry board with flour and placed the dough at its centre.

'Now you need to roll it out to about a quarter of an inch,' she said, miming the thickness with her fingers before handing Jenny the rolling pin.

Jenny placed her hands on each end and pressed it into the dough, using her entire strength to move it forwards and backwards but instead achieving a large dent.

'This is why I use half lard,' her mother said, placing her hands softly over Jenny's and applying some extra force. 'It makes it easier to roll.'

Eventually the pastry resembled a cold, smooth sheet, and she couldn't resist stroking it, flour coating her fingertips.

'Now for the best bit,' said her mother, placing a cutter on the sheet of pastry and making faint imprints. 'You want to squeeze as many of these out of the pastry as possible, nice and close together.'

Jenny pressed the cutter into the pastry so that it sank through the dough until it hit the board. Tapping the neat shape out with her fingers, she admired its symmetry in the palm of her hand.

'Beautiful,' said her mother.

Eventually, all that was left on the board was a tracery of leftover pastry. Her mother gathered it into a ball with a sense of urgency, and repeated the process until they were left with a piece the size of a dice.

'Can I eat it?' she said.

Her mother nodded, a dimple appearing in her right cheek.

'It's not very sweet, is it?'

'No,' said Jenny, squashing the bland slug against the roof of her mouth. 'I still like it though.'

They draped each round into the tin, pressing it into the corners and adding a teaspoon of mincemeat.

'Do you want to know a secret?' said her mother, leaning close so that she could smell her perfume. 'If I have any going spare, I put a thin disc of almond paste under each lid. It's why your father loves them so much.'

Jenny painted the circumference with water and pressed on the lid, forming a neat little mound in the middle which her mother pierced with a fork.

She felt the sinking disappointment that it was all over, when one round caught her eye.

'You can make that one into a jam tart, if you're quick,' said her mother, retrieving the jam from the pantry.

'I think I might save it for Father Christmas,' said Jenny. 'He might have had too many mince pies.'

Her mother posted them into the hot oven and Jenny sat with her body pressed against it, her cheeks scarlet as a sweet fug filled the house.

'Mummy,' she said, her brow creased with concern, 'will there be a Christmas message this year, now that we have no King?'

'I should think Elizabeth will do it, now that she's our Queen,' said her mother. 'You funny thing. Jam teaspoon?'

Jenny's face lit up as her mother handed it to her like a lollipop.

Pressing the cold dome against her tongue, she savoured its strawberry sweetness. There was nowhere happier.

The moon was bright against the night sky, and they sat around the fire with plates of cold ham, scotch eggs and

Waldorf salad, sipping warm glasses of mulled wine as they laughed and chatted with a glow that was unique to Christmas Eve.

The room was cloaked in the earthy smell of spruce as the Christmas tree stood proudly in the window wearing memories that told the story of the family. There were old forties decorations that had belonged to Margot; faded colourful baubles with inverted gold centres which looked like they had been moulded on the spike of a lemon squeezer. There was a salt dough star tied with a red ribbon, hand painted by Poppy with generous lashings of metallic paint, her initials etched into the back. On a lower branch sat a crepe paper snowman, dishevelled but precious, fashioned out of the same cotton wool balls that Rose probably used to remove her make-up.

Jeremy was telling Bernard about his cycling escapades. He was a wiry man of intense energy who spent the week working as a solicitor and the weekends dressed in Lycra, his piston-like legs powering him along winding country roads and up impossible hills. Poppy was squirming with excitement, intent on stealing Bernard's full attention away from her father with interruptions such as *Uncle Bernie, would you like to come and see my den?*

Jenny understood why Poppy loved him so much. He had a wonderful way with children in that he spoke to them as if they were his peers. He never put on the patronizing voice of feigned enthusiasm or commented on their appearance, but instead listened to them with the same integrity he would give to any adult.

Whilst Poppy led Bernard around the house as if she were walking a good-natured but tired Labrador, Rose coaxed conversation out of Max who had, it seemed, developed into a teenager since last Christmas.

'Tell Aunty Jenny about the award you won at school,' she said, tucking her thick blonde hair behind her ear as it sprang back in the enviable way that Quinn hair did.

Max bounced his knee up and down, avoiding eye contact so that she might as well have been naked.

'I won the maths award for the highest grade in the year,' he said, as if it was punishable by death.

She was quietly shocked to hear that his voice had found a strange new pitch, like a trumpet playing the wrong note.

'That's wonderful, Max,' she said, remembering him as a little boy, standing on a stool in her kitchen as she made jam tarts and he made 'pastry robots' with the offcuts.

'So you're enjoying school, then?'

Max flicked his mop of hair further across his forehead as he subtly retrieved his phone from his pocket.

'S'all right,' he said, smiling at something on the screen before responding at an extraordinary speed.

'He's going to be choosing his GCSE options soon,' added Rose, vying for his attention, 'aren't you, Max?'

He nodded. 'History, music tech, Spanish and photography.'

'Photography?' said Rose, sitting up a little straighter. 'Since when?'

'Since my mates are doing it . . .'

'You shouldn't base your future on what your friends are doing –'

'Spanish . . .' said Jenny, watching as Max picked at his short slivers of nail, 'what a great language to learn. It will be nice to have a variety of different subjects.'

'Exactly,' said Max, glaring at his mother from beneath his hair, the shadow of a first-time moustache on his top lip.

Jenny had watched Rose become a mother as if it were the most natural thing in the world. There were Christmases when Max had been hanging from her leg as she put together the Christmas dinner, all whilst having a tiny baby tucked underneath her jumper. There were moments where she pulled a breadstick out of her handbag like a wand, using it as a distraction technique for Max on the brink of tears, or conjured a colouring book out of nowhere as a bargaining tool whilst she tried to enjoy a meal. Jenny wondered if everyone so seamlessly developed these skills, and if Jeremy had grown to love Rose even more for it.

After supper came the moment they had all been waiting for: the unveiling of Jenny's Christmas baking. Poppy's eyes lit up and she clapped her hands together like an excited seal at the sight of the tiffin. Jenny felt a warm sense of satisfaction as she watched Poppy devour it, nibbling the biscuit away until she was left with just the smooth chocolate top, savouring every last bite.

'You've made more this year than ever – it'll last us for weeks!' said Jeremy, tasting everything with his eyes.

'Oh look,' said Rose, her hand hovering above the chocolate log. 'Poppy, Max, this one here was your Granny Margot's favourite.'

'Nice,' said Max, cutting himself a generous wedge and then devouring it as if it were his first encounter with sugar, barely coming up for air.

'You're the best baker, Aunty Jenny,' said Poppy with chocolate teeth.

'It's her superpower,' Bernard replied.

Jenny stared into the vast American fridge, their kitchen the polar opposite to her own, all straight lines and spotlights with nothing hanging off its hinges or balanced on its runners.

'Do we need a glass of milk?' said Poppy, as she pulled a carrot from the salad drawer. 'He might be thirsty by the time he gets here.'

'I think he'd prefer a drop of sherry,' said Bernard, perched uncomfortably on a bar stool behind the island – a far cry from his velvet armchair. 'What do you think, darling?'

'I agree,' Jenny replied, 'everyone will leave him milk.'

She accompanied Poppy to the fireplace, absorbing the magic of her unwavering belief, before pulling the lid off the tin of homemade mince pies so that a poof of icing sugar followed. She watched as Poppy's hand hovered above each one in careful consideration, eventually making her selection.

'These mince pies have a secret ingredient, so I'm sure he'll like them.'

'What is it?' said Poppy, as Bernard appeared with a glass of sherry.

'There's a thin disc of almond paste under the lid; it makes all the difference.'

'Are you awake?' said Poppy through the crack in the door, in a whisper that was intended to wake them.

'Just about, Pops,' replied Jenny, checking her watch

through foggy eyes. 5:45 a.m. That was an early start even for Bernard.

'Merry Christmas, darling,' he said, his voice a deep rasp as he reached for his glasses. 'I think we'd better get up.'

Jenny pulled on her dressing gown and followed Poppy down the stairs, Bernard, Rose and Jeremy in tow as if they were taking part in a dishevelled conga line, still heavy from sleep. It seemed Max had reached the age where the desire to stay in bed outweighed the excitement of opening a stocking at the crack of dawn. It was still dark outside and an icy mist hovered in the air, glittering in the glow of the street lights. Even at the age of seventy-seven she felt the tingle of believing, as if a spell had been cast which made everything on Christmas morning look like the best version of itself.

Poppy paused outside the living room door. She turned around, her eyes wild with anticipation.

'Shall I go in?' she said.

They nodded and she clicked open the door. The air was warm with pine and lit only by the light of the Christmas tree, colourful gifts in intriguing shapes spilling out from underneath it. In the fireplace stood a large structure cloaked in a tartan blanket, far too big to fit in the swollen stocking beside it.

'He's been!' she said, rushing over to the mysterious shape.

Jenny watched Bernard as Poppy pulled back the blanket, his eyes bright behind his glasses which were reflecting a thousand fairy lights.

'A doll's house!' gasped Poppy, as she peered into the

tiny rooms which smelt of fresh paint and wood shavings. It was a Victorian-style house with white framed windows and a roof that folded backwards to reveal little attic bedrooms.

Bernard reached for the switch and clicked on all of the tiny ceiling lights at once, bringing it to life. Poppy wriggled with glee at her little world ready to be filled with inhabitants that would be as real to her as Father Christmas.

'Margot Manor,' she said, pointing to a hand-painted sign above the front door.

Rose and Jeremy drew closer, gathering around to read it.

'Thank you, Father Christmas,' said Rose, glancing towards Bernard and putting her hand on her heart as if to show him that it was full.

Christmas Cake

In a whirlwind of walking boots and winter coats, Jeremy tried to herd the family out of the front door for a walk by regularly announcing the time. On any other day of the year this would require no fuss, but today was Boxing Day, so it was an event. Rose wrapped up pieces of Christmas cake in tin foil and made a flask of tea, whilst Max half-heartedly searched for his welly socks which had mysteriously disappeared from their home in the toe of his wellington boots.

'I'm not sure I can come,' he said as he flicked his hair to one side, causing a rare sighting of his eyes which were swollen with sleep. 'I can't find my socks.'

'Don't be ridiculous, use my spares,' said Jeremy, bowling a pair towards him so that they rolled the length of the hall, a disgruntled Max following closely behind.

Eventually they made it out, blades of frozen grass crunching underfoot as their noses fizzed with the first blast of crisp morning air. Jenny looked back at Bernard walking hand in hand with Poppy, as he explained to her the secret powers of dock leaves when trying to relieve a nettle sting. Surrounded by family, Jenny was reminded that he thrived as part of a pack and yet had lived life in a pair.

'You know, I remember Uncle Bernard explaining that very same thing to me as a little girl,' said Rose, 'on one of our camping holidays.'

'You remember those holidays?' said Jenny.

'Of course I do,' Rose clapped her gloves together, 'some of my happiest memories. Ice creams, cricket on the beach, fish and chips . . .'

Jenny thought of the years that they had taken Rose camping in the summer holidays to give Margot and John a break, but more than anything because they enjoyed it. She would fill the car up with tins of biscuits, flasks of soup, bread, baked beans – Bernard would joke affectionately that they were going for six days, not six months. She remembered the three of them under canvas at night listening to the hoot of the owls and the rustle of the trees, and how Bernard would convince Rose that he had spotted what he called a 'sea fairy', causing great excitement. In the morning there would often be a seashell hidden somewhere in the tent that she had left behind.

'Do you remember the year of the storms?' said Rose, putting her hand to her mouth as she relived it. 'And the tent leaking?'

'Yes!' said Jenny. 'We ended up sleeping in the car, didn't we?'

Rose nodded, 'Except Uncle Bernie slept in the tent to give us more space.'

They walked for a moment in silence, lost in their individual memories as their steps became synchronized.

'What's on the cards for next year then?' said Rose.

She thought about the application deadline, a spark of excitement swiftly snuffed by the date: 11th January.

'I'm not sure, really,' she said, relieved to be walking so that her face was hidden, '. . . although it's a big year for Bernard and me; it's our diamond wedding anniversary in October.'

'Of course,' said Rose, her arms swinging by her side. 'Are you going to have a party?'

'I expect we'll do something, but we've got to get there first.'

Rose laughed. 'If you've managed fifty-nine years, surely you can put up with him for another few months?'

Jenny chose not to correct her misunderstanding, for fear of sounding morbid.

'What about you, any big plans?'

'I think it will be quite work focused,' said Rose, the toes of her wellingtons now wet and shiny. 'I'm hoping to be made a partner this year.'

'That's brilliant,' said Jenny, as she pulled a rag of tissue from her sleeve and blotted her nose. 'I'll keep my fingers crossed for you, although I'm sure you won't need any luck.'

'Thank you,' she said. 'My main concern about stepping up is it's a real balancing act between challenging myself and being present for Poppy and Max.'

Jenny nodded as if she understood.

'Sometimes I think Poppy is still so little and Max needs me more than he would like to admit, especially with his exams coming up.'

She searched for some wise words, for some experience

to draw on, but instead felt herself shrinking smaller and smaller, punctured by a pin of inadequacy.

'I've never been all of the things that you are,' she said, sensing that she should say something, 'so my thoughts are probably of little use, but you've got two wonderful children and a brilliant career, so trust your instinct. It's got you this far.'

She looked back over her shoulder at Bernard and Poppy in the distance as they leant over a fence to study a molehill.

'Thank you, Rose, for sharing your family with us.'

'Aunty Jenny,' Rose said, stroking her arm with her glove, 'you know we consider ourselves beyond lucky to have you both.'

'Wait!' called Jeremy, wafting his right hand in the air as he caught up with them. 'I think we should slow down a bit; it's taking Bernard a while to catch up.'

'I did notice he was a little more unsteady on his feet than when I last saw him,' said Rose, lowering her voice as lines appeared across her forehead. 'He is eighty-two, Jeremy. I did think we should have done the other walk, the shorter one.'

Jenny felt an ache in her chest, Rose's words compounding a painful truth.

'Why have we stopped?' said Max, meandering towards them with his hands pushed deep into his pockets so that his shoulders looked permanently shrugged.

'We're just waiting for Uncle Bernie to catch up,' said Rose, 'so we can all walk together.'

As Bernard approached, his breathing sounded laboured.

'Are you all right, darling?' Jenny said, watching as he reached for a tree stump.

'Fine,' he replied, looking away so as to divert attention. Pulling his inhaler out of his pocket, he put it to his mouth, his chest heaving so that he sounded like a human accordion.

'Uncle Bernie has an inhaler!' said Poppy, her excitement levels rivalling that of Christmas morning. 'I'm desperate for an inhaler . . . my friend Jessica has one.'

'Tea break?' said Rose, to which they all heartily agreed, perching around the stump as they looked out across the fields.

'Who would like some Christmas cake?' she added as she struggled to unwrap it using her gloves, persevering as if it were a party game.

'Aunty Jenny,' said Poppy, tugging at her arm and pointing to something beneath the trees.

As she searched the horizon, a deer emerged wearing his proud, twisted antlers like a crown on top of his head. He looked through the December mist like a mythical creature, and one by one walkers stopped in their tracks. Gradually the crowd of onlookers grew and so did the herd, their elegance highlighting the clumsiness of the humans as they stared gormlessly back, swaddled in coats and scarves. Two audiences of different species staring at each other in utter wonder.

Jenny grew distracted by a little boy amidst the crowd. He was no older than two and his fine hair curled to a point in the nape of his neck.

Rose eventually managed to unwrap the cake, dividing it

between the group. They passed around the flask of steaming tea but she politely declined. Everything from a flask tasted slightly savoury as if the soup that it had once contained had left a permanent stain.

The little boy was now toddling through the crowd, gathering speed like a rolling car. She scanned the body language of nearby walkers, trying to work out who he might belong to.

'This is delicious, Rose,' said Bernard, reminding her to take a bite.

Immediately she knew he was just being courteous. It was, in fact, overdone. The outside edge was blackened and it fell apart like clumps of wet sand. The dryness wasn't the worst thing, though; the worst thing was the unwelcome surprise of a gritty currant like gravel between her teeth.

'Thank you, Uncle Bernie, it's Mum's trusty recipe,' Rose said, and Jenny felt a pang of guilt. Thank goodness people couldn't hear your thoughts.

'I only like the top bit,' said Poppy, detaching the layer of royal icing and biting into it like a piece of chalk.

'That's not very kind, Poppy. Mummy worked hard to make that,' said Rose, her eyebrows raised.

The little boy had now made a break from the crowd and was running directly towards the deer, their stance suddenly ominous as their antlers loomed. She could hear the thud of her own heart as she watched his legs move faster and faster, as if danger had its own magnetic field.

'I'll eat yours, Pops,' said Max, holding out his hand as he polished off his own piece in one.

Without warning she shot after the little boy, her mind

barely registering what her legs had just decided to do. As she drew closer, she reached for the tip of his hood, grabbing it so that he fell backwards with a thud.

There was a three-second delay before he let out a piercing scream.

'I'm sorry,' she whispered as he looked up at her, a tiny stranger with unfamiliar green eyes and a yellow crust framing his nose. He caught his breath in rasps, growing silent as they stared at each other, both equally shocked by what had just happened.

'You shouldn't have pulled his hood, you could've strangled him,' snapped his mother, as she swung him on to her hip and his crying resumed.

'I'm sorry,' she said, retreating, her eyes fixed to the ground in the hope that she might become invisible. As she returned to the group she could feel her cheeks burning.

'Well done, Jenny, I've never seen you move so fast,' said Bernard, with a chuckle.

'Well, I'm glad you found it funny,' she snapped, an uncomfortable silence washing over the group.

As they walked back through the fields making polite conversation, she longed for home, to hide the part of her that had been seen.

A deep inky blue stained the sky and cat's eyes shone like scales on the road ahead as they drove home to Kittlesham, another Christmas complete.

Her thoughts were amplified by the quiet of the car, fragments of the day flashing through her mind: the shock in the little boy's eyes, the anger in his mother's. She pictured

Bernard as he fell behind on the walk, Rose's words squeezing her heart as they confirmed her fears. At this point, each day was a blessing.

She turned to him, overcome by a sudden impulse to tell him about the competition, about her hunger for something more, but as she teetered on the edge of admission, he took a deep breath and began to whistle. Guilt silenced her. Why couldn't she, like him, just be content with a smaller life? She thought of what she had said to Rose – *trust your instinct, it's got you this far* – and yet she never allowed herself the same advice. She clenched her fists, banishing the voices from her mind. Time was slipping away and the finality of it fluttered in her chest and gripped her bones.

It was now or never. She had to go for it.

Lemon Meringue Pie

Jenny usually considered January the worst month of the year; the excitement of Christmas was over and yet the promise of spring still felt so far away. This year however felt different; she had a deadline to meet.

Her mouth watered at the thought of the sharp citrus filling, firm like cold custard, sweetened by weightless swirls of meringue. Paired with the buttery pastry, it was the perfect trio of texture and flavour, and her father's speciality. Nothing quite matched the smell of his lemon meringue pie baking in the oven, hot clouds of lemon curd filling the house.

Delicately lifting the slack sheet of pastry, she draped it over the fluted dish and pressed it into the grooves with her fingertips, the jagged edges relaxing over the sides. She ran a knife around the circumference so that they dropped limp on to the worktop, the most satisfying of tasks. Pricking the base with a fork, she posted it into the fridge to chill, leaving her a neat window of time to go to the shops for yet another box of eggs.

As she rummaged through her handbag, she pulled out

her red leather purse. It was bursting at the seams with everything but money: Poppy's first passport picture, an old school photo of Max, and a tiny cut-out of Bernard from a holiday photograph taken shortly after he'd sold his carpentry business, at the start of his retirement. She looked closely at his joyous face which was the colour of a hazelnut, a stark contrast to his now sallow complexion. Behind it were shopping lists and postage stamps, but the note section was completely bare. She had spent her entire weekly allowance and it was only Wednesday.

'Bernie!' she called.

He appeared wearing a puzzled expression. He was generous yet sensible with money and their books were always balanced.

'I just need to pop to the shops to get some more eggs but I've run out of pennies. It never used to be this expensive to bake . . .'

'I think it's because you're making three cakes a day, darling. Not that I'm complaining, but do you think you might be . . . overdoing it?'

She thought about this for a second, struggling to disagree. It was a challenge to explain the sheer quantity of baked goods she had churned out of late. She was creating at a much faster rate than the two of them could consume, the freezer was full to the brim and almost all of the neighbours had received gifts wrapped in greaseproof paper.

'Well, it was my new year's resolution to cheer everyone up in January,' she said, still searching through her purse, 'and I've promised the local nursing home a lemon meringue pie. It's one of the old boys' favourites.'

'That's very noble of you,' he said, dealing out his

pension like playing cards. 'I haven't spent much this week so you can have mine.'

She felt a stab of shame as she put his money in her purse and headed off to the shops. But *Britain Bakes* had slowly and silently taken over her every waking thought, forcing its way into the centre of her orbit. As she lay in bed at night she wrote shopping lists in her mind and when she woke in the morning she would deliberate between madeleines and fondant fancies.

Jenny stirred to the comforting sound of newspaper pages grazing bedsheets as Bernard folded them into a more manageable size. Inhaling the savoury musk of their morning bodies, she reached for her cup of tea, noticing the date printed below the headline. It was 9th January, two days before a date which brought with it a silent pain as it rolled around each year – this year with a new significance. Usually she would spend the day focused entirely on getting through it, quietly enduring her own personal grief which never lessened with the passing of time as she had once been told it would. She rubbed the soft cotton sheet against her top lip as a plunging sensation sank straight through the core of her, hollowing her out.

She took a sip of tea. Today was her last chance to post the application form in order to make the deadline.

'I've got an indoor bowls match with Ann and Fred today, darling,' said Bernard. 'Do you fancy coming along? We could all go for lunch afterwards?'

She paused.

'I'd love to, but I've got a list as long as my arm of jobs to do, thank-yous to post and all sorts . . .'

'Can't it wait?' he said, his voice hopeful.

She leapt out of bed as if she hadn't heard.

Bernard headed off to his bowls match in a white jumper and the sort of trousers which crackle with static. She thought how unlike himself he looked in anything other than corduroy trousers, a shirt and a wool jumper.

She opened their wardrobe in search of her half-finished application form which was hidden in a hat box on the top shelf. Using her dressing table stool, she strained to reach it, briefly distracted by one of his suits. It was the one he had worn to Rose and Jeremy's wedding many moons ago, a brave shade of cream with a noticeably slimmer waistband. The suit was Bernard in his early sixties. He'd never wear it now, she thought to herself as she put the sleeve to her nose and inhaled the must of stale fabric, but beneath it the woody trace of his aftershave. Clothes had a way of capturing a moment in time and staying frozen there forever whilst their owner ripened, changed. She imagined clearing his wardrobe after he had gone, each shirt, each bow tie, a memory of him. The idea of folding his life into charity bags was unthinkable.

She reached for the hat box and lifted the lid. Folded on top of her best black hat was the application form which she had printed some weeks ago. It had lived in here but also in her mind, a seed of hope that had grown and grown until she could no longer contain it.

She decided to do it in the kitchen, the place where she did all of her best work. The Formica worktop was cream and speckled like the shell of a quail's egg, and she joined the dots together with her finger as she considered her answers, writing them out on scraps of paper before making them permanent in the green ink of her fountain pen.

How good do you think you are at baking? How good would your family/friends say you are?

Over Christmas, my husband described baking as my super-power. I know that he is biased but I truly consider it the only thing that I am any good at. I grew up in a family that put baking at the heart of every occasion. In the weeks leading up to a birthday we discussed the theme of their cake so meticulously that it became bigger than the event itself. I am from a long line of people who have considered baking one of life's greatest pleasures, something to be shared, and I realize now, remembered by. I know myself to be a good home baker and one that rises to the challenge.

She struggled to rate her own abilities; it was the most unnatural exercise. Would she appear arrogant, or worse, delusional? On the other hand, if she rated herself too modestly, she might not stand a chance. She gave examples of her most successful bakes in each category, rating them instead by the reactions of her friends and family.

Pies:

Uncle Stanley's Cherry Brandy Pie – named after my uncle because he was so enamoured by it that he had seconds, thirds and fourths, and then had to retire from the table bent over in pain. His gluttony was frowned upon at the time but in retrospect, it was quite the compliment.

She smiled as memories returned to her, each one sparked by a different bake, but the further down the application she got the less about baking the questions became. Her pen ground to a halt, leaving a blot of ink on the page.

What is your greatest ambition in life?

In seventy-seven years, nobody had ever asked her this question. She didn't think of herself as an ambitious person, having never excelled academically, achieved career success or raised a family of her own. Until recently, she had never considered that great ambitions were something she could have.

For once, she thought, *I'll just be honest.*

I've spent my life being led less by great ambition and more by small victories. The perfect swirl in a Swiss roll, the smooth pink dome of an expertly turned-out summer pudding, cutting into a Baked Alaska to find the ice cream has remained cold. I would say my biggest achievement is my marriage to my husband Bernard – it's our diamond wedding anniversary this year and I love him dearly. However, whilst he is graciously settling into the winter of his life, I have started to question what I have done with my own. When my day comes, I stand to leave behind nothing on this earth except perhaps a few recipes in my kitchen cupboard. Applying for Britain Bakes *is the first time I've really embarked upon a great ambition and I'm seventy-seven. All of that is to say, I recently realized that if not now, then never.*

She squeezed each answer into the allocated box, filling it with her best emerald handwriting which had grown a little shaky over the last couple of years. She checked the clock: 4:15 p.m. She had lost track of time. The last post was at 5 p.m. and Bernard would be back soon.

She folded the pages neatly into the envelope alongside an assortment of photographs both old and new: a black-and-white picture from her father's fortieth birthday of his delighted face as he stood before a cricket pitch made from sponge and coloured icing. She also put in some more recent pictures, including the one of herself which Bernard had taken on Christmas Eve, proudly surrounded by her festive bakes like a teacher in a class photograph. She closed and reopened the envelope in an attempt to capture how it might be received, before deciding that time was of the essence.

Running her tongue along the sweet edge of the envelope, she pressed it down with force, copied out the address and attached a stamp. As she pulled on her winter coat and walked towards the front door, a Bernard-shaped outline appeared in the glass, followed by voices.

She glanced at her watch: 4:30 p.m.

'Afternoon, Jenny,' said Ann, a chirp to her voice. Fred smiled vacantly next to her as if she were a ventriloquist and he her puppet.

'I've invited Ann and Fred for a celebratory piece of cake and a cup of tea, since we have so much going spare,' said Bernard, rubbing his hands together. 'We won the match!'

'Oh. Congratulations!' she said, her lack of enthusiasm betrayed by her eyes.

'Were you heading out?' said Ann, inspecting her from top to toe.

'I've got some thank-you letters to post. But by all means come in – I won't be long.'

49

Ann's eyes travelled down her arm and paused at the large, brown envelope in her hand.

'Just the one?'

Her limbs tingled with urgency.

'I'm . . . keeping them all in one big envelope,' she said, edging it behind her back and stepping aside.

To her great relief, Ann trotted towards the kitchen with Fred following obediently behind her. Bernard leant against the front doorframe, his brow furrowed.

'You don't need to post thank-you letters now, right this minute, do you? I can post them later this evening if you'd like?'

Usually she would have handed it over, dashed inside and made a pot of tea. Today, she did not have time for this.

'Here,' he said, holding out his hand. 'If you give them to me, I'll put them in my coat pocket so that I don't forget.'

She moved the letter closer to her chest.

'I want to make the last post. I will be ten minutes, Bernie, you go and put the kettle on.'

With that, she dipped under his arm which was propping open the front door, and scurried off into the village before he could register what had just happened.

4:55 p.m. Her shoulders grew tense as if she were wearing a coat hanger. She cut through the frosty January air at great speed, her feet clawing against the soles of her shoes so as not to slip on the frozen ground. As she neared the local school, she heard a huddle of children leaving an after-school club, clutching PE kits, lunch boxes and book bags. She looked at the parents and wondered if their greatest ambitions were walking right next to them.

As she turned the corner to the postbox, a postwoman was crouched down, emptying it.

'Wait!' she called, her scarf flying behind her. The postwoman looked over her shoulder, her nose pink with cold.

'Don't worry, dear, you've got time,' she said.

Jenny pulled out the heavy envelope and dropped it into the post bag so that it landed with a thud amongst the hundreds of others. The bills, the invitations, the condolences. She felt a flash of excitement as it struck her that the postwoman had no idea what was in her envelope. What would she think if she told her? Perhaps there were other application forms in there, ones from younger, more adventurous contestants, who were better at baking bread.

As she thanked the postwoman and headed home, she remembered the abrupt fashion in which she'd left Bernard, who was probably struggling to locate the cake tin and hadn't put the milk in a jug. It was for the greater good that she didn't tell him just yet. She'd probably never hear back anyway, and there was no need to burden him with thoughts that she might be dissatisfied with their life, that she might want something just for herself.

Shortbread

Jenny knelt under the stairs, reaching for the cold slab where the butter was stored. She felt its weight in her palm as she peeled back the greaseproof paper, noticing the soft yellow imprint of fingers from the last time it was used. She studied the delicate oval shape of them and felt her throat tighten as it dawned on her whose they were. Overcome by a dull wrench of longing, she wondered how it could be, that before her very eyes were the fingerprints of hands that she missed so much. Hands which made her feel safe as they held her own, and which washed her hair on a Sunday evening before weaving it into neat plaits. Hands which were last seen holding the handlebar of a bike as it was hit by a car.

She stared down, absorbing the precious piece of her that she had found.

'We haven't got all day, Jennifer. Your father has requested shortbread so we need six ounces. Is there enough?' called Aunt Ethel, as she tipped the ground rice into the mixing bowl in one agitated sweep.

'No,' she said, biting her lip in an attempt to stifle her tears. To use it would be to lose a little more of her, and it was all she had left. 'It's all gone.'

She felt Aunt Ethel move closer, inhaling her sour breath as she leant over her.

'Why are you telling lies?' she said, her rough hands reaching over as she scooped up the remaining butter with her stubby fingers.

She wanted to grab her arm, to snatch it back, but instead she watched in horror as Aunt Ethel returned to the kitchen, pulled it into clumps and dropped them into the mixing bowl.

'Are you going to help or just stand there?' she said, nudging the stool with her boot so that it scraped against the tiles.

'I'll help,' she said in her quietest voice, stepping on to the stool.

'You need to work the dough with your hands,' said Aunt Ethel, trapping her between her thick arms as she pummelled the butter into the dry mixture.

Jenny held her breath until she moved away.

Lowering her hands into the bowl, she squeezed the ingredients between her fingers, conjuring the memory of her mother behind her, her warmth, her perfume, her twinkling rings on the windowsill. The house had been cloaked in a heavy silence since she had gone, her singing replaced by the ticking of clocks.

Aunt Ethel was her father's sister and his complete opposite. In fact, the only thing they really shared was a surname and a sweet tooth. Since her mother's passing, Aunt Ethel had taken it upon herself to support her father by attempting to fill her role, much to Jenny's contempt. Time spent with her aunt felt as if she were in a permanent state of waiting. Waiting for her father to come home from work. Waiting for her grandparents to visit. Waiting for her mother to walk in through the door so that she could bury her face into her soft neck.

The mixture was now a dense, golden dough which she pressed into a ball, her hands coated in a film of grease. She took a pinch and snuck it into her mouth, smoothing away the evidence. Delicious. She *took another, the butter melting on her tongue. Just one more, she thought, taking a generous lump.*

'What are you doing?' said Aunt Ethel, as she appeared next to her, wearing her mother's blue cardigan. It looked ugly, wrong, as if it had been stuffed with straw, and she remembered her mother knitting it, fury twisting in her stomach as she pressed the dough on to the roof of her mouth.

'I'm checking that it's right,' she said, as her aunt snatched the bowl away.

'If you eat the mixture, there won't be enough for the shortbreads,' she said, her voice clipped.

Jenny narrowed her eyes, a rage burning in her throat.

'Mummy let me taste the mixture,' she said.

'Really?' Aunt Ethel's face grew tight. 'Well, I don't.'

It had been two weeks and five days since Jenny posted her application form, and she knew this because she was counting. She pressed the shortbread mixture into the bottom of a cake tin with her hands, before smoothing it out with the back of a tablespoon. Her lips were pursed as she focused on getting the surface flat enough to satisfy even Bernard's spirit level, before patterning the top with pricks of the fork. She used the prongs to decorate the edge, twisting the tin as she worked her way around it like the second hand of a clock, her attention snatched by the ringing of the phone.

'Bernie, can you get that?' she called, the silence that followed reminding her that he was in the garden. She slid her shortbread into the oven, her glasses steaming up as she rushed to answer it.

'Hello, Jennifer Quinn speaking,' she said, grabbing the phone just in time.

'Oh, goodness.'

She lowered her voice.

'Yes, I did fill the form in myself . . . I just didn't expect to hear from you.'

She looked at herself in the mirror, her lined skin reminding her of tissue paper that had been used over and over again. *Is this really happening?* she thought, as she sank into the chair beside the telephone table, gripping her left hand between her knees.

'Yes, yes, I've got time. I've actually got shortbread in the oven as we speak.'

She paused, the enthusiasm of the young lady on the other side of the call putting her at ease.

'Yes, I bake every day, I've done so for as long as I can remember. Cakes are my speciality, but I've made it my aim to get better at bread.'

'I live with my husband, Bernard,' she said, remembering to keep half an ear out in case he walked in. 'Almost sixty years, it's our diamond wedding anniversary this year.

'Yes, he's well fed indeed.'

She laughed, before pausing with a jolt, aware of her volume.

'I've never been good at tests, but I'll give it a go.'

She sat up poker straight, threading a strand of hair between her lips.

'Well, I think that could be one of two things. If you open the oven door before it's ready and let the heat out, or if you add too much bicarb . . . or, I suppose, if you leave the mixture to settle for too long before you put it in the oven.

'I believe it's proved when it doubles in quantity, and gradually springs back when you prod it.'

She gripped the phone between her ear and shoulder, using her hands to twist her hair tightly into a clip, the pain of it a welcome release.

'Genoise is a traditional sponge recipe, but the eggs are beaten with the sugar until they are light and fluffy before the flour is folded in, then some oil or butter added. Joconde ... I'm sorry, my mind has gone completely blank.'

She could feel her cheeks flushing, so she shook the neck of her blouse to create a draft.

'It's ground nuts, almonds! Joconde is made with ground almonds.'

She forced a deep breath as she listened, nibbling the inside of her cheek.

'It's got butter between each layer; the official word has escaped me.'

It felt as if she were searching for items in her baking cupboard, ones which she knew she had but just couldn't lay her hands on.

'Laminated!'

She leant back in the chair, letting out a sigh of relief.

'Croissants have yeast in them, puff pastry doesn't. I suppose because croissants need to rise more than puff pastry.'

The back door slammed shut.

She could hear the poppers of Bernard's coat being ripped apart as he hung it up and exchanged his boots for slippers. The soles clicked against the floor as he walked into the kitchen.

She quickly stood up and rearranged herself, as if she were an actress and had changed roles.

'Darling, I think something's burning?'

She grew aware of the tinge of bitterness crawling down the hall.

'I'm just on the phone, Bernie, I'll be two minutes. Can you get it out?'

'Sorry,' she said in a whisper, 'I've just burnt my shortbread. I probably shouldn't be telling you that . . .'

'Yes, I'm free on Wednesday.'

Excitement ignited in the pit of her stomach, creeping the length of her like a lit fuse. She felt around in her handbag for a shopping list, writing the address down on the back of it.

The oven door slammed shut. She lowered her voice as Bernard passed through the hall and made his way up the stairs.

'It's in the diary. So what do I need to bring with me?'

'You'll send an email . . . brilliant. Yes, the one on the application form. Thank you, goodbye.'

She put the phone back on the hook as if it were as heavy as a stone and leant back against the wall, releasing a deep sigh of relief.

For a moment the future wasn't somewhere that she feared, a place promising only old age and loss, but instead a place of hope and possibility. It became somewhere she wanted to tread.

'Everything okay, darling?' called Bernard from the study, the moment quickly dissipating as it dawned on her that he was just seconds away from receiving an email from *Britain Bakes*.

She sped up the stairs, bursting through the door.

'All fine,' she said, her eyes darting past him towards the screen. 'What are you up to?'

'Rose has emailed asking if we can look after Poppy on Wednesday – she has an inset day at school and they're both at work. I was thinking we could stay the night and take her to see the dinosaurs at the Natural History Museum, perhaps the changing of the guards at Buckingham Palace?'

'Lovely . . .' Her face grew pale as the double booking dawned on her. 'This Wednesday?'

'Indeed,' he said, gathering some pages from the printer and tapping them jovially into a neat pile. 'That's all right, isn't it?'

'Yes, that's great,' she said, rooted to the spot. 'Would you mind if I jumped on the computer, darling? I need to quickly look up a recipe.'

She heard the trill of an incoming email. Her hand squeezed the back of his chair as she watched on helplessly.

He turned to the screen.

'Spam,' he said, opening an email from an energy company and promptly deleting it.

She loosened her grip on the back of his chair, which creaked as he stood up.

Once Bernard had left the room she shut the door of the study, his enthusiasm weighing heavily on her conscience. If she had truly believed this to be a good idea, then wouldn't she have just been honest with him in the first place?

The trill of another email. She clicked it open.

Dear Jenny,

Thank you for applying for *Britain Bakes*. We are delighted to invite you to our London audition on Wednesday 2nd February. Please find directions and timings in the attached document. You will be required to bring with you the following three bakes:

– 12 x identical individual bakes of your choice

– 1 x cake of your choice

– A loaf of bread (made using the attached recipe)

Selected candidates will then be required to participate in the 'Blind Bake Challenge' which will take place in the afternoon. This involves copying a bake, but without a recipe. The details of this will be given to you on the day, should you be successful in the morning audition.

If you have any questions, please don't hesitate to contact us and we look forward to meeting you in person on Wednesday.

She read it again, the words like green shoots. She pressed print before deleting it and folded her secret into her pocket. She wasn't ready to part with it yet.

Bread and Butter Pudding

For the first time in the history of their marriage, Jenny was downstairs before Bernard.

It was 5 a.m. and she felt as if she were trespassing, as if the house did not belong to her before 8 a.m. and this was his territory. She stood in the kitchen in her dressing gown, her reading glasses perched on the end of her nose and the throb of tiredness behind her eyes. This week felt like one long, continuous day and she had left it until the last minute to make a bread loaf for her audition in London.

First things first, she thought, taking a large gulp of tea and switching on the radio, choosing some classical music to soothe her nerves. She had decided to stick to what she knew, and last night had made a Black Forest gateau and twelve identical Lincolnshire sausage and caramelized onion rolls.

She opened the fridge and took out a bowl of dough wearing a floral shower cap. It was something she remembered her mother doing and she quite enjoyed how putting a hat on an inanimate object gave it a personality.

Removing the hat, she inhaled the tang of yeast, satisfied to find her dough had doubled in size overnight. She glanced at the recipe which *Britain Bakes* had sent her. It was sparse and contained a list of ingredients but very little instruction or indication of how this white loaf should look. A bloomer? A baguette? A plaited loaf?

She opened her recipe book and flicked through it in search of inspiration, stopping at one that was so faint it was barely visible, titled 'Wartime Loaf'. It was made with wholemeal flour and treacle, a sobering reminder of a time when white flour was in short supply after the war. She considered the supermarket shelves as they were now, groaning with choice, and wondered what her parents would make of it. To the right was a recipe for potato farls written in block capitals, an indication that it was her father's. It was his ingenious way of turning leftover mashed potato into a delicious bread to be enjoyed for breakfast the next day. There was something dense, bland and comforting about potato bread, and it was as close as she could now get to him on this earth.

She turned the page. Written in pencil was *Queen Elizabeth II – Corination Crown Buns*. Judging by the spelling and the little crowns that had been drawn above the Os, this was one of her grandmother's recipes. Folded between the pages was a faded photograph. Her eyes narrowed as she held it up to the dawn light, her face softening as she realized what it was. It pictured a sea of families, all attending a coronation street party, huddled around a table in their best frocks. She spotted herself as a little girl, nestled behind her father's leg. It was not long after her mother had died and their smiles were hollow, struck through with grief. At the centre of the feast, she spotted her grandmother's bread crown, the inspiration she had been looking for. She might be the full stop to the family tree, but through her these precious family recipes could be taken to the starry heights of national television.

She pressed her fist into the dough, watching it deflate as she stretched and pulled the air out of its soft flesh. Dividing it into five pieces as per her grandmother's sketch, she rolled them into soft, round ovals and arranged them in a circle on the baking tray. She noticed an additional instruction *(CLOSE NEIGHBOURS but not touching),* smiling inside as she duly arranged them. She had to be at her audition by eleven thirty and she still hadn't told Bernard that she couldn't spend the day with him and Poppy.

Several hours passed before her loaf was finished and she studied her creation on the cooling rack. The one in the photograph was shapely and impressive, making hers look flat and underwhelming in comparison. Her heart began to thud so that she could almost see it through her blouse. There wasn't time to make another, but there was no way she could turn up to her audition with this. *What can you do with bread that's no good?* She thought to herself, clicking her fingers as her brain whirred . . . *bread and butter pudding.*

She switched the oven back on so that it lit up like stage lights, lining up cream, currants, eggs and nutmeg along the worktop. Slicing the bread into careless chunks, she buttered it as fast as she could, arranging it in the bottom of a dish. It wasn't what they had asked for, but who on

63

earth didn't enjoy the spongy sweetness of custard-drenched bread with a chewy browned crust?

'Morning, darling,' said Bernard, his nose red from the heat of the shower as he excavated his ears with a towel. 'We better get cracking, we don't want to be late for Pops. Do you think you can be ready in thirty minutes?'

Her stomach sank all the way into her slippers.

'Bernie . . .' she said, her eyes focusing anywhere but on his. 'I've got the most terrible headache.'

'Oh dear,' he said, as his rigorous towel drying ground to a halt. 'Have you taken anything for it?'

'Yes, earlier this morning. Look, I think that perhaps you should go ahead so that we aren't late.'

He dropped his chin, his brow pinched.

'I might feel better for a couple of hours of extra sleep, and then I'll just get the train later and join you?'

He put his hand on her forehead and she was sure he could feel the cogs turning in her mind.

'I don't know if that's a good idea all on your own. It's not the easiest journey; there's a change –'

'I know.'

He blinked in mild surprise.

'Jenny,' he sighed, pausing to find his words. 'I'm not sure getting up early to bake will have helped. I worry you're overdoing it and wearing yourself out . . . you were up late last night making sausage rolls . . . they are delicious, but Poppy is going to have a lovely day regardless –'

'How do you know they're delicious?' she said, suddenly still.

'I was unusually hungry after you'd gone to bed, probably all of the delicious smells as I was drifting off, so I had one as a midnight snack. Anyway, my point is, I just worry you're putting too much pressure on yourself and I don't know that it's good for you, or entirely necessary.'

Her head started to thump. She had made twelve identical sausage rolls, as per the instructions. This was a complete disaster.

'You should've asked.'

He looked at her as if she were a complete stranger.

'I'm sorry, Bernard. I'm going to have to go back to bed. I will meet you at Rose's this evening . . . if I'm feeling better.'

'I should cancel,' he said, shaking his head. 'I don't want to leave you here if you're unwell. It's not right.'

'Absolutely not, it's just a headache. You're right, I'm burning the candle at both ends. I will go back to bed but you must go and see Poppy.'

'Okay,' he said, his tone deflated, 'if you insist.'

She swiftly finished her bread and butter pudding and got back into bed, one eye on the clock as she listened to the orchestra of knocks and thuds as he opened and closed drawers, noticing that he had lost his usual whistle.

Jenny slid down the seat of the taxi as it weaved through the London streets, her eyes searching the crowds for Bernard and Poppy. She glanced at her watch. They would probably be on their way to the Natural History Museum by now. She recrossed her legs, a restlessness thrashing around inside her as if her nerves and her conscience were engaged in a brawl. She just couldn't get comfortable.

As they slowed at a traffic light, an older gentleman sitting alone in the window of a coffee shop caught her eye, his expression vacant and his skin grey. His walking stick was propped against a bar stool and he looked incongruous amongst the exposed lightbulbs and the complicated coffees. Around him people were chatting and laughing, and she ached at the thought of all the things he might have to say and the tragedy that they would remain inside, for lack of a person to share them with. She thought of Bernard, afraid of him ever finding himself alone in the window of a coffee shop.

'Are you just visiting?' said the taxi driver.

For some reason, the plastic screen that divided them felt like a confessional.

'Yes,' she said to the back of his head, hugging her tins in close, 'I'm going to an audition.'

She was so far from home, so anonymous, that the words left her mouth before she had a chance to stop them.

'Are you an actress? Anything I might know?' he said, peering at her in the wing mirror.

'*Britain Bakes*,' she said, looking for his reaction.

His eyes grew bright, meeting hers so that she averted her gaze.

'Congratulations, madam. My wife loves that show. So when am I going to see you on the telly?'

'Oh no, it's very early stages. I probably won't get on it, but the opportunity presented itself and I thought, I'm seventy-seven, why not give it a go?'

'Why not, eh? I'm a firm believer that age is just a number. My wife will be very excited when I tell her.'

He pulled up outside what looked like a college, the streets populated by young, professional-looking people holding takeaway coffee cups as if they were accessories. She imagined the high-flying jobs they might have, the promise of a future radiating from them.

'Here you go, it's just in there,' he said, jumping out of the taxi to open the door for her, as if she'd earned VIP status already. 'Best of luck, madam.'

She stepped out, pulling her various bags over her shoulder. As she followed the signs to reception, she grew aware of her headache which in the interest of karma was now becoming very real.

'Are you here for the audition?' said a girl, glancing towards her clipboard through thick-rimmed glasses, a walkie-talkie attached to her jeans. 'Jennifer Quinn?'

She was taken aback that this complete stranger knew her name, especially when she was nowhere near home.

'Yes, I am. *Britain Bakes*, eleven-thirty?'

'Great, right on time. If you'll follow me,' she said, marching down a path lined with iron railings. 'I'm Carys, by the way, I did your phone interview.'

'Oh, right,' she said, following Carys and wondering if this might be what starting university felt like: a nauseous mix of pride and terror.

'So remind me, where have you come from today, Jenny?'

'A little village called Kittlesham.'

'Copy that.'

'Pardon?'

'Sorry, someone just said something on comms,' she replied, gesturing towards her walkie-talkie. 'How was the journey?'

'Not bad at all, thank you. What do you do, Carys?'

'I'm a producer.'

She nodded, not entirely sure what that entailed, but recognizing it from the credits.

'I was the person that first read your application. Your husband must be so proud; I remember reading he's a big fan of your baking.'

It wasn't until now that she had allowed herself to consider whether Bernard might feel proud should she make it on to the show. She had been more focused on keeping her secret hidden safely away until she knew the outcome.

She followed Carys up an institutional staircase which had a smell unique to places of education, a lingering mixture of a thousand activities: acrylic paint, floor cleaner and wood. As they turned a corner into one of the classrooms, she was met with what appeared to be the most intimidating bake sale ever. In the centre of the room was a large table covered in creations of all shapes and sizes: cakes topped with intricate sugarwork flowers, impressive plaited loaves and the odd reassuring slip-up, including a Swiss roll that had split down the middle.

Around the edge of the room, staring directly at the table, sat a nervous line of bakers making small talk. She tried to match the owners with their bakes, only to be surprised when a burly gentleman, whom she had paired with the plaited loaf, stood up to collect twelve perfect rainbow macarons and made his way into an audition room.

'I've got a confession,' she said to Carys, looking down at her feet. 'My loaf went wrong and so I turned it into a bread and butter pudding at the last moment. And I'm afraid there are only eleven sausage rolls. I made twelve but my husband didn't realize what they were for, and so he ate one as a midnight snack.'

To her great relief, Carys giggled.

'Just explain that in your interview,' she said, glancing down at her phone before quickly putting it back in her pocket. 'Perhaps your husband eating one is a testament to your baking?'

'Perhaps,' said Jenny, not convinced that that would cut it.

Heading towards the centre of the room, she felt acutely aware of how out of place she must look. What was she doing here auditioning for a TV show? She could feel the eyes of strangers watching to see what this old lady had brought to the table.

She peered into her tins one by one, checking on her bakes as if they were babies in a cot. The Lincolnshire sausage rolls were a little shaken but they looked satisfyingly equal, and smells of pastry and sage escaped through the open lid. She arranged them on a plate and placed them on the table. There was definitely a hierarchy of bakes and she felt conscious that perhaps she had gone too simple. They weren't a patch on the immaculate bundt cake next to them which looked almost ornamental, but perhaps a little more refined than the garish blue cupcakes to its right. Nothing edible should ever be blue.

As she opened the second tin, her face fell. The top layer of her Black Forest gateau was slumped against the side and her neat cream rosettes were now smeared in cherry pie filling which had made its way up the sides of the tin, resembling a crime scene.

'Is everything okay?'

She looked up to see a young man with kind chestnut eyes and a boldly patterned shirt, reminding her of the

69

eighties. His ears were like brackets around his face, just like Bernard's, peeping out of his shiny black hair.

'No, not really,' she said, shaking her head. 'This was a Black Forest gateau this morning and now it just looks like . . . a mess. It hasn't survived the train journey.'

She could feel the corners of her mouth pulling downwards.

'I think I should go home,' she said, her shoulders rounded with disappointment, 'I shouldn't even be here.'

'No, I think we can salvage it,' he said, looking into the tin as if he were a doctor giving a second opinion. 'I've got a plastic knife and some napkins in my bag?'

Jenny and the young man with kind eyes spent the next fifteen minutes knelt on the floor of the waiting room, performing what looked like open heart surgery.

'I'm Azeez, by the way,' he said, his eyes fixed on the cake as he tidied the cream with a knife.

'Nice to meet you, Azeez, I'm Jenny. Thank you for this.'

'It's not a problem,' he said, rummaging around in the depths of his pockets, 'it could've happened to any of us.'

He held out his hand to reveal a Flake bar. 'Do you think it might help if you crumble this on top?'

'It's worth a try, if you don't mind,' she replied, proceeding to crush it beneath her fingers, covering up the mess that she had so neatly piped just hours before.

'I think this is the best we're going to do,' she announced, before adding her rescue mission to the table.

'At least you've got a story to tell them in the interview,' said Azeez. 'You work well under pressure!'

'I don't know about that,' she shrugged, 'but you certainly do.'

'What shape did you make your loaf?' he said.

She shook her head, 'To be honest, I sliced it up and buttered it . . .'

Azeez laughed.

'No, really, I did,' she said, her chest tight. 'Bread isn't one of my strengths and it looked terribly dense. I didn't have time to do another so I turned it into a bread and butter pudding.'

Before they had a chance to discuss it any further, her name was called and she collected her bakes. He flashed her a thumbs up as she left.

Walking into the audition room felt as if she'd been summoned to the headmistress's office. Her heart raced as she stood opposite two grave-faced ladies. The one on the left had drawn on her eyebrows so that she looked permanently surprised, contradicting the dour look in her eyes. On her right stood a lady whose hair had been washed through with pink dye, so that it made it hard to look at her without your eyes drifting upwards. They introduced themselves as home economists.

'What have we got here then?' said the lady on the left.

'Before we start, I just want to explain that I had a bit of a disaster on my journey down, and two others before I'd even left the house. I made one of my old faithfuls, a Black Forest gateau, but it turns out that they don't travel well. The top was originally piped cream and cherries,' she said, presenting the cake. 'I tried to revive it on the floor of the waiting room.'

The ladies blinked, giving little away.

'And talk me through what happened here?' said the lady with the pink hair, gesturing towards the pudding dish.

'Well, I appreciate that it's not what you asked for,' she said, clasping her hands together. 'All I can say is that bread is something I'm working on. On this occasion, I didn't feel it was good enough to bring here, so with limited time I turned it into a pudding.'

'Right,' the lady said, scribbling something down on her notepad, 'and where do you think you went wrong?'

'It was too dense, I didn't get enough air into it.' Certain that she had nothing more to lose, she continued, 'To be honest, where it really went wrong is my insatiable sweet tooth. I only truly enjoy baking things that I can taste along the way, and so I don't practise bread nearly enough . . .'

The pink-haired lady pressed her lips together, a look which said that it was not the answer she was hoping for.

'And these sausage rolls, there are only eleven?'

She felt as if she had forgotten her homework, her excuses pathetic.

'Well, there were twelve originally, I promise, but my husband ate one. He didn't realize what it was for . . .'

The ladies nodded silently and took them away for tasting. She watched her bakes disappear like pets being led away by a vet, her control loosening before her eyes. This was the problem with baking, she thought to herself. When you make a meal you can taste it as you cook, but with a cake you can't check whether it's any good until the moment of truth.

After ten uncomfortable minutes, the ladies returned. She searched their faces for any sign of enjoyment, but none was visible. The only reassurance she could glean was from the neat triangular gap in the cake where the first slice had been taken. It must've stood up, she thought. She looked at the sausage rolls and saw to her relief that golden flakes of pastry had splintered on to the plate where one had been cut, a good sign. There was also a large chunk missing from the pudding. Small wins.

'So, talk us through how you made each of these,' said the lady with surprised eyebrows.

She began to relax as her mind returned to the familiar safety of her kitchen. She described the process as if she were driving around roads she knew like the back of her hand, and before long she was engaged in an in-depth discussion about the perils of refrigerated eggs.

'It hardens the fat so I always keep them on the worktop,' she explained, and the home economists nodded in unison. She thought she might even have seen a smile from one of them.

'Thank you, Jenny. If you'd like to go through to the casting director, he's just down the corridor in room six, on the right.'

She followed the signs towards the room which was in a newer part of the building, wringing her palms as she twisted her ring. It smelt like new carpet and coffee, everything a shiny shade of white or grey, the door a huge pane of glass which meant that anyone walking past momentarily peered in.

'Nice to meet you, Jenny. I'm the casting director,' said a man with a Yorkshire accent, a manicured beard and a biro perched behind his ear. 'Thanks for coming today.'

He fiddled with the back of a camera, before standing

73

behind it and observing her. 'We're going to just pop this on, if you don't mind.'

She tucked her hair behind her ears and pulled forward her pearls.

'Does the cake you made today have any particular meaning to you?'

She thought of the recipe book with the cassock-blue cover that she had written long ago.

'Baking is an expression of love, I suppose. Recipes hold a lot of sentiment to me and Black Forest has always been my go-to birthday cake; it's a family favourite . . . If for some reason I can't make a birthday, I make sure my Black Forest gateau can.'

'And how often do you bake, in an average week?'

'Oh, every day. It's part of my routine, that feeling of accomplishment. I'm from a generation that grew up making things, we learnt it from our parents. It used to be cheaper to make than to buy.'

She sat up a little straighter and cleared her throat, aware of the camera.

'You mention family a lot in your application form – are they a big part of your baking?' he asked, glancing at his phone.

'Yes, absolutely. I have a collection of family recipes which were like school books to me; I learnt everything from them. Many of the recipes have outlived the dear people that wrote them, so when I follow the instructions it's a memory as well as a bake.'

He pressed his lips into a smile, placing his phone back on the table.

'And do you have any grandchildren that you bake with?'

She paused, taking a sip of water from a plastic cup which collapsed in her grip.

'No, I don't,' she said, looking at the freckled backs of her hands. 'It's just me and my husband Bernard. We have a great-niece and -nephew, Poppy and Max. I bake with them sometimes, more Poppy now Max is a teenager.'

He moved awkwardly in his chair, recrossing his legs.

'When you're as old as I am, it dawns on you that you have reached a point in life where any day could be your last. As I mentioned, Bernard and I don't have a family of our own, and it recently occurred to me that I might be leaving nothing behind when the day comes. I have never achieved anything of note ... but I do hope to leave behind my recipes.'

She knew immediately from the look of concern on the man's face that she had said too much.

'Sorry, that's not what you asked.'

'No, not at all,' he replied. 'Tell me about your husband, Bernard.'

'I met Bernie at a dance, back when people went to dances. It's our sixtieth wedding anniversary this year, our diamond. He's had a full cake tin all of his life,' she said, her smile extinguished by guilt.

'And what do you think you would bring to *Britain Bakes*?'

'Well, I'm not the most modern baker. I've never made a rainbow cake or a red velvet and I struggle with bread,' she said, realizing that this was the opposite of what he'd asked. 'But I'm well versed in the classics and I'd certainly bring some old family favourites. I also love a challenge, so I will give anything my best shot.'

He took the biro from behind his ear and rolled it between his palms, 'Anything else?'

She hadn't said enough.

'It's sometimes easy to feel left behind at my age, as if the world has a future and you have no place in it . . . but I hope to discover that there is meaning and adventure still to be found.'

There was a long silence as he scribbled something down, and she sat with her words, feeling increasingly uncomfortable with each second that passed.

'Thank you, Jenny,' he said, putting down his pen and jumping to his feet to turn the camera off, '. . . for making the journey, and for the time you've taken to answer our questions, and for your baking.'

She nodded, fumbling for her coat.

'I hope you don't have plans this afternoon, because I would like you to stay for the Blind Bake audition.'

She froze, her arm caught at an awkward angle in her sleeve.

'Really?' she said, aghast.

'Really,' he replied.

'Well, that was intense,' said a young girl as they filed out of the audition, her eyes wide as she blinked into the camera on her phone, her head angled slightly to the right.

'I'm sorry,' said Carys, attempting to intercept her with a wave, 'you're not allowed to –'

'I know, don't worry, I won't post it yet,' she said, her tone defensive. 'I'm just documenting it for later down the line.'

'I'm afraid you're still not allowed to film any of the audition process,' said Carys.

The girl rolled her eyes, pushing her phone back into her pocket.

'What are you documenting?' said Jenny.

'My journey, for my brand.'

Confused, she decided to abandon that line of questioning. 'I'm Jenny, by the way.'

'I'm Sorcha,' she said, twisting her ponytail into what looked like a shiny piece of rope. 'How did you think that went?'

'Better than this morning,' said Jenny. 'I'm not used to digital scales, but luckily I've made many Victoria sponges in my time, so I knew the quantities . . .'

Sorcha tilted her head. 'But how do you measure things?'

'With cast-iron ones,' she said, miming scales with her arms, 'weights on one side, and ingredients on the other.'

'Seriously? How would you manage if you actually got on to the show? I thought only Victorians used those.'

'Yes, well, I'm not sure. I'm certainly in the minority,' she said, exposed as an ancient imposter. 'Enough about me. How did you find it?'

'It's television at the end of the day,' Sorcha said. 'The baking went well, but really it's about the whole package.'

'That's all for today, folks,' said Carys, reappearing with her clipboard and her enthusiasm. 'Don't forget your Tupperware, it's all on the table in the waiting room. If you'd like to follow me, I'm heading there now.'

Relieved to say goodbye to Sorcha, Jenny followed Carys down a corridor, the strip lights contrasting against the dark sky. It was later than she'd realized and Bernard would likely be back at Rose's by now, probably questioning her whereabouts. What if he had called the house phone and she hadn't answered? She had been so focused on the audition that she hadn't thought about that.

'You know only the final thirty-two made it to the afternoon audition, right?' said Carys.

'No, I didn't,' she said, looking down at her tassel loafers which were peeking out of the bottom of her wool coat. She wondered how on earth she had found herself in the final thirty-two of anything at seventy-seven, other than the waiting list for a new hip.

'Carys, you don't happen to have a phone I could borrow, do you? Just so I can let my husband know I've finished.'

'Of course,' said Carys, pulling one out of her pocket.

It had no buttons.

'I'm afraid you will have to dial the number for me.'

She relayed Rose's home phone number to Carys, who typed it in so fast that her fingers barely moved. With each ring she felt increasingly tense, searching for what she might say if he answered. There was no point in telling him the truth, not before she knew the outcome for certain.

It stopped ringing and went to answerphone.

'Hello, it's Jenny . . . I'm just letting you know I'm on my way . . . I will be with you in about an hour . . . I hope you've had a lovely day with Poppy, see you later, bye.'

She returned the phone to Carys who led her out of the building, explaining that she should hear within the next month if she had made it on to the show.

'Thank you,' she replied, but it didn't feel like enough.

'Thank you for letting me have a go, Carys. I never dreamt I'd do what I've done today, and I'll remember it forever.'

Carys put her hand to her heart.

'It's a pleasure. My fingers and toes are crossed for you.'

As she stepped out into the dark London street, an icy chill carried with it a fine flurry of snowflakes which hit her cheeks and melted. She felt as if a part of her had been ignited, a fragile flame of ambition. To want something, she realized, was to make yourself vulnerable to losing it.

9

Omelette

'Thank you, ladies,' said Jenny, as she collected the fresh eggs from the chickens, holding each one for a couple of seconds as she savoured its delicate warmth. After rations had ended, most of the neighbours had given theirs up, but Jenny and her father had found it impossible to part with 'the ladies', as they called them, and their regular gift of fresh eggs. They had become a part of their small family.

Returning to the kitchen, she cracked two into a hot pan, spooning fat over them as they sizzled, a palest pink skin forming over the yolks. She jumped from side to side, imagining the handle into a dance partner whilst humming to Victor Silvester. She had spent the morning typing to his music at college as a way of keeping pace, and it played on a relentless loop in her mind.

She recognized the rhythm of her father's footsteps as he approached the front door and the way he tapped lightly before he opened it, even though it was his house. What he lacked in height he made up for in character, and rooms were always warmer for his presence.

'Just in time,' she said, as she transferred the eggs on to the bread, a trail of fat marking their path.

He hung up his coat, balancing his trilby above it, and took a seat at the kitchen table where a steaming cup of tea was waiting for him.

'Thank you, Jen. Something smells delicious,' he said, rubbing his hands together as a fried egg sandwich appeared in front of him. As he lifted it to his mouth he paused, watching as she skipped back to the stove.

'You're in good spirits,' he said, a tickle of mischief in his voice. 'Not a young man, I hope?'

She looked over her shoulder and shook her head, her eyes playful. 'I've got some good news.'

He took a bite of his sandwich, drops of ochre decorating the plate. 'Go on . . .'

She joined him at the table, knitting her hands tightly together. 'I've been offered a job at Lady Jane's, the clothes shop in town.'

'You're not leaving your secretarial course, are you?' he said, leaning back in his chair. 'I know you're struggling with the shorthand, but you'll get there. Once it clicks you'll never be out of a job, I really th –'

'Don't worry, Daddy,' she said, 'it's a Saturday job.'

'Ahh.' He took a sip of hot tea, 'In that case, well done!'

'What it does mean is that I can afford to get some extra tuition for my shorthand, which should help me get up to one hundred and twenty words per minute. Just think – I'll be able to join a typing pool, become a secretary, have a career of my own!'

She crossed her legs, the top one bouncing with excitement so that she nudged the table, creating ripples in the tea.

'A few of the girls in my class visit a lady once a week; they say it's done them the world of good so I'm going to save up and join them.'

'I think that's a wonderful idea,' he said, mopping the plate with a crust.

'There's a girl that went to our college and she's recently got a job as a secretary to a company director.' She lowered her voice as if telling him a secret, 'I've heard she earns five pounds a week.'

'That's a jolly good wage for a young lady,' he said, kind creases appearing around his eyes. 'So when do you start?'

'This Saturday.'

He glanced at the clock before leaping up and pulling on his coat, draining the last sip of tea.

'I better get back to work,' he said, patting his pockets. 'I'll see you this evening.'

As he reached the door, he paused as if he had forgotten something. 'Jen . . .'

'Yes?'

'I'm very proud of you, you know. And your mother would be, too. Our golden girl.'

Outside the front door of Rose's house, Jenny applied her lipstick in the brass reflection of the door knocker. She took a deep breath to calm her mind, which was replaying her Black Forest gateau rescue mission, the moment when she got through to the afternoon audition, the relief she felt when the Blind Bake was a Victoria sponge. As she knocked, she tried to remember how everyone else's had looked in comparison, but she couldn't quite conjure the image. Relief washed over her as Bernard's outline appeared in the glass.

'Where on earth have you been?' he said, his eyes round, bewildered. 'I was starting to worry.'

'Sorry it's so late, I've been in bed most of the day . . . I've almost slept it off,' she said, her head throbbing in protest as she dropped her tins to the floor. 'Did you get my message?'

'I did, yes,' he said, rubbing the side of his neck with his hand before returning it to his hip, 'a good couple of hours ago.'

'Where are Poppy and Max? Are Rose and Jeremy still at work?' she asked, searching for a distraction.

'They've gone out for supper; I told them to have an evening off whilst we are here. Max is at a friend's, and I'm afraid you've missed Poppy; she's fast asleep in bed.'

He paused, folding his arms with an air of concern. 'Are you sure you're okay?'

'Yes, fine. Just tired.'

He stooped to retrieve her bags from the floor, hanging her coat on the hook.

She scrunched her nose up as she entered the kitchen, hit by a sulphuric cloud. On the hob was a large saucepan and she marched straight over to it, nudging the yellow pool with a spatula. It looked to her like a cross between scrambled eggs and an omelette, dotted with the occasional fleck of eggshell. Somehow, it was both sloppy and charred at the same time.

'Is this your supper?' she asked.

A deep line formed between his eyebrows as he scratched his head.

'Yes,' he said, 'I was trying to make an omelette.'

'Oh, Bernie,' she said as she scraped it into the bin, 'for a start this pan is far too big –'

She stopped herself, sensing that it probably wasn't the time.

Bernard placed her bags on the kitchen table, falling silent as he peered into tins and opened Tupperware.

She was alerted by the snap of a lunch box.

'There's a big piece of bread and butter pudding missing here . . . and the cake? And half a sausage roll?'

Her mind whirred as she dropped some butter into a small pan and watched it slide across the hot surface.

'I got a little peckish on the train,' she said, 'I'd not eaten all day.'

She felt his eyes studying her movements as she cracked the eggs against a bowl, pulling open their shells before beating them together with a touch of pepper. Once the pan was piping hot she poured it in with a hiss, watching it contract and turn opaque, spitting tiny flecks of butter.

'Tell me about your day in London. How is Poppy – did she have fun?'

'It was great, darling, you would have loved it.' He rubbed his eyes underneath his spectacles. 'She was especially interested in the huge dinosaurs, and then to top it all off, one of her milk teeth fell out.'

'Did she manage to keep hold of it?'

'Yes, it's by her bed. She's hoping for a visit from the tooth fairy.'

She grated some cheese and pulled a handful of chives from the pot on the windowsill, cutting them into the omelette so that they fell in bright green splinters. Folding it into a perfect half, she pressed it down with the spatula, cheese oozing into the pan.

When they finally sat down to eat, she watched Bernard in a focused bubble of hunger, each forkful trembling towards his mouth. There was something vulnerable about him tonight, the unsteadiness of his jaw and the droop of his neck. It was as if she had caught a glimpse of him without her.

Before she got into bed, she had just enough energy to do one last thing. She found a pound coin in her purse and polished it with vinegar to make it shiny.

Tiptoeing up the stairs, she gently nudged Poppy's bedroom door open so that it was just wide enough for her to sneak in. It smelt of fresh washing and Olbas oil, perhaps lingering from a winter cold. Every surface was covered in trinkets: bracelets from party bags, hair clips and a varied assortment of teddies, one of which was wedged awkwardly into the kitchen of her doll's house. Through the darkness, she was certain that she had never seen anyone look as peaceful as Poppy did right now; her half-moon eyelids had a lilac sheen and she punctuated her dreams with sighs of contentment.

On her bedside table sat a tiny silver pot. Holding her breath, Jenny lifted the lid and tipped into her palm a small, sharp tooth. It was jagged and uneven with the dot of a brown root at its centre. As she held it in her palm, it struck her that she had never been the tooth fairy before.

She remembered the thrill of a gummy gap and the metallic taste of blood, unique to a milk tooth hanging on by a thread. She thought about how she had never held her own child's little tooth in her hand, or heard their footsteps in the morning as they ran towards her bedroom to show her what they had found under their pillow. It wasn't just the landmark moments of motherhood she had forgone, but the everyday ones too: holding hands on the walk to school, hearing about their day as she bathed them, tucking them into bed at night.

She slid the pound coin under the corner of Poppy's pillow and tiptoed out of the room.

'Sweet dreams, little one,' she whispered, shutting the door behind her.

Toast and Marmalade

Jenny woke up in the guest room at Rose and Jeremy's house. She opened her eyes to the slope of the ceiling, the stripe of the blinds, the smell of their laundry which was different to her own. For a long moment she had no idea where she was, and then yesterday returned to her in vivid waves: the hot lights, the curious cameras, the clang of utensils. If she hadn't been aching from the exertion of it all, she would have wondered if it had even happened.

Poppy's feet thundered down the stairs, followed by the muffled undulations of Bernard's voice as he reacted to her tooth fairy news. Pushing her feet into her slippers and threading her arms through the sleeves of her dressing gown, Jenny headed downstairs to join them.

'Is Aunty Jenny feeling any better this morning?' she heard Rose say, as she approached the kitchen door.

She stopped upon hearing her name.

'I . . . don't know,' said Bernard.

She strained to listen amidst the clatter of crockery, rooted to the spot.

'How do you mean? Is something wrong?'

'Something isn't quite right, Rose,' he said, lowering his voice, '. . . and I've got no idea what it is or how to fix it.'

She was wide awake in an instant, overcome by a prickling awareness that she shouldn't be listening, and an inability to stop.

'What's been going on?'

'Well, it's a lot of tiny things that sound like nonsense, but when you know someone as well as I know Jenny, you just *know* that something isn't right.'

'Like what?'

The fridge door opened and closed and a glass of juice was poured.

'She's often tired, she's never spent so much time on the computer . . . it's as if she's researching something . . . and she's baking as if it's about to go out of fashion, often at the crack of dawn.'

A knife grazed the surface of a piece of toast.

'I know it all sounds trivial, but something's going on. And she never used to get up before me.'

Hunger growled in her stomach and she hugged it tight in an attempt to stifle it.

'But she's always baked a lot, hasn't she?' said Rose in a concerned whisper.

The lid of a jar made a dull pop as it came loose.

'Yes, but this is different. She's always baked for *us* but she's currently making enough to feed a small army, and when I ate one of her sausage rolls the other night, she told me off. It sounds silly but it isn't like her at all, and there were plenty left.'

She felt a twist of guilt. All she needed to do was walk in and they would stop, but curiosity paralysed her.

There was a crunch of toast between teeth.

'And yesterday!' he said, the toast obstructing his words. 'She was in bed with a headache all day. Then, when she called to say that she would be late, it was from a strange number.'

She squeezed her eyes tightly shut. How could she not have thought of that?

'I overheard a phone call recently too . . .'

She strained to listen, taking shallow breaths.

'Who with?' said Rose.

'I don't know who it was with, but she said she's never been good at tests. I could only hear bits. She said other things like *laminated* and something else about her mind going completely blank . . .'

'What does she mean by laminated?'

'Well,' he said, his voice flat with worry, 'when I looked it up, it's a sort of blood clot.'

The colour drained from her face.

'Do you think –'

'Yes,' he paused, 'this is my concern . . .'

'That she's ill?' said Rose.

She bit her lip as her chest grew tight, ensnared in her own lies.

'Oh, Uncle Bernard. But you're such a pair, you share everything, why would she keep that from you?'

'Well, this is just it. We're such a pair that I can only think that she doesn't want to worry me.'

'But would she go to the doctor's without you? It's a

huge thing to keep from someone that you love . . . I just can't imagine her doing that – you do everything together.'

She wanted to disappear, her true self plummeting against their vision of her.

'No, I don't think she would. But then it would explain her spending time on the computer researching symptoms, the strange phone call to the doctor, disappearing for appointments.'

'I suppose,' said Rose, as a teaspoon chimed against the side of a cup, 'but it doesn't explain the baking, or the early mornings.'

'Well, if she can't sleep she might get up and bake. It has always been an outlet for her; perhaps it's a distraction.'

Silence followed.

'I think you need to ask her about it; we're assuming the worst here.'

'I know, you're right. It just feels ridiculous to ask her if she's ill when we know each other better than we know ourselves. It's as if I'm suggesting she's hiding –'

'Aunty Jenny!' said Poppy, appearing behind her.

She jumped, spinning around to face Poppy as the conversation in the kitchen ground to a halt.

'Look,' Poppy said, holding out her palm to reveal a shiny pound coin.

'Is that from the tooth fairy?'

Poppy nodded, admiring it in her hand.

'It's beautiful and shiny – she must've been very pleased with your tooth,' Jenny said, grateful for her company as she walked into the kitchen.

'Good morning.'

'Morning,' replied Rose and Bernard in unison.

'Did you sleep well, darling?' Bernard asked.

'Yes, thank you,' she said, hovering by the kettle.

She watched as Jeremy marched into the room and proceeded to make a very complicated bowl of porridge, involving blueberries and packets of seeds.

'Help yourself to toast and marmalade,' said Rose, her wet hair twisted into a towel on top of her head.

'Thank you. How was your evening? Did you go anywhere nice?'

'It was lovely! We went to the Italian around the corner. It's been so long since we went there, just the two of us,' said Rose, her blue eyes small and blinking without any make-up on.

'I'm glad,' she said, as she dropped a slice of bread into the toaster, conscious that she was being watched. Pressing it down, she caught sight of Bernard pushing crumbs around the plate with his finger, and she wished she had never started keeping a second secret. Living with the first was enough.

'Five times five?' said Bernard, as they walked Poppy to school, their arms swinging as she linked them together.

Her eyes narrowed as she searched for the answer.

'FIFTY-FIVE!'

'Not quite,' he replied, 'let's count it together. Five, ten, fifteen, twenty, twenty . . .'

'FIVE! Twenty-five?'

'Well done,' he said.

Jenny was thankful for the distraction that Poppy was providing, staving off any difficult conversations.

'Four times three?'

'Four, eight, TWELVE!'

'Yes!' he said. She felt him attempt to catch her attention, but her eyes remained glued to the pavement.

As they turned the corner, little red uniforms could be seen approaching from all directions and the chorus of faraway screams grew louder. The school gates were surrounded by crowds of adults waving and fussing, interrupted by a bell which cut through the chaos so that the children ran into several lines like a piece of choreography.

'Bye, darling,' said Bernard, giving Poppy a tight squeeze, 'see you soon.'

'How soon?'

'Very soon,' said Jenny, giving her a kiss.

They watched and waved as she ran towards the line, her rucksack bobbing in time with her hair as her coat flapped behind her like a cape. For a moment, as they watched her disappear into the classroom, it was as if they were living a life that never was.

As they left the school gates, the silence between them grew loud, uncomfortable.

'Darling . . .' he said.

She felt herself withdraw.

'Yes?'

'I don't know quite how to say this,' he said, each word laboured, 'but is there something you're not telling me?'

'How do you mean?' she said, her eyes fixed firmly ahead so as not to be read.

'I know I said you were overdoing it the other day, but what I meant was you just don't seem quite . . . yourself.'

She stayed silent, letting him continue.

'You're not keeping anything from me, are you? Anything about your health?'

'My health?' she said, relieved that this wasn't technically a lie. 'No, darling, I'm fit as a fiddle as far as I know.'

He nodded, although his mouth remained a worried line.

'That's good, then,' he said.

She would tell him soon, she reasoned, but only if she was successful. What was the point in confessing her ridiculous ambition, if it were all to amount to nothing? In the meantime she would be energetic, easing his concerns without saying a word.

Cut and Come Again Cake

She had never meant to fall for Ray. He was much older than her, almost thirty when she was just sixteen, but when she was in his presence something happened; it was chemical, thrilling, all-encompassing. Like bindweed, affections had grown before she even realized she was caught in their grasp.

It was five minutes to five. Her hands grew hot as she counted the day's takings and cross-checked them against the till roll. She was aware of every inch of herself, the position of her feet, her hair, as if she were cashing up on the stage rather than in the back room of Lady Jane's. As the bell above the door chimed, blood rushed to her cheeks.

'Are you still open?'

Her shoulders dropped; it wasn't him. 'Sorry, madam, we're closed. We open again at ten o'clock on Monday morning.'

The door rattled shut. She continued counting the pounds, shillings and pence, a metallic film clinging to her fingers. It was five o'clock, he would usually be here by now.

The bell chimed again. She straightened her posture, looking down so as to appear occupied.

'Hello, dear, is Mrs Smith around?'

She looked up to see the gentleman that owned the cobbler's across the street.

'I'm sorry, she's not. Would you like me to pass on a message? I'm going that way on the way home.'

'It's all right, dear, it can wait until Monday,' he said, her hopes dashed for Saturday evening as it grew rapidly less exciting with each slam of the door.

She placed the last couple of ten-shilling notes on the pile, writing down a total of thirty-five pounds and underlining it twice. They had sold a couple of the shift dresses and the boxy wool jacket in the window; Mrs Smith would be pleased with that. Dropping it all into the bottom of a brown envelope, she folded it over and pushed it into her handbag where she noticed a squashed slice of cut and come again cake wrapped in greaseproof paper, left over from her lunch. Eating it now would create the perfect delay on the off chance that he was late, she thought, as she unwrapped it and sank her teeth through the soft sponge, the plump raisins. It was simple but delicious and she savoured every bite.

Dusting the crumbs from her lap, she switched off the lights. It struck her how different the shop looked in the dark, transforming from a bright and busy space into a lifeless room of rails.

The bell chimed. Her heart lurched.

'Thieving from the till, Jen?'

She turned to see his silhouette in the doorway, a hot wave of excitement rolling the length of her. He was neat with broad shoulders and a thick head of dark hair which, if you looked closely, was greying at the temples.

'Of course not,' she said, searching for a smarter combination of words but losing her entire vocabulary.

'Good day?' he said, closing the door behind him and leaning *against it with the assurance of someone who knew all their best angles.*

'Busy, thank you,' she replied, aware of his body in proximity to hers, as if they were attached by strings.

He moved closer in sauntering steps.

'Poor thing. How about I take you for a drink on the way home?'

As much as she tried to repress it, a flicker of a smile appeared at the corners of her mouth so that she had to pretend to check her handbag.

'I have to drop the takings off at your mother's on the way home, and she'll be wondering where I am.'

'Don't worry about that,' he said, placing his hand on the counter. It was a hand of perfect proportions and she felt herself flush as she imagined it touching her.

'We can drop them off on the way.'

She combed her hair through her fingers, avoiding his gaze. 'What about . . .' she lowered her voice, 'Margaret?'

The corner of his mouth curled upwards to form the sort of smile that you give a child, a handsome dimple appearing in his left cheek.

'Miss Eaton, my wife is not yours to worry about. Besides, she's visiting her parents this weekend.'

My wife. The words tainted her exhilaration with shame. The measure of her happiness had become inextricably linked with his presence, and his visits had grown increasingly frequent. From the first time she met him, his attention was like a searchlight, his eyes following her as she worked. She had grown to crave it so intensely that when she was away from him she felt as if she existed in darkness.

'All right,' she said, reaching for her coat, 'just one drink.'

He held the shoulders as she wriggled her arms into the sleeves, her skin prickling as she felt the closeness of his body and the smell of his aftershave.

'Jen,' he said, his dimple reappearing, 'try not to hold my hand until we get to the pub.'

'Ray, I've never —'

He put his finger to her lips with a smirk, the smell of stale tobacco lingering even after he had removed it. He made her feel so many opposites, so alive and yet so restrained, yearning for his touch and yet painfully shy.

As she locked the door of the shop behind her, they walked towards his mother's house and she imagined what it might feel like to walk next to him legitimately, hand in hand, without trying to appear invisible.

After the audition, life returned to normal. February slipped by in a fog of crisp mornings, dark afternoons and hearty suppers. There were no more surprise calls or undercover auditions and she buried the memories beneath the distractions of everyday life, although they did tend to resurface during her quieter moments. Life returned to normal, almost.

She opened her recipe book in search of something for Valentine's Day tea. Ann and Fred would be here in a couple of hours and she didn't have the ingredients for anything fancy, so she did exactly what her mother would've done: a Cut and Come Again Cake. She leafed through, eventually finding the loose piece of yellowed cardboard upon which it was written, her mother's original quantities amended with her own adjustments.

She sifted together the salt, flour and mixed spice, the cloves tickling at her nostrils. Rubbing in the butter, she looked back to the recipe and noticed that next to *milk* her mother had written *save the top for trifle*. She couldn't help but hear her voice, picturing her straining the cream from the top of the milk. She would then whip it together and pipe it on to the trifle for Sunday tea, never wasting an ounce.

She cracked an egg, holding it high as gravity pulled it into the bowl.

'This makes a basic but moreish fruit cake. It was my mother's go-to if we had guests for tea,' she said, glancing towards the window. 'When butter was scarce, we used to spread it on afterwards rather than using it in the mixture.' Life could take away opportunities, but never your imagination.

Pouring in the dried fruit and peel, she remembered an ingredient that definitely contributed to the 'come again' factor. Glacé cherries. Thank goodness she always had a spare tub of them in her baking cupboard. As she cut each one in half, steeped in syrup, she admired the happy shade of red. There were very few things in life that were better than cutting yourself a slice of cake and realizing that you had won the cherry lottery; that your piece had the most generous allocation. As a little girl she would pluck them out with her fingers and save them until last, leaving large pink craters in the sponge.

She fought her way to the back of the cupboard, where her heart-shaped tin had found itself in the most difficult corner through lack of use. Filling it with the speckled mixture, she pushed it to the edges and sprinkled some brown sugar on top for a little crunch.

'Come and look here, darling,' called Bernard from the garden, as she slid the cake into the oven.

Pulling on her coat, she walked towards him as he stood with his hands on his hips staring at the ground, steam rising from his collar as he caught his breath.

'Just look at those,' he said proudly, pointing towards a patch of green shoots wearing snowdrop bonnets. They multiplied before her eyes.

'Even at eighty-two, it always comes as a wonderful surprise,' he said.

She knew exactly what he meant.

'Spring must be just around the corner,' she said, before clapping her hands together. 'The cake's in the oven and Ann and Fred will be here shortly, you know what they're like.'

'Always early,' he agreed, dusting the dirt from his knees.

'I better go and make myself look presentable,' she said, conscious that she should look her best to counteract any lingering worries he might have.

Jenny peered into the oven to find that her cake had risen so well that the heart shape made it look swollen with love. She grabbed a tea towel and took it out, the chain of her best amber necklace prickling with heat. The doorbell rang. It was an antique doorbell which emitted a shrill, stress inducing *brrr-inggg!* as you twisted it.

'One moment,' she called as she staggered with the cake to the worktop, misjudging its weight.

Brrrr-ringgg!

'Coming!' called Bernard as he bundled down the stairs, one arm in his red wool jumper.

She heard him open the door, followed by Ann's tiny shoes clip-clopping down the hall.

'Afternoon, Jenny,' she said, her blue eyes narrowing. 'You look rather smart.'

Unsure whether it was an observation or a compliment,

Jenny grew conscious of her navy twinset, her matching amber jewellery, her copper eye shadow.

'Thank you,' she said as she put together a tea tray. 'I thought I'd make an effort for Valentine's.'

'What's this?' Ann said, hovering above the cake tin.

'It's a cut and come again cake.'

'How old-fashioned. My mother used to make those. I haven't seen one for years, decades even.'

Jenny's smile pulled taut like a washing line.

'Smells good in here,' said Fred, rubbing his hands together as he returned to his usual position: just behind Ann and a little to the left.

'Fred, you can carry the tray through for Jenny, can't you,' said Ann, in a tone that was definitely not a question. He jumped to attention and did as he was told, the best china chinking together in time with his unsteady hands.

The warm spice of the cake had permeated the living room, which was dappled with early spring sunshine. Bernard put his Frank Sinatra record on and she noticed the collar of his pink gingham shirt underneath his jumper, which she knew he had picked out especially for the occasion.

'Isn't she clever?' he said, admiring the heart-shaped bake whilst she poured the tea.

'Who'd like some?'

'Myself and Fred would, please,' said Ann.

Jenny slid the knife through the telling first slice, imagining herself to be a *Britain Bakes* judge. To her relief it held together in the perfect triangle jewelled with bright cherries, the fruit evenly distributed. There was one slice which had won the cherry lottery. She handed it to Bernard.

'Delicious, this, Jenny,' said Fred, crumbs clinging to his top lip.

Ann gestured towards them with her napkin so that he sent them flying in all directions with the back of his hand.

'So what number Valentine's Day is this for you two?' said Bernard.

Ann looked up to the ceiling as if she hadn't thought that far back in a long time. 'Fifty-three years in March.'

'Congratulations, that's no mean feat.'

'I had a job in the local library. Fred used to come in every weekend without fail to exchange his books ... I thought he must be so well-read, but when I asked him about the books, he didn't have much to say at all.'

Jenny exchanged a passing smile with Bernard. It was funny how all these years later, she could imagine a young Fred with his bag of books and his few words.

'Well, I hadn't read them,' he said, chasing a cherry around his plate with a fork. 'My mother told me there was a nice young lady working at the local library, so I went to see for myself.' He caught the cherry and popped it straight into his mouth. 'And she was right.'

'How many times did you ask me to the pictures, Fred?' said Ann, eyebrows raised. 'Seven,' she answered, before Fred could get his words out. She looked to them for a reaction, her mouth moving as if she were sucking a raisin. 'And here we are, three children and five grandchildren later, and to think they might never have existed if it weren't for Fred pretending to read books.'

Jenny watched as Fred fumbled in his trouser pocket for

his phone. He eventually pulled out a leather case that folded open like a diary, proudly presenting a picture of all five grandchildren huddled on a sofa, a sea of red hair.

'Tom, Isabelle, George, Toby,' he said, pointing at their faces with clumsy fingers, 'and little Ellie on the end there.'

'Wonderful,' said Bernard, 'just look at that hair.'

'That's my mother's red locks, everyone used to call her ginger. It skipped two generations and then, just like that, they've all got it,' said Ann, pushing the phone towards Jenny. 'Tom is just like my father. Brilliant with numbers.'

She studied the photograph of all that Ann and Fred had made. Although they were no older than five or six, it struck her that they were little time capsules of all those who came before them, mirrors of their ancestors who had lived through wars and fallen in love and, by a stroke of luck, survived. That red hair, an aptitude for maths, was in fact an age-old gift from someone that they had never met, but without whom they would not exist.

'That must be so comforting, to look at Tom and see so much of your father,' she said, returning the phone to Fred.

'It is,' said Ann, 'there really is nothing like it. Although there's no time to make Valentine's cakes; it's a full-time granny daycare with five . . .'

Jenny felt her heart drop, exposed as someone who had nothing of greater importance.

'I feel that sometimes with Poppy, my great-niece. I look at her when she's chatting away and I see –' Bernard paused, his throat catching on his words – 'I see my sister.'

She reached out under the table and put her hand on the soft cord of his trousers.

'Would you like another slice?' said Jenny, glancing towards Fred as he pushed his phone back into his pocket.

'Would I, Ann?' he said.

'A sliver,' she replied, taking a sip of tea. 'Where did you both meet?'

'We met at a co-op dance in the swinging sixties,' said Bernard, a smile encompassing his whole face. 'I spotted Jenny from across the room and I knew immediately that I couldn't leave without speaking to her.'

'Had you spotted him, Jenny?' said Ann.

'My friend had but I hadn't – not until he asked me to dance – but thank goodness he did.'

'Was Bernard your first love?'

'Well . . . I think my first love was baking,' she said, igniting polite laughter. 'I think it's your last love that really counts.'

The garden was a whispering darkness as she washed up the pots, struggling with a stubborn tea stain which had lined the spout of the teapot and was impossible to shift. The fruit cake heart looked a little sad, half demolished on the worktop. At least it had been enjoyed, she thought, especially by Fred who had managed to siphon off multiple 'slivers' over the course of the afternoon.

'Darling,' said Bernard from the hallway, his tone wavering, unsure. 'There's an answerphone message for you . . .' his voice trailed off.

She paused before ripping off her rubber gloves and peering around the door.

'I didn't hear it ring,' he said. 'It must've been when we had the music on earlier.'

'Who's it from?' she said, her calm exterior slipping.

'I'm not sure, Andy someone? From a company I've never heard of . . .'

She walked towards the phone as if it were an unexploded firework, expecting that Bernard would leave. Instead he remained by her side, studying her closely. In an attempt to appear unfazed she decided to listen to it, pressing the phone tightly against her ear so that no sound could escape. It was the casting director with the manicured beard, asking for her to call him back.

She returned the phone to the hook.

'Well, who was it?' he said.

As she looked up, it struck her that the contours of his face were steeped in long, worried shadows so that he looked older than he had done even before Christmas. It was cruel to keep this from him any longer.

'I haven't been entirely honest with you, Bernard,' she said, the words leaving her lips before she had formed the sentences in her mind.

His eyes grew round with fear.

'It's nothing to worry about,' she said, taking his hand in hers. It was warm, his skin papery, and she loved it so very much. 'I'm not unwell, but you're going to think I'm completely ridiculous.'

He hung off her every word.

'And there's almost no point in even saying anything now because it might be all over anyway.'

'What is?' he said.

'I . . . I've applied to be on *Britain Bakes*.'

He paused, his face crumpling in confusion.

'*Britain Bakes*? The baking programme? On the telly?'

'Yes.' She blinked through her embarrassment. 'I didn't mention it because I'm ashamed to even want it.'

Silence ensued as he rubbed his forehead.

'When?' he said.

'Well,' she stroked her top lip with the silk of her sleeve, 'I applied just after Christmas and I've been, sort of, doing auditions since, really.'

'Auditions? Where?'

'One was on the phone, and the other in London.'

'London?!'

Now she had started, she couldn't stop.

'I got all the way to the final round,' she said, a shiver of excitement shooting through her, 'so I'm waiting to hear . . . which is what this answerphone message is probably about.'

'Final round?'

She nodded, sobered by the memory of the squashed Black Forest gateau, the missing sausage roll, the bread and butter pudding.

He continued to rub his forehead as if he were massaging the details into his mind. Eventually he looked at her.

'I knew it. I *knew* you weren't yourself,' he said, his mouth pressed into an unreadable line, 'only, I thought you were ill. I was worried about you, Jenny. You *knew* I was.'

His face twitched as one-by-one, pieces of the puzzle clicked into place.

'The masses of baking . . . missing our day with Poppy . . . telling me off for eating that sausage roll . . .' He looked wounded. 'That was all, lies?'

'Well,' she said, tilting her head as she chose her words, 'white lies . . .'

'White lies?' There was a crackle of agitation in his voice as hurt flashed across his eyes. 'I don't understand why you couldn't just tell me – I mean, we share everything.'

Guilt cut through the centre of her like a sharp knife.

'I know,' she said, 'I am so sorry.'

They stood in uncomfortable silence, feeling for a moment like the strangers they once were, long ago. She searched for something to say to make it better, but he was right. There was no excusing what she had done.

'Come here,' he said, engulfing her in a hug which felt rather like embracing a climbing frame.

'I'm a terrible person,' she said into his jumper.

'You're not,' he said, her body softening in his arms, 'but we mustn't keep things from each other, Jenny. We're all we've got.'

A salty tear made its way down her cheek as she listened to the thud of his heart. He didn't know the half of it, she thought.

He drew back to look at her, a crack of light returning to his eyes.

'I suppose you ought to call them back?'

'Oh, I don't know,' she said with a shrug. 'It's a bit late on a Friday night, they'll all have gone home now.'

'They might not. At least give them a try?'

She took a deep breath and picked up the handset, her heart racing as she listened to the message again, dialling to return the call.

It started to ring.

Bernard leant in, reading her face.

She was poised, ready to introduce herself at any moment, only to be greeted by the robotic tones of an answering machine.

'Hello, it's Jennifer Quinn . . .'

Bernard's eyes lit up.

'. . . just returning your call, haveagoodweekendbye.'

She slammed down the phone.

'Answerphone?'

She nodded.

'Go on then,' he said, as they returned to the kitchen, 'I want to hear all about it . . .'

'Well,' she replied, pulling her rubber gloves back on, 'I'm not sure where to start.'

12

Baked Alaska

Her hands stroked the velvet of the seat as the lights went up for the interval. It was like waking from a dream, a dream where she had been admiring Holly Golightly's beauty and gazing into Paul Varjak's eyes.

'Wow,' she whispered to Sandra, who was sitting to her right with her mouth slightly ajar, 'I think this might be the best thing I've ever seen . . .'

She had met Sandra on her first day at technical college after they had found themselves wearing the other's fur collar coat by accident. Given that Sandra was significantly taller than Jenny, the mix-up was immediately obvious. Sandra had marched towards her wearing a particularly tight one, whilst Jenny stared down at herself in a state of bemusement. Being the eldest of five, Sandra was never backwards in coming forwards and her home life was the opposite of Jenny's: a loving chaos of shared bedrooms, sibling politics and busy mealtimes. She envied the hustle and bustle of it, almost as much as Sandra envied the solitude of hers.

'You say that every time we go to the pictures,' Sandra laughed, 'but I must say I do agree. She's so stylish . . .'

Their eyes snapped to the spotlight at the very same moment, as if they had seen an angel. It was in fact a lady wearing a tray of ice creams.

'Fancy one?' she said, her taste buds squeezing at the thought.

'Absolutely,' said Sandra, counting out six pence from her purse.

Jenny weaved her way to the aisle, quick on her feet so that she didn't find herself short of time and going without. The ice cream was of equal importance to the film.

'What can I get you?' said the lady.

'Two vanilla cups, please,' she said, handing over the warm pennies from the palm of her hand.

She returned to Sandra and wasted no time in removing the paper lid and sinking her tiny wooden spoon into the creamy coldness, cherishing every mouthful.

'It tastes the best in the pictures, doesn't it?' she said, chiselling her way around the edge where it was melting in the heat of her hand.

Sandra made a hum of agreement, licking her lips.

'How's Lady Jane's?' she said, breaking for a moment as she twirled the spoon between her fingers.

'I really like it,' said Jenny, 'and I've nearly got enough saved for my shorthand lessons, which is a relief.'

'Once your teacher's taught you, please can you teach me?'

'I'll try, but I think it will take me a while to get the hang of it,' she said, the spoon hanging from her lips as she sucked it. 'Just think, once we're secretaries we can afford to go to the pictures every weekend.'

'And don't forget the dances!' said Sandra, now scraping the tub. 'It would be nice to find a boy to get me out of the madhouse . . .'

There must have been something about the way Jenny smiled that Sandra immediately noticed.

'What?' she said, her attention diverted from her ice cream as she lowered the tub to her lap. 'Have you met someone?'

Jenny looked at the curtain, her cheeks flushing.

'You have,' said Sandra, 'you're bright pink!'

'Shhh!' Jenny looked around, leaning closer. 'There's someone at work, but —'

'A boy? At Lady Jane's?'

'Well, he's the owner's son. He pops by sometimes when I'm working . . .'

Sandra repositioned herself in her seat as if Jenny were now the screen.

'Why have you not mentioned this before? What does he look like?'

'Well, he's very handsome,' she said, her stomach fluttering at the thought. 'He's a little older . . . and he has the most lovely dimple on his left cheek.'

Sandra blinked, her eyes hungry for details.

'So are you courting? And how old is older?'

'Nearly thirty, I think,' she said, spooning the last liquid dregs into her mouth. 'I don't know, it's complicated.'

'Thirty!' She was struggling to remain subtle. 'Why is it complicated?'

Jenny glanced around, gesturing for Sandra to lean closer. 'He's . . . he's married.'

Sandra gasped.

'Jenny,' she said, her eyes flaring, 'have you kissed?'

'I didn't know at first,' she said, a rush of heat flooding her face so that she was grateful when the lights dimmed, the quiet chatter dulling to silence.

'You have,' Sandra hissed, pinching her thigh, 'I can tell.'

Jenny shook her head, looking back to the screen. As the curtains opened and it burst into life, she could sense Sandra's eyes on her but she stared stubbornly forwards, a sickly knot tightening in the pit of her stomach.

*

No matter how hard she tried, Jenny could not sleep. She clicked open her emails, the sharp throb behind her eyes reminding her that she should be in bed at 4 a.m. and not wide awake. There was one from Rose with a picture of Poppy holding a certificate that she had won for her hard work in art lessons. Below it was a newsletter from the tennis and bowls club and below that was an advertisement for half-price men's trousers. Nothing from *Britain Bakes*. She headed back downstairs, carefully avoiding the creaky floorboards that were hiding beneath the carpet.

As she opened the kitchen door, closing it gently behind her, she inhaled the warm drift of the sponge which was resting on the cooling rack. Lightly placing the back of her hand on it, she decided it was cool enough for the next stage of her insomnia-fuelled baking mission, the goal of which was to make Bernard one of his all-time favourite desserts: Baked Alaska.

She looked back to the recipe, following her note to add a few tablespoons of orange juice to the top of the sponge. She found that it could be too plainly sweet without it. Once the orange juice had soaked in, she covered it with tinned mandarins which slipped between her fingers like goldfish.

The meringue crown was going to be the biggest challenge in the dead of night, she thought to herself, as she plugged the gap under the door with a hand towel so as not to disturb Bernard. Holding her breath, she drilled the hand whisk into the puddle of egg white, which miraculously transformed into a snowy light foam. Gradually adding the sugar, a pinch of salt and the cream of tartar, she watched them spin together, Bernard's words replaying in her mind: *We mustn't keep things from each other, Jenny. We're all we've got.*

She knew that the 11th January had been a sign, but she hadn't expected it to make the past so present in her mind. Not after all these years.

She took the vanilla ice cream from the freezer, the coldness gluing her fingertips to the tub. Once she had filled the sponge with custard-yellow globes, she covered it with clouds of glossy meringue, noticing that she had written, _must_ _be thoroughly covered with no gaps, or else the ice cream will melt_ _in the oven_, accompanied by a worried-looking face. This, she recalled, was based on a previous mistake at a dinner party. She remembered cutting the first slice, ice cream flooding the plate. Baked Alaska was a science experiment.

After intricate spatula-based sculpting, she stepped back to admire her work: the sea anemone of the baking world. It would have to live until lunchtime in the freezer, when she would surprise Bernard with it.

'Morning, darling,' said Bernard, placing a steaming cup on the side table next to her, 'have you been here all night?'

'Morning,' she said, her confusion dissipating as she realized where she was. 'I couldn't sleep so I came down here to do some baking in the night. I must've nodded off on the sofa.'

Her eyes prickled as he pulled back the curtains and light poured in through the windows.

'I thought the kitchen smelt delicious. It wasn't my snoring, was it?'

'Well, you were snoring, but no more than usual.'

As she stood up, she felt as if she were wearing a chain vest rather than a floral nightie. She knew what this feeling was, as much as it pained her to admit it.

'Bernard,' she said, taking a sip of tea, 'I feel old.'

He turned to her and grinned.

'How old?'

She paused for a second, her joints groaning as she stretched.

'Ninety-nine.'

'Oh, that's no age. Only double figures?'

'How old is old, then?' she said, looking at him as if it were a cross-examination.

He thought about this for a moment.

'I think you can be old at twenty-five, if you're that way inclined. You have a very healthy appetite for life, darling.'

'Do I?' she said, her neck fused in the position she had slept in.

'Well, you've spent the last two months auditioning for a television show. It's hardly knitting in your slippers, is it?'

A twitch of a smile flickered across her face.

'What you need to remember, Bernard Quinn, is that what some people call "a healthy appetite for life", others call "losing the plot",' she said, and they laughed. They laughed so much that she developed a stitch in her right-hand side which prevented her from standing up straight, making them laugh even more.

'Bernard,' she said, catching her breath, sobered by a sad thought. 'Do you ever think about if one of us . . .'

'One of us, what?'

'If one of us was, well, left on their own.'

Bernard looked out of the window, pushing his hands into his dressing gown pockets. 'I suppose I have done before, yes.'

'And?'

'It's very sad, but there is little point in dwelling on the things we can do nothing about,' he said, his lips forming a heavy smile. 'Besides, it's a price I'm willing to pay.'

'How do you mean?'

'Well, I know that you can't have one without the other,' he said, 'and we'll only be grieving for something which has been our greatest joy.'

She could feel her throat tighten as she stood up, wrapping her arms around his waist and burying her face into the fusty fleece of his dressing gown. She held on to him, listening to the creaks and groans of his stomach and the beat of his heart.

'I think you should go and run yourself a bath,' he said, gathering himself with a sigh. 'That always makes you feel better.'

She headed upstairs and did just that, hot water gushing from the tap as she added a glug of bubble bath. Clouds of steam rose from the surface and clung to the bathroom mirror as she pulled her nightie over her head and folded it on to the bathroom chair.

She looked down at her body, stroking her arms so that they gathered to form wrinkles, reminding her of custard skin. Everything had grown victim to gravity, her breasts resembling pockets hanging heavy from her frame, marbled with the green of her veins and speckled with the memories of summer holidays. In growing older, she had learnt to appreciate her body, judging it with a kinder set of eyes. It had worked beautifully for her for seventy-seven years and for that she was very grateful.

She tucked her hair into her bath hat and lowered herself inch by inch into the hot water until she was fully submerged, the bubbles tickling the underside of her chin. Bernard's toiletries were lined up by the sink, his old razor and brush both an extension of him. Every morning like clockwork, after he had read his paper in bed, she would hear him in the bathroom, tapping his razor three times on the side of the sink before swilling it in the basin. This would happen at short intervals before she heard the squeal of the shower as it burst into life. For as long as she had known him, he had been a man of routine. Life without him would feel as if the clocks had stopped.

'Darling!' he called from the bottom of the stairs. 'There's someone on the phone for you.'

Pulling herself up, she stepped out of the bath, wrapped herself in a towel and headed towards the bedroom, a trail of drips marking her path.

'Hello, Jenny speaking.' she said, noticing that Bernard was still listening on the other end.

'Hello, Jenny, it's Andy, from *Britain Bakes*.'

'Oh, hello, Andy. Sorry I missed your call yesterday – we had guests over and I didn't hear the phone.'

'Not to worry and sorry to call you on a Saturday. I know it's taken a while for us to get back to you. I just wanted to say thank you for coming to the audition . . .'

Her heart was in her mouth as she watched the droplets of water run down her skin and congregate in the creases.

'Not a problem.'

'We were impressed with everything you baked, particularly your maverick attempt at a bread loaf.'

She held on to the wall to steady herself, the cogs turning in her mind.

'. . . your bread and butter pudding,' he added.

'Oh! Well, I like to be resourceful,' she said. 'I thought that was me gone, if I'm honest.'

She thought she heard a noise on the other line, but she couldn't be sure.

'Well, I'm delighted to tell you that it didn't stop you from impressing the team, and you've made it into the final eight.'

She clutched her bath towel which was now somewhere below her armpits, unable to compute the numbers, the word *delighted* ringing in her head.

'Final eight?'

'Yes, congratulations. You're a contestant on this year's *Britain Bakes* – providing you'd like to be, of course.'

She heard the click of the receiver, followed by a thunder of footsteps as Bernard raced up the stairs faster than she'd ever heard in all her years of knowing him.

'Are you . . . sure?'

Andy laughed.

'Of course we're sure, you were brilliant. We're really excited to welcome you into the *Britain Bakes* family. Carys is absolutely thrilled – she has been rooting for you since she first read your application form.'

'God bless her,' she said, as Bernard appeared beside her signalling a frantic thumbs up.

'Sorry if I'm quiet, I absolutely can't believe you've chosen me . . .' she said, feeling exposed in her bath hat as she tightened her grip on the towel, her skin dotted with hundreds of tiny goosebumps, '. . . thank you.'

'It's well deserved. Thousands applied, so you've done incredibly well. I will leave you to enjoy your weekend and the team will be in touch on Monday with the filming schedule and all the details, but I just wanted to let you know the good news.'

'Thank you . . . so very much.'

'One thing, don't mention it to anyone. Your name will be announced in the press after filming has finished, but before then it has to be top secret. I will send you another NDA to sign, but in the meantime, anyone that doesn't absolutely need to know, shouldn't know.'

'NDA?'

'Non-disclosure agreement.'

'Ah, not a problem,' she said. 'Other than Bernard I've not told a soul.'

'Lovely, enjoy your weekend, Jenny.'

'You too, goodbye.'

She hung up and Bernard grabbed her shoulders, before scooping her into his arms. She was completely stunned as her tired mind tried to process the last sixty seconds.

'Jenny, you've done it!' said Bernard, squeezing her so hard that she thought she might burst. 'You've bloody done it!'

She opened her mouth but no words came, only tears.

13

Gingerbread All Saints Church

There had been several occasions in the last few months where Jenny found herself next to a sink piled high with baking utensils, red-faced and on the brink of dropping out of the competition. Today, however, wasn't one of them. She had just executed a successful recipe for biscuit week and the house was filled with the fug of warm spice.

She heard Bernard's key in the lock, followed by the rustle of shopping bags as he arrived home from yet another trip to the supermarket. Recently he was almost permanently stationed there, dutifully scouring the shelves for her latest culinary requests.

'I think I've got everything,' he said, his breathing heavy as he dropped the shopping bags to the floor, sliding his house keys on to the worktop. 'What time are *Britain Bakes* arriving again?'

'Any minute now,' she said, watching him closely as she waited for him to notice.

He began to unpack the bags item by item – eggs, sugar, buttermilk – when it caught his eye. On the table stood what looked like an architectural model of a church, constructed out of deep amber biscuit, the details drawn in fine white icing, complete with stained-glass windows made from colourful marbled sugar.

'All Saints . . .' he said.

She clapped her hands together, 'You recognize it!'

'Of course I do. It's incredible.'

He moved closer to study it, pointing to a tall character standing at the church door.

'Is this supposed to be me?' he said, his mouth curling with mischief. 'I thought I had far more delicate features?'

'Oh, Bernard!'

The doorbell rang. She smoothed her blouse and tidied her hair.

'How do I look?' she said, her eyes bright, anxious.

'Gorgeous.'

They both went to the front door, where they could see the shadow of several figures through the glass.

'This looks like them,' she said, collecting herself before opening the door.

'Hello,' said Carys, her hair tied into a sprout on top of her head, reminding Jenny of a burst pipe.

'Hello, Carys,' she said, giving her a tight squeeze. 'Welcome to Kittlesham. This is my husband, Bernard.'

Bernard looked a little stunned, and it dawned on her that it must be strange to see her being so familiar with someone he had never met. Their adulthood had mostly been a shared experience, so much so that if one of them had forgotten a name or a place from the past, the other would be there to fill in the gaps. This was a reminder of something she had done alone.

He held out his hand.

'Hello, Bernard, I've heard a lot about you,' said Carys, returning his handshake.

'Good things, I hope? Do come in, let me take your coat.'

Behind Carys was a stream of people carrying heavy-looking flight cases, each giving a polite 'Hello Jenny, hello Bernard' and a nod as they walked past. They proceeded to open the cases, pulling out black poles which extended to form tripods three times their original size, clipping on what looked like floodlights. It was as if the circus had come to town and set up in their kitchen.

'So, the plan for today,' said Carys, summoning them both close, 'is to film the bit of the show where you will be first introduced. It's sort of a "slice of life", so the voice-over will say something like "Jenny lives in Kittlesham with her husband, Bernard" and we will see a little clip of you in situ.' She pushed her glasses up her nose and tilted her head, 'Does that make sense?'

'Perfect sense.'

She glanced towards Bernard whose eyebrows had knitted together in concentration, relaxing briefly as they shared a flicker of excitement.

'I'm beginning to wish I'd got the kitchen done – never did I think it'd be on television,' said Jenny, glancing apologetically towards the tired cupboards.

'Well, I'm glad you didn't,' said Carys. 'It's just . . . so you. And I love the daffodils.'

Bernard's face lit up.

'From the garden,' he said.

Carys turned towards a gentleman wearing a pair of headphones and a bag full of buttons and lights.

'Can we get them both miked, please?' she said.

'Hello, I'm Graham,' said the man, attaching a tiny clip to Bernard's collar. 'If you could just thread this down your shirt and then I will clip it to your trouser pocket, underneath your jumper.'

'Anti-shine?' said Carys, looking at Bernard as if it were a question he was usually asked.

A look of panic flashed across his face, as Carys reached up and dusted the top of his head with her brush, snapping the powder shut. Jenny repressed an urge to giggle. There was a first time for everything.

'We'll start with you, I think, Jenny. If you'd like to pick a recipe book off the shelf there and flick through it. Then if you just start measuring out some flour and sugar in your beautiful scales . . .'

'Does it matter which recipe?'

'No, not at all, anything will do. You don't have to actually make it.'

Looking around, she wasn't sure that there had ever been so many people in their house. Bernard looked like a stranger in his own home as he stood on the periphery, taking it all in.

'Shall I go?' she said.

'Yes, when you're ready,' said Carys. 'Just ignore us.'

The room fell silent. She reached up, plucked her recipe book from the shelf and flicked through the pages, aware of the lights, cameras and strangers that surrounded her. She had baked in her little kitchen a thousand times before but suddenly the intimate felt public, as if a magnifying glass were hovering above her every move.

'Great, keep going, we're just going to get a shot of you from the garden,' said Carys.

A man carrying a camera headed out of the back door and she noticed Bernard wince as he positioned one of his big black boots in the flower bed.

'This is great, thank you. If you could just look out of the window for me . . . keep stirring . . .'

The man outside did a thumbs up and Bernard looked visibly relieved as he returned his boot to the lawn.

'Perfect. Now let's repo to the living room,' Carys said to the crew. 'Bernard, it would be great to have you reading the paper when Jenny walks in with one of her bakes. Have you got anything, Jenny?'

'I've got a curd tart, some lavender shortbread and a couple of fondant fancies in my tins?'

'Let's go with a mixture of the three and a pot of tea,' said Carys, whilst the crew deconstructed the circus and rebuilt it in the living room.

'Bernard, if you could just sit down as if you're going about your day, maybe reading the newspaper, then when Jenny comes in just react as you normally would.'

'Understood,' he said, lowering himself into his armchair, exposed under the bright light that had been positioned above his head so that it highlighted every freckle of his eighty-two years. The room hushed. He picked up his paper and unfolded it in an unnatural manner.

'Sorry,' said Carys, swapping his newspaper for another one. 'We've actually only got clearance for the *Kittlesham Herald* so you'll have to read that, if that's okay?'

'Not a problem, dear,' he said.

'And in three, two, one . . .'

Jenny emerged slowly from the kitchen holding a plate of treats and their best Royal Albert tea service, which was rattling so intensely that it was ringing. He raised his eyebrows in feigned surprise and put down his paper.

'Deeeee-licious,' he said, slapping his hands on his knees and beaming.

She noticed Carys glance in the direction of the man in charge of the microphones, who shook his head.

'Right, let's try that again,' she said, so that the crew started chatting. 'I think Jenny, if we have the tea already on the table then it might be better for sound if you just walk in with the cakes.'

Jenny nodded, setting the tray aside to reapply her lipstick.

'. . . and Bernard, I don't actually think you need to say anything. Just try and act natural.'

'Okay, dear,' he said, picking his newspaper back up.

'And again in three, two, one . . .'

She came around the corner with the plate of treats. In trying to be silently expressive, Bernard lowered his paper to reveal his face, which was making a shape she had never seen it make before.

'Are you all right?' she said, slightly alarmed.

'Right, let's try something else,' said Carys. 'Just a second.'

A hushed conversation ensued between Carys and the serious man watching on the screen.

'I thought you were having a stroke for a second,' Jenny whispered in Bernard's ear.

He dropped his head and his shoulders began to shake

as he tried to harness the peal of laughter which erupted from him and infected the crew.

'Sorry,' he said, wiping a tear. 'It's a good job it's you going on television and not me. I think I've murdered my role as a hungry husband.'

'So,' said Carys, glancing at the clock, 'I think to make this feel more natural, we should have you both doing a crossword puzzle together on the sofa. Then, Jenny, if you pour the tea for you both, and Bernard, if you reach forward and take one of the cakes.'

They both nodded. Bernard folded the newspaper around the crossword page, which was incidentally his favourite, and the man with the camera knelt down on the rug in front of them, a trail of mud from his boots on the carpet.

'Okay, go for it.'

She picked up the teapot and steadily poured the tea, creating tiny bubbles which clung to the sides of the cup. Bernard took this as his cue to reach for a shortbread.

'Much better,' said Carys, 'now just carry on as if we aren't here.'

Bernard took a sip of tea, dipping his shortbread for three seconds before taking a bite – the optimum amount of time before there was a biscuit casualty.

'Here's one for you, darling,' he said. 'Five across, six letters. A Lancashire cake.'

'Eccles.'

'Well done,' he said, as they continued to answer questions, painfully aware of their audience.

After what felt like the longest ten minutes of their lives, Carys jumped up.

'Great. That's a wrap!' she said, as the crew broke into conversation and began folding the circus back into flight cases.

'Sorry,' said Bernard, 'I don't think I was the best at that.'

'Not at all, it's difficult getting used to being on camera,' said Carys. 'Are your recipes almost ready for submission, Jenny?'

'They're nearly there,' she said, a lilt of excitement in her voice.

She looked at Bernard, missing him even though he was standing right next to her.

'She's going to be brilliant,' he said, winking at Carys who returned a smile.

'You'll miss her, I bet?'

'Terribly,' he said, 'but she's spent sixty years looking after me, it's about time she did something for herself. Heaven knows, I might even learn to cook!'

'Thank you, Carys, for everything,' said Jenny.

'Not a problem, you make things very easy for me. I'll be in touch tomorrow about the next couple of weeks,' she said as she zipped up her jacket. 'Actually, you might want to start thinking about setting up some social media, with some of your baking on it.'

It was as if Carys had just suggested she participate in a space mission.

'Is that this tweeting business?' said Bernard.

'Yes, Twitter, Facebook, Instagram. I mean, it's not mandatory but it's a good way of making the most of the opportunity. Some of the previous contestants have even got publishing deals.'

'Goodness,' she said, the recipe book that she wrote sixty years ago flashing through her mind. 'I'm not sure they'll be very interested in me.'

'You'd be surprised.'

The van outside rumbled into life.

'Right, I better head off. Thank you for today and I'll see you very soon,' Carys said, embracing her as if she were her own grandmother.

They stood in the doorway waving goodbye, watching the circus grow smaller and smaller until it disappeared. Bernard put his arm around her shoulders and pulled her close. She had always fitted perfectly by his side.

'It's all very exciting, isn't it?'

She shook her head, staring out across the street.

'It just doesn't feel real . . . It's as if I've borrowed someone else's life; it's all a big mix-up and they've got the wrong Jenny.'

He squeezed her.

'They've got exactly the right Jenny.'

14

Lime and Mascarpone Cheesecake

'Poppy, would you like to help me decorate the cheese-cake?'

'Yes, please,' she replied, wriggling with excitement. She had grown since they last saw her, her features more prominent. Her missing milk tooth, which she had exchanged for a shiny pound coin just a few months ago, had been replaced by a white tombstone which took centre stage when she smiled.

'So this is what we're aiming for,' Jenny said, showing her a picture of an eighties cheesecake recipe, displaying an extravagant crown of frosted grapes and chocolate leaves.

'Are they real?'

'They're chocolate, but we make them from real leaves, yes.'

Poppy screwed up her nose in confusion.

'You'll see, come with me,' Jenny said, heading out to the garden.

Rose, Bernard and Jeremy were wrapped up in the spring sunshine, chatting over a pot of tea whilst Max sat on the periphery, looking at the phone in his lap. She could feel the presence of her secret as if it were a person, waiting to be acknowledged.

'So we need to pick about twenty rose leaves. Try to avoid the ones that the creatures have nibbled.'

'Like this?' said Poppy, holding up a leaf covered in little brown holes.

'Exactly, we don't want those ones.'

She watched as Poppy's little hands navigated the branches.

'Mind the thorns,' she said, pulling back a leaf to show her one, 'they're as sharp as needles.'

She returned to the kitchen to melt some dark chocolate, watching Poppy through the window as she inspected each leaf with deep consideration. Her company was the most welcome distraction, keeping Jenny mostly in the present moment and away from the fear of the upcoming weeks.

'Done it,' Poppy said, appearing by her side with two handfuls of leaves.

Jenny fetched her a stool, looping an apron over her head and pleating it over and over at the waist to stop it from trailing on the floor. As she tied a double bow in the small of her back, she felt as if she were looking at herself, yet somehow she had become the grandmother figure that was tying the apron.

They rinsed the leaves carefully under the cold tap, patting each one dry with a tea towel.

'So, what we need to do is cover the back of this leaf with the melted chocolate. Do you know why we use the back?'

Poppy shook her head.

'Because later we are going to peel these leaves off, and the back has a more prominent pattern on it than the front.'

She had lost Poppy's attention to the shiny bowl of chocolate.

'Sweep them through the chocolate like this,' she said, demonstrating the movement as if she were painting nails, before laying the leaf chocolate-side-up on the grease-proof paper, 'so they're completely covered.'

Jenny watched as Poppy picked up the biggest leaf and pulled it through the chocolate so that it left a five-second trail, her fingertips white as she pinched the stem.

'Like this, Aunty Jenny?'

'That's perfect.'

She put the tray of leaves in the fridge before cracking two egg whites, juggling the orange yolks between their shells.

'We need to dip each grape into the egg white,' she said, demonstrating, 'give it a shake, and then roll it in the sugar.'

'Like glue and glitter?'

'Like glue and glitter,' she smiled, as Poppy picked up the first grape and dipped it into the glue, reminding her of a time not so long ago, before the pressure of baking a masterpiece.

'Darling, are you joining us?' called Bernard.

She took a deep breath, pretending not to hear. She knew exactly why she was being summoned. Sharing the secret would make it feel terrifyingly real, the pressure multiplying with each person that knew.

'Darling?'

'I think Uncle Bernie's calling you,' said Poppy.

'Thank you, Pops,' she said, her stomach fluttering. 'Will you be all right doing these if I go outside?'

Poppy nodded, rolling a grape through the sugar and placing it carefully on the plate.

As she approached the table her vision grew faint like a photograph bleached by the sun.

Bernard looked towards her, clasping his hands. 'We have a bit of exciting news.'

An expectant silence fell over the table. If she had been much younger, people might have looked at her middle. Max put down his phone whilst Rose and Jeremy sat up a little straighter.

'It's Jenny's news,' he said, radiating pride. 'You tell it, darling.'

'Well,' she said to the teapot, 'I'm going to be a contestant on *Britain Bakes*.'

The table stared back at her as if she'd had a dramatic new haircut.

Max broke the silence first, 'The TV show?' he said.

'Yes,' she nodded, 'in a strange turn of events, they've offered me a place.'

'Jenny!' said Rose, leaping up and throwing her arms around her, 'Congratulations! When does it start? How long have you known? I've got so many questions . . .'

'I applied just after Christmas. Nobody knew, it was a silly sort of a . . . secret.'

'You know when I thought she wasn't well?' said Bernard, shaking his head in disbelief. 'That's because she was auditioning and I'd got completely the wrong end of the stick.'

Rose nodded slowly, as everything started to make sense.

'How on earth did you keep it from Uncle Bernie?'

'Well, I didn't expect it to come to anything.' She swallowed. 'I suppose I was a bit embarrassed, being seventy-seven. There's also a sort of pressure that comes with it, isn't there, if other people know?'

She could feel all eyes on her.

'I know what you mean,' said Jeremy. 'I didn't tell anyone the day of my driving test.'

'Yeah, and sometimes I just don't mention it when I've got an exam at school,' said Max, so that Rose looked concerned for a second, before choosing to let it go.

'I *knew* your Christmas baking was a little more complicated this year,' she said. 'I knew it!'

'So when does it start? Will you have to go away for filming?' said Jeremy, always keen to know the practicalities.

'It starts, well, next week. I'll be in a hotel a couple of days a week, and then I'll be at home practising in between.'

'I think this might be the most exciting thing that's *ever* happened,' laughed Rose. 'Can you believe it, Uncle Bernie?'

Max nodded in agreement, grinning to reveal the shiny metal of a brace.

'I'm not surprised that she got on to the show, but I do think I will be pinching myself when I actually see her on the telly.'

'This is mad,' said Max, as he tapped his foot, 'Aunty Jenny's going to be famous.'

'No, I'm not,' she said, 'no one will be fussing over me. I could go home in the first week.'

'So, who else knows?' said Rose.

'Just you. We aren't allowed to tell anyone except our

nearest and dearest; it won't be announced until after the show has been filmed.'

'The TV crew came over the other day to film us at home,' said Bernard, animated.

'What? They've been here?' said Max, as if he had just found out they were undercover agents. 'Like, in this house?'

'Yes,' said Bernard, 'we just had to go about our everyday business, except we were sort of acting. I was terrible.'

'Acting?' said Jeremy, as he poured them each another inch of tea.

'Well, you know, Jenny had to pretend to do some baking and then we did the crossword. Sounds simple, except there were people and lights and cameras everywhere. Jenny was a natural.'

Everyone looked a little stunned, as if their minds couldn't quite process it.

'Fin-ished!' shouted Poppy, to Jenny's relief.

She leapt up, returning to the safety of the kitchen where Poppy greeted her with a scowl.

'What is everyone being silly for?' she said, her bottom lip protruding.

'How do you mean?'

'In the garden. Everyone is being silly. I heard you.'

'Oh, that was because I have been keeping a secret, and everyone found out about it.'

Poppy thought about this for a moment. 'You shouldn't keep secrets.'

'And why's that?'

'Because it makes them grow bigger,' she said, with such conviction that Jenny was lost for words. 'What is it?'

'I can tell you, but then *you'll* have to keep it a secret.'

She thought about this for a moment, her soft brow pinched. 'Okay then.'

'I've entered a baking competition that's going to be on the telly,' Jenny said, 'but people aren't allowed to know yet.'

'Oh, right,' said Poppy, refreshingly unfazed as she pointed at the plate. 'Are these okay?'

'They're brilliant, Pops,' she said, tapping the frosted grapes which had already formed a sugary crust. They piled them one by one into the centre of the cheesecake.

'Now for my favourite part,' she said, taking the tray of leaves out of the fridge, which looked as if they were covered in droplets of morning dew. She gently peeled back the stem like a sticker, revealing beneath it a perfectly symmetrical web of veins imprinted in the chocolate. No matter how old she was, this little joy never lost its wonder.

'Wow,' said Poppy, studying it in her palm.

Together they positioned them around the nest of frosted grapes, creating an eighties dessert in all its flamboyant glory.

'High five,' said Poppy, holding up her hand as they admired their masterpiece.

She met her hand with five wrinkled fingers.

'That was too quiet,' Poppy giggled, clapping their hands together and making her feel very old indeed.

As she picked up the cheesecake and headed out into the garden, she imagined herself in a week's time, holding her bake and walking towards the judges. The fear and the excitement were indistinguishable as they wrestled in her stomach, interrupted by the hollow pop of a champagne cork.

'To Aunty Jenny!' said Jeremy, as they all raised a glass of bubbles.

'To Aunty Jenny,' they echoed, their eyes on the cheese-cake.

'Look at you, you're going to be great,' said Rose, squeezing her arm. 'I just know it.'

As she looked around the table at the excited faces that she loved so much, she felt a new kind of warmth. Beneath the fear and the worry, was a feeling like the sun on the back of her neck. For a rare moment, she felt as if she had made her family proud.

As she placed slices of toast in the toast rack and put the marmalade on the breakfast table, the house groaned in the way it did when it was full, as taps turned on and off and little feet scurried along the landing.

'Morning,' said Max, his eyelids swollen with sleep as he joined her at the table. 'I've made you something . . .' His fingers moved faster than the speed of light as he held out his phone.

'I need my glasses,' she said, retrieving them from her case and pushing them on to her nose. 'What is it?'

'Your socials,' he said, his voice dropping a few keys. 'Your username is *MrsQuinn'sRiseToFame* – Jennifer Quinn and Jenny were taken. I've already posted some of the pictures of things you've baked.'

'Goodness me,' she said, feeling completely illiterate to the strange new world in which she now apparently existed. 'Is it not a little presumptuous . . . rise to fame?'

'Don't overthink it,' said Max. 'My username is *Max-LovesCheese*.'

Jenny looked at him, perplexed.

'But you don't even like cheese!'

'I know,' he said, with a shrug, so that she couldn't help but be tickled by him.

'Well, thank you, Max,' she said, tapping the picture of her chocolate log, trying to get a closer look. 'That's very kind of you.'

'Careful,' he said, smiling so as not to reveal his braces, 'you'll like your own post.'

She twisted her hair between her fingers, nibbling at the inside of her mouth as she wondered what exactly he meant by this. Under each photograph he had written several disjointed words, such as #*bakes, #baking, #cake, #chocolate*.

'What are these words?' she said, her eyes narrowing behind her glasses.

'Oh, they're hashtags, they help people search for things.'

She looked for something familiar, for a frame of reference from which she could navigate through what he had just said.

'Don't worry. If you send me the photos that you want to post, I can run it for you if you like?'

She breathed a sigh of relief, tucking the twisted lock of hair behind her ear.

'Thank you. I'm good on email, but all of this is a step too far,' she said, pouring him a glass of orange juice.

'No worries,' he said, drinking it in three glugs.

'Morning,' said Rose, joining them at the breakfast table. 'What are you two plotting?'

'I've set Aunty Jenny up on social media,' he said, sliding his phone towards her across the table.

'Wonderful,' she said, flicking the screen. 'Well done, Max.'

'He's kindly offered to help me with it, thank goodness,' Jenny said, spreading a thick layer of marmalade on her toast.

Rose returned the phone to Max. 'I wondered, do you fancy going shopping today, just you and me? I thought you might want to get a few new clothes for *Britain Bakes*?'

'That would be lovely,' she said, finishing off her tea.

'So what's on the list? Have they said anything about what you should wear on the show?' said Rose, offering Jenny a mint from her handbag as they moved up the escalator and into the mouth of the department store.

'I think I can wear anything I like. They just said no stripes or checks and nothing with big logos on it ... which shouldn't be a problem,' she said, sickly sweet perfume clinging to the back of her throat as people with immaculate complexions sprayed scent cards and handed them out to shoppers.

'Do you need any new make-up, whilst we're here?'

'I suppose I'm going to have to do something –'

'Can I help you at all?' said a lady with eyelashes as thick as broomsticks, standing behind a counter of shimmering pallets as if she were in the driving seat of a spaceship.

'I'm not sure. Maybe a lipstick?'

She looked at Rose who pulled a face as if to say, *why not?*

'We've got some great new products that have just launched today. If you'd like to sit up here I can show you,' the assistant said as she pushed a lever and a silver stool shot upwards. She reached for a circular mirror on an extendable arm and tilted it towards Jenny's face. It felt oddly intimate to have her make-up done in the middle of a shop floor for all to see.

'So what sort of products do you usually use?' she said.

'Well, a bit of powder, blusher, lipstick and mascara . . . eyeshadow for best.'

'I've got a new range that I think will really suit you.'

Jenny closed her eyes tightly as the lady dotted something cold across her eyelids, the bangles on her wrist clattering together each time she dipped the brush into the pot. She could feel the lady's warm breath on her cheeks as she tugged at her lashes with what felt like a miniature comb, before clamping them in some sort of device.

'What do you think?' she said, flicking a switch so that the mirror lit up.

She blinked her eyes open, taking a second to adjust to her magnified face.

'Goodness,' she said, noticing only a hundred deep lines, which split into fainter ones like streams from a river. Her irises had developed a bluish hue like the wings of a beetle and her lashes were now thinning stubs which this lady had managed to miraculously bend towards the sky. She remembered applying block mascara as a young woman, mixing it with saliva and painting on doe-eyes, imagining herself to be Elizabeth Taylor or Audrey Hepburn.

'Look at your lashes,' said Rose, before picking up the mascara and inspecting it.

'I've got another product that will really bring out your cheekbones, just a second,' said the lady, disappearing behind the counter.

'I can't wear this much make-up when I'm baking, Rose. It will be halfway down my face after an hour in the kitchen,' she said under her breath.

Rose nodded, her eyes following the lady as she returned shaking a glass bottle.

'This is our new highlighter,' she said, dabbing Jenny's cheeks with a cold sponge. She tilted the dreaded magnifying mirror towards her again, revealing a copper sheen which made her feel fit for the pantomime.

'I think what she'd quite like is a new lipstick,' said Rose. 'Pinks? Reds? Neutrals?'

'I usually go for pink, occasionally red; something pretty for summer would be lovely,' said Jenny, her back beginning to ache from the stool.

The lady rummaged in her apron pocket, pulling out a pencil and carefully drawing around the edge of her lips before filling them in with a poppy red gloss. It tickled. Jenny stared down at her knees so as to avoid her gaze, her sweet scent cloying.

'Striking, isn't it?' she said, stepping back to admire her work.

'I love that,' said Rose.

She smiled into the mirror, catching a glimpse of her ivory yellow teeth.

'It's long lasting too, so it stays on for twelve hours.'

'That could come in very useful,' said Rose, with a wink.

'In that case then, I'll go for the Poppy and the Tulip, please,' she said, reaching her toes back towards firm ground.

She pulled out her purse and handed over some crumpled notes to the lady with the lashes.

'There you go,' said the lady, returning a shiny cardboard bag complete with a ribbon. 'Enjoy.'

She linked Rose's arm as they walked towards the escalator.

'Do I look ridiculous?' she said.

'No, you look fabulous, but yes, I agree. It's not baking make-up,' she smiled, 'if such a thing exists!'

As they walked into the womenswear section, navigating the maze of plastic hangers and spring florals, they communicated by making small noises of appreciation, as if they were watching the world's most underwhelming firework display. Gradually they drifted further away from each other, like sniffer dogs following scents, their eyes taking them around different corners. She wished, when she had worked at Lady Jane's all those years ago, that she had taken full advantage of the fact that absolutely anything would have looked good on her. Now, she picked up garments, admired them and put them back on the rail.

'Can I help you, madam?' said an alarmingly loud voice.

She spun around to find that a shop assistant was looming over her.

'I'm okay, thank you,' she replied, distracted for a moment by her severely asymmetrical haircut.

'Are you lost?' the assistant said, stooping slightly as if she had found a toddler in the supermarket.

'I'm with my niece, thank you,' she said, looking around for Rose.

'Where is she?'

'I'm not sure . . . she won't be far away,' she said, pretending to admire a shapeless roll-neck jumper in an attempt to end the conversation.

'What does she look like? Can you describe her?' the woman said, drawing attention from the other shoppers.

She could feel her cheeks burning.

'I'm fine. Thank you,' she said, but the more she tried to assert herself, the less convincing she sounded.

The lady tucked the short side of her hair behind her ear, forcing a smile.

'What are you looking for, dear?'

She took a deep breath. Perhaps she just needed to give this lady something to do and then she would leave her alone.

'I'm looking for blouses.'

'Blouses, okay,' she said, as if she had finally got some sense out of her. 'Follow me.'

Jenny begrudgingly followed her, weaving through the hordes of people and clothes, having a heated conversation in her head where she told her that she might look like an old lady who doesn't know her way around a department store, but in fact very soon she would be watching her on television.

'Aunty Jenny!' called Rose, waving with her arms full of clothes and hangers.

'Is that her?' said the lady.

'Yes,' she muttered, her jaw clenched.

'Everything all right?' said Rose, looking from Jenny to the lady.

'She looked a bit lost, bless her, but at least we've found you,' she said, doing that forced smile thing again.

Jenny kept her mouth firmly shut as the lady disappeared back between the rails.

'I wasn't lost,' she said, when the lady was out of earshot. 'That woman was talking to me as if I'd lost my marbles. Do I look that ancient?'

'Of course not,' said Rose, holding out her arms which were draped with clothes so that they looked like wings. 'I've found some things I think you'll like, comfy enough for the kitchen but elegant too.'

'Thank you,' she said with a sigh. 'It's no fun growing old, Rose.'

'Well, I've got a feeling that any day now it's about to get incredibly fun,' she said with a grin.

Jenny was reminded of her sixteen-year-old self on the precipice of life, about to dive into what she hoped was a career, a first love. As she stood in the department store, more than sixty years later, she recognized that very same ledge from which she was about to jump.

Quiche Lorraine

Jenny whisked together the cream, eggs, salt and pepper with the vigour of a jockey in the Grand National. Next to her the bacon rashers whistled and popped in a pan with the onions, contracting as they cooked, infiltrating every corner of the house with a mouth-watering fog. Once ready, she layered everything into the pastry case with a generous helping of cheese and posted it into the oven, setting her timer for twenty-five minutes.

Whilst she waited she took a piece of cardboard, cut from a box of porridge oats, and listed Bernard's meals for the next couple of days alongside their cooking instructions. She couldn't bear the thought of him living on beans on toast.

'I'm loading up the car, darling,' he said, peeping his head around the door as he buckled under the weight of her suitcase.

'Careful,' she said, dashing to help. 'I think we need to treat ourselves to those cases with wheels on.'

'I'm fine,' he said, his face saying otherwise. 'Anything you need from the kitchen?'

'Just my scales, please.'

He put down the suitcase, picking up the scales with bent knees as if they weighed a ton, his elbows jutting out as he navigated the awkward shape.

'They're letting you use these old things?'

'They've approved them, thank goodness, my old friends.'

As he carried them out to the car, she wiped down the worktops with a stale dishcloth, feeling a fond ache towards this little room which she had barely left over the last couple of months. The tired melamine cupboards, the yellowing tiles around the oven, the kettle whose lid was glued shut with a white crust of limescale so that you had to fill it up through the spout. It was home, and its dearness grew heightened with her parting.

Interrupted by the timer, she opened the oven door to a buttery breeze. The top of the quiche had formed a golden skin and she tapped it lightly. There was a slight resistance, so she switched off the oven for the last time, tracing the faint shapes where the numbers had once been.

The car rumbled into life outside.

'Goodbye, little kitchen,' she said as she pulled on her coat. She picked up her book of family recipes and closed the front door behind her.

'Ready to go?' said Bernard as he leant over to open the passenger door.

'As I'll ever be,' she said and they pulled away, home shrinking behind them until they turned a corner, and it was gone.

'I've left a quiche Lorraine for you in the oven; the cooking instructions are all written out for you on the top,' she said, the fields outside merging into a green blur.

'Thank you, darling.'

'I'm only going for a couple of days anyway,' she said, with an unconvincing air of calm. 'I'll be back in no time at all.'

'So what's the theme this week?'

'It's cake week.'

'What does that involve?'

'I'm doing miniature rhubarb and custard drizzle cakes for the Baker's Dozen Challenge,' she said, massaging her temples, 'and a chocolate and orange Battenburg for the Baker's Delight . . . then who knows whether I'll make it through to the Blind Bake.'

She sank deeper into her seat.

'Well, I'm only jealous that I won't be the one eating it,' he said, as he changed gear with a clunk.

Her eyes jumped between the trees, flicking from side to side.

'I'm not a joke, am I, Bernard? They wouldn't have put me in the show for a laugh?'

He was quiet for a moment, so that she thought he hadn't heard her.

'Jennifer Quinn,' he said, tightening his grip on the wheel, 'stop doubting yourself.'

The butterflies in her stomach felt more like wasps.

'And anyway, I'll still love you,' he said, catching her eye, 'even with a soggy bottom.'

Her face twitched into a reluctant smile.

She switched on the radio in search of a different sort of noise to fill her mind. Instead, it became a backdrop to her thoughts as she was transported to her kitchen, kneading dough and piping macarons and filling éclairs. Her eyelids grew heavy as she sculpted chocolate icing with a

spatula and crimped the edge of a pasty with two fingers . . .
push and twist . . . push and twist . . . her body surrendering to the draw of sleep.

Before she knew it, the car was slowing and Bernard
was leaning forward in his seat, straining to read the sign
before him, one hand on the wheel and the other on her
knee as he tried to wake her.

'I think we're here, darling,' he said. 'Bramley House
Hotel.'

Her throat ground against itself as she swallowed.

'Yes, that's it. That was quick.'

She took a sip of water and pulled down the sun visor,
searching her handbag for her lipstick.

'Stay in the car for just a second,' she said, clutching his
knee. 'I can't get out like this.'

She filled her lips with crimson, catching sight of other
people in the mirror as they got out of cars, said goodbye
to children and carried suitcases towards the reception.

'Everyone's half my age, at most,' she said, as she wound
her lipstick back into its tube, clicking on the lid.

'But half your experience,' he replied.

As they stepped out of the car, he wrestled her suitcase
and scales out of the boot and they made their way across
the car park, exchanging polite smiles with the other families as she tried to deduce which of them was the baker.

'Anyone for *Britain Bakes*, if you head to the meeting
room on the left you will be given your room keys. You
can leave your bags here,' shouted a young man wearing a
Britain Bakes T-shirt, pointing to a row of luggage trolleys.
There was an excited buzz in the air as people darted past
her in shoals.

Bernard heaved her bag on to the trolley, her adrenaline turning to dread as each second brought them closer to him leaving.

'Good luck, darling,' he said, holding out his arms.

This was it. She inhaled the smell of wool, aftershave and home, gripping him tightly and not letting go.

'Enjoy yourself. You'll be brilliant,' he said. 'I'm so proud.'

She nodded, reluctantly drawing back.

'Thank you, I'll do my best . . . and I'm a phone call away if you need me.'

With that, she picked up her handbag and walked towards the meeting room, unable to look back over her shoulder. If she had done, she would have seen that he waited until she had completely disappeared before he left, his hands pushed deep into the pockets of his cords, his eyes glittering with tears.

She pushed open the door to room 207 with some force, as it fought against the fluffy carpet. It smelt of synthetic lemon and she was struck by the size of the bed, overcast by a six-foot upholstered headboard, the sort she imagined that royalty might have.

Spotting a kettle on a tray in the corner, she flicked it on to make a cup of tea whilst carefully unpacking her new clothes, sliding them on to hangers in the hope that the creases would drop out by the morning. She poured the boiling water into the mugs, adding a plastic sachet of milk to each which created a shiny film on the surface of the tea.

'For goodness' sake,' she said, as she removed the

teabags, realizing that she had made not one but two cups, one a little stronger than the other.

There were small habits that you picked up when you had spent considerably more of your life with someone than without, primarily that you do everything in pairs. In many ways, she considered their relationship her proudest recipe and one which had been tweaked and modified over the course of a lifetime as they each grew a deeper understanding of the other. Shaking an egg to work out whether it was out of date, sensing a mood from the way he spread the butter on his toast, or adding a pinch of salt to chocolate to balance out the flavours. Knowing him so intuitively was part of the fibres of who she had become.

Just as she finished her last gulp, she realized that she had ten minutes before everyone was meeting in the restaurant downstairs for their first night supper. She quickly made her way to the lift, which jolted to a stop on the first floor.

The door pinged open.

'Jenny!'

For a couple of seconds her mind strained to place his dark eyes, the kind shape of his smile. It was the boy who had helped her resurrect her Black Forest gateau in the audition.

'Azeez!' she said, feeling an urge to throw her arms around him, a wave of relief coming over her at the sight of someone familiar.

'So it worked, then? Our DIY rescue effort?' he said, as he joined her in the lift.

'Yes,' she said, 'thank you so much for that. I might not be here if it wasn't for you . . .'

He smiled.

'How have you found the practice time?' she asked.

'So stressful, honestly. The breakdowns have been coming at regular intervals. I feel so sorry for Ashley.'

'Is Ashley your girlfriend?'

'My boyfriend.'

'Oh, sorry.' She felt a creeping embarrassment at having made such an assumption.

'How did you find it?' he said, eyebrows raised as he tidied his hair in the mirrored walls.

'I'm relieved you've said that because I found it very similar; at points I was close to dropping out. My husband has been back and forth to the shops almost every other day; he's apparently emptied the baking aisle.'

'I'm not surprised. It's so nice to finally speak to someone that's been going through all the same stuff, you know? No one else really gets it, do they?' he said, as the lift sprang to a halt on the ground floor and they stepped out, heading into the restaurant together.

'Jenny, Azeez, welcome,' said a couple of enthusiastic strangers. 'How were your journeys?'

They exchanged a shared glance, hoping the other might know who they were.

'Good, thanks,' said Azeez, holding out his hand. 'What are your names, sorry?'

'Laura and Matt, casting team. I forget you don't know us; we've got pictures of you up on the wall in the office so we automatically feel like we know you.'

Before she could comprehend the idea that her picture was up on a wall in an office, she heard a *Hello, Jenny!* followed by Carys almost skipping towards her. She'd had a fringe cut since she last saw her, which had been meticulously styled so that it barely moved.

'How are you?'

'Well, thank you, dear. Lovely to see you.'

'Azeez, I'm Carys. I don't think we've met,' she said, hugging him like a long-lost friend before turning back to Jenny.

'The last time I saw you was when we were doing VTs. I loved your house by the way, it's so cute,' she said, closing a gap in her fringe with her fingertips.

'They went full architecture student with my VT; they had me on the floor of my bedroom drawing straight lines, using protractors and flicking through sketchbooks,' said Azeez. 'Of course I have never actually sat on the floor of my bedroom like that in the entirety of my degree.'

'Artistic licence,' winked Carys.

'An architecture student,' said Jenny, 'so your biscuit week will be something to behold, then?'

'You would hope so,' he said, a mischievous glint in his eyes, 'but architects aren't traditionally trained in gingerbread, much as I wish we were.'

A waiter appeared with a tray and offered them each a glass of fizz. The bubbles raced to the top, disappearing in a multitude of tiny explosions which tickled her nose as she took a sip.

'Shall we sit down?' said Carys, leading them over to a large dining table.

'This reminds me a bit of starting university,' said Azeez, as he pulled out her chair.

'I can imagine that. I mean, I didn't go to university, but I thought it might be a little like this.'

'Except everyone knows your name here, and we're drinking champagne,' he said, his eyes scanning the sea of new faces, 'and only one of us will get the degree.'

The seats around them started to populate with the crew and contestants, the room developing an excited hum which grew louder as the drinks circulated. There was a vicar who looked in his fifties with round spectacles, and Sorcha who she recognized from her audition, with the sort of dark curls that usually only film stars manage to achieve. There was a drama teacher whose voice was set at a pitch which cut through everyone else's, and a shy-looking young farmer. They exchanged stories of how they had come to apply for the show, their biggest disasters during practice and the perils of keeping it a secret. It struck her that although they all led very different lives, were varying ages and from completely different backgrounds, they shared a unifying love of baking.

'Welcome, bakers,' said a lady with an air of authority, before chiming a teaspoon against the side of a glass. She was notably small, her clothes tailored to her neat waist.

'My name is Sarah, one of the executive producers, and I'm delighted to welcome here today the eight best amateur bakers in the country. We had over twelve thousand applications this year, so it's a huge achievement, and you are all now a part of the *Britain Bakes* family!'

The room roared and Jenny felt a tingling sensation in the pit of her stomach. *Twelve thousand applications.*

'Andy, our wonderful casting director, is going to read out the names of our bakers. Please stand up when your name is called so we can put a name to a face,' said Sarah, pushing a piece of paper towards the man with the mani-cured beard from her audition.

'Azeez Patel!' said Andy, and he stood up next to her, beaming from ear to ear. She clapped a little harder for her new friend, who sat back down and fanned his face with a napkin.

'Paul Dixon!'

A man rose to his feet who she'd overheard was a fire-fighter, his shirt clinging to his muscles so that it looked as if it might have been sprayed on.

Her pulse raced in anticipation of her own name, as one by one they stood up.

'Angela Sutton!'

A larger lady pushed back her chair so that it toppled over, causing a small kerfuffle which she attempted to smooth over by shrieking with laughter.

'And last but not least . . . Jennifer Quinn!'

She froze like a rabbit in the headlights, a surge of adrenaline propelling her to her feet.

'Thank you,' she said, holding her right hand up in an attempt at a wave, before sitting back down in her seat with a thud.

'So, a bus will come and collect you all from the hotel at five-thirty in the morning and take you to location,' said Carys, once they had all finished supper. 'It's an early start but you'll get used to it, I promise.'

'I'd better get to bed then,' Jenny said, glancing at her watch.

'I'll come with you,' said Azeez, as they said their good-nights and left the buzz of the restaurant for the quiet hotel corridors. She could feel a tired ache behind her eyes as they followed the arrows in search of their room numbers.

He paused for a moment before stooping down to give her an unexpected hug.

'See you bright and early, dear,' she said, pressing the key card against her door.

'Sleep well,' he replied, disappearing towards the lift, and as he did so she remembered that he was on the floor below. He must've taken a detour to walk her to her room.

As she stood in the bathroom in her nightie, she stared into the brightly lit mirror, removing her make-up with cotton wool balls. *This was it*, she thought, it was really happening. She got herself a glass of water and climbed into the huge bed. The sheets were taut as she fought her way underneath them.

She switched off the bedside light and turned on to her side, looking across at the untouched sheets next to her, the pillows plump and pristine. Stretching out her leg, she forced her foot between the cold cotton covers, where usually it would meet Bernard's warm body, the right to her left. She closed her eyes, picturing the back of his head which she had watched turn from brown to snowy white, the rustling of his book as he turned its pages and then the back and forth of his snore like waves against the shore. These familiar routines usually blended into the noise of the everyday, but tonight they left a deafening silence.

Rhubarb and Custard Drizzle Cakes

She was walking towards Sandra's house on a wet Thursday morning when the feeling came over her. She narrowed her eyes as the first drops of rain blew in gusts towards her face, her feet moving quickly, her chin tucked into her coat. Slowing down, her jaw tensed and her mouth grew watery. She searched for somewhere, anywhere, before darting behind the closest tree. The dark, twisted shape of its roots turned her stomach and she doubled over, tears streaming down her cheeks as her body heaved itself empty.

Her mouth was sour as she leant against the tree trunk, the cool droplets of rain now a comfort against her skin. Opening her satchel, she rummaged in its depths, pulling out a crumpled paper bag, worn as thin as a rag. Inside she was relieved to find that she had one rhubarb and custard sweet left, the pink and yellow stripes joyful beneath its dusty surface. The church bell chimed; she was late. Popping it into her right cheek, she continued to walk, the sweet rhubarb countering the acidity in her throat.

As she turned the corner, she spotted Sandra perched in her usual place on the wall outside her house, her hair wild as it danced in the wind. She tapped at her wrist, lowering her feet to the pavement.

'Hurry up,' she called, gesturing with her long arms.

Jenny attempted to speed up, her feet lifting her off the ground every couple of steps so that she looked as if she had developed a limp, the sweet clattering against her teeth.

'Sorry,' she said, leaning her hand on the wall as she caught her breath.

'Morning,' said Sandra, attempting to tame her hair with a clip that was gripped between her teeth. 'We're going to be late for book-keeping if we don't run. Come on!'

With that, Sandra headed off down the road, each of her long strides making up three of Jenny's as their satchels slapped against their legs.

The feeling was coming, again.

'I can't,' she said, her breathing jagged as she slowed down. She dived behind a nearby bench, doubling over, the back of her throat burning.

Sandra's footsteps ground to a halt.

'Are you all right?' she said, gathering her hair away from her face. 'Was I too fast?'

Jenny was aware of her fumbling in her pocket, handing her a tissue.

'I don't know,' she said, using it to dab at the corners of her mouth. 'It happened earlier too, but it usually stops.'

'Usually?' said Sandra.

Jenny took a deep breath, the relief of being empty washing over her.

'It's happened a couple of times recently.'

'Don't you think you should see a doctor?' Sandra said, with an assertiveness that came from being the eldest of five. 'I can come with you, if you like?'

Jenny shook her head, the skin on her arms tightening into

pimples. 'I'll go home and rest. If I don't feel any better I'll make an appointment.'

Sandra sighed before readjusting her satchel.

'I'll walk you home,' she said.

'I'll be fine,' Jenny glanced at her watch. 'Go! You'll make the first lesson if you run. Take notes for me . . .'

She sat on a hard chair in the waiting room, submerged in the potent smell of TCP as she watched a mother distract her ruddy-cheeked toddler by fashioning a puppet out of a handkerchief as he screamed at the top of his lungs. Further down sat an elderly lady and her husband, her face gaunt and green. She couldn't help but feel they were waiting for bad news.

'Miss Jennifer Eaton,' called Dr Walker, peering around the door. His tie was so tightly knotted that it caused his shirt to gather around the collar, his forehead similarly creased into a well-worn frown as he peered over his spectacles.

She stood up, relieved to be away from the screaming as he ushered her into his cool, quiet room, closing the door behind her. He had been their family doctor for her entire life and yet he never greeted her with any familiarity, so that she wondered whether he recognized her at all.

She took a seat in front of his desk and they sat in silence for a moment whilst he polished his spectacles with his tie and put them back on the end of his nose.

'So,' he said, looking down at his notes, 'Miss Eaton. What can I do for you today?'

On the few occasions when she had been unwell enough to pay Dr Walker a visit, he had always been so impassive that she'd felt foolish for involving him in the first place. When she was nine, he had been called out to pay her a home visit after she'd developed a hacking cough that had left her bedbound. Dr Walker had arrived with his doctor's bag and without batting an eyelid, prescribed lozenges and bed rest. Her father had remarked that if she'd had half a leg missing, he would have done the same. She had no doubt that today would go a similar way.

'I've been feeling sick, mostly in the mornings, but it tends to go away during the day, or after I've eaten.'

'Feeling sick?' he said, shuffling his papers, 'or being sick?'

'Both,' she said, her mouth stale as she looked into her lap.

'I see. And have you noticed anything else unusual recently, aside from the sickness?'

She thought about how it hurt to sleep on her front, her chest tender, but explaining that to a man felt uncomfortable. Besides, it didn't seem relevant.

'No,' she said, 'just the sickness.'

She waited for him to tell her to go home and rest, but instead he sat up a little straighter, raising his eyebrows.

'Are you menstruating regularly?'

Her cheeks flushed.

'Yes, usually,' she replied, picking at her nails, '. . . I'm a few weeks late this time.'

He clasped his hands together and placed them on his desk in a fashion that was notably dramatic for Dr Walker.

'Is it possible that you could be . . . with child?' he said, his voice curling up at the end of his sentence.

She remained silent, her throat tightening so that she couldn't speak.

'Miss Eaton?' he said, pushing his spectacles further up his nose.

'I hadn't thought –' she said, shifting uncomfortably in her seat, 'I hadn't thought I could be –'

'It really is very simple,' his eyes glimpsed her left hand. 'Have you had sexual intercourse?'

She studied the grain of the wood on his desk, the knots dark, ominous.

'Is that a yes?'

'He said it would be okay if –'

'If what, exactly?'

'He said if he . . .' she searched for the appropriate words but there were none, 'if he took the kettle off before it boiled.'

Her words hung in the silence, mocking her.

'Usually in this situation, you would make quick plans to marry,' he said, rolling a pencil between his palms.

She sank deeper into the chair.

'If that isn't a possibility, then there are two options,' he said, 'one that I would openly advise.'

'What is it?' she said, her voice quiet.

'Adoption,' he replied, scribbling something in his notes.

'And the other?'

He paused, looking up at her with a cold stare.

'I'm sure you can use your imagination,' he said, before continuing to write.

She slipped her hand underneath her cardigan, feeling the warmth of her stomach. A shiver ran the length of her spine.

Jenny opened her eyes to a very different sort of morning than the one she was used to. The chorus of Bernard's whistle, the rumble of the kettle boiling and the thud of the newspaper as it landed on the doormat had been replaced by a piercing alarm, *05:00* flashing in bright letters through the darkness. Like a parachute coming in to land, it took a couple of seconds for reality to hit as it dawned on her that she was in a hotel and that today was her first day on *Britain Bakes*.

As the birds began to trill their good mornings, she pulled on her best blouse and trousers with the powder-blue cashmere jumper that Rose had picked out. Putting on her new red lipstick in the bathroom mirror, she noticed that her hand was shaking. *It's as simple as eggs, sugar, butter and flour,* she told herself.

Shutting her bedroom door, she headed to the hotel restaurant, fuelled by an energy which made her feet move surprisingly quickly considering the time.

'Morning,' said Azeez, waving for her to join him. 'Please tell me you're as exhausted as I am? It feels like the middle of the night . . .'

'One of the few benefits of growing older, my dear,' she said, picking up a pain au chocolat and pouring herself a tea, 'is that you need less sleep. How are you feeling?'

'Nervous, excited, sick,' he said, sipping his drink, the crease of his pillow still imprinted across his cheek. 'You?'

'Similar,' she agreed. 'We've got ten minutes, shall we join the others?'

As they approached reception, she spotted some of the faces from last night. The vicar was checking his watch at regular intervals, too distracted to fully engage in the small talk that Paul the firefighter was attempting to make. Behind them, Sorcha was making a peace sign with her fingers into her phone camera. Jenny couldn't help but notice her emerald-green wrap dress and she felt incredibly plain in comparison, with her limp silver locks and muted blue jumper.

'Here we go, eh?' said a warm voice from behind, followed by the sort of laugh that comes from the very centre of your soul and makes your whole body shake. She turned around to see the contestant who had knocked over her chair last night.

'I feel as if I'm about to get on a school bus,' said Jenny.

The lady let out another chortle so that Jenny quickly concluded that she must be one of those people who had a natural ability to generate laughter on demand.

'I'm Angela by the way,' she said, resting her hand on her chest as she caught her breath. 'Sorry, remind me of your name?'

'Jenny,' she replied, noticing that the minibus had arrived.

As they populated the seats, they compared how they had slept and speculated about who the first guest judge might be. Gradually it quietened as nerves took hold and they stared out of the window at the dawn sky. She reached into her handbag for the mobile phone that Bernard had given her for whilst she was away, pressing the power button so that it pierced the silence with a mortifyingly loud tune.

'Wow,' said Azeez with a smirk, 'is that the nineties calling?'

There was a titter amongst the other bakers and she couldn't help but smile as she nudged him with her elbow. There was an envelope on her screen. She opened it and it read GOOD LUCK DARLING. LOVE FROM BERNARD X. She reread it, drawing every last ounce of comfort from it before switching the power off and pushing it back into her handbag.

'There!' said Angela, tapping on the window with her fingernail, 'There it is!'

The bus turned a corner and crunched down a gravel driveway so that they all sat up a little straighter, leaning like flowers towards the light. She could see manicured gardens, huge rustling trees and an incongruous Porta-kabin as she searched the horizon for something familiar. Then, there it was. At the heart of the estate with the sun rising behind it, stood the iconic manor house she had seen so many times on the television. As they drove in through the gates, it looked even grander than she had expected.

Stepping off the bus, she felt as if she had a dough hook in her stomach, twisting her insides together to form a heavy knot.

'Good morning and welcome, bakers. If you'd like to come with me,' said Carys.

Azeez squeezed Jenny's arm and they followed Carys around the side of the manor, like ducklings to water.

Morning dew licked at the toes of her loafers as Carys led them to the rear of the house and through an orchard, towards a huge limestone building signposted *The Stables*. As they approached the door, she pushed it open, inciting a collective gasp. It was a grand but rustic barn conversion with cream brick walls and exposed oak beams which ran the length of the roof, strapped with studio lights. It was starkly lit, much brighter than it looked on screen, like walking into an operating theatre.

She recognized everything as if it were an old friend: the enormous dresser covered in jars and utensils, the twinkling fairy lights looped from the rafters, the personal-ized workstations each with their own hob. In the corner of her eye she spotted one with a floral skirt, her cast-iron kitchen scales on proud display and looking particularly worn amongst the shiny new equipment. That must be her kitchen, she thought, her insides fizzing. She could already tell which one was Sorcha's, the front of it covered by a wall of artificial roses.

'The kitchen is through there,' said Carys, pointing towards a heavy, sweeping curtain through which she caught a two-second glimpse of plastic supermarket crates and industrial steel sinks, like a ladybird spreading its wings to reveal the shock of the inner workings.

'And that's the gallery,' she said, signalling towards the other side of the room, 'but you'll never need to go in either of those areas; we don't want to spoil the magic.'

'What's the gallery?' Jenny said to Azeez in a whisper.

'I think that's where the director sits?'

'Oh,' she nodded, 'I didn't even think about that.'

Carys left the barn and crossed the gardens towards a small marquee which was dotted with chairs and refreshments, the air damp, earthy.

'This is the green room, where you will spend *a lot* of time . . .'

'I can't believe that the set was once the stables,' said the young farmer as he sank into a chair. 'Looks nothing like the stables I'm used to.'

'The home economists will come in shortly and check with each of you that you have the correct ingredients for today's bakes,' said Carys, raising her voice above the chatter. 'Don't be afraid to say if you don't – we have a runner permanently stationed at the local supermarket.'

Angela laughed, but Jenny was quite sure that Carys wasn't joking.

'One other important thing: before you put anything in the oven, please shout "going in" so a camera can catch it.

Likewise, before anything comes out of the oven, get into the habit of calling "coming out" as we need all of the big moments to be on camera.'

There was an air of delirium as they all lined up like children outside a classroom whilst a gentleman talked them through where to walk and stand. She felt as if she were underwater, watching everything from inside a diving suit, immersed and yet separate.

'And . . . off you go!' he shouted, as they walked back through the orchard and across the lawn, coming to some stone steps which she navigated with extreme caution so as not to go flying at the first hurdle.

As they entered the barn, the hairs on her arms stood on end. She weaved her way towards her workstation, which was thankfully nestled in the middle of the others. She couldn't hide, but at least she wasn't on the front row. On her worktop sat a folded piece of stiff cotton, the colour of cake mixture. She looped it over her head and watched it tumble down to her knees, tying a knot in the arch of her back as her mother had done, many years ago. Never before had an apron felt so monumental, as if she were putting on armour ready to go into battle.

She pushed her hands deep into the front pocket, as silence washed over the room. To her relief Azeez's workstation was in front of hers, each side of it a bold colour, perhaps inspired by his taste in shirts. She deduced from the placement of the fridges that they would be sharing.

When the judges entered, it felt as if everything before this moment had been a dress rehearsal. Amanda, whom she had long admired, looked breathtakingly elegant. Her clothes floated behind her as they hung from her tall, slim frame, and her silver hair was styled into a neat bun at the nape of her neck so that it somehow looked like the precious metal itself, not a strand out of place. There was something feline about her high cheekbones and lightness of foot. On television she kept her cards close, communicating mostly through the subtleties of body language, a tilt of the head, a raised eyebrow. In person, she had an other-worldly presence which silenced the room as she entered.

Behind her followed a young man with a bun on top of his head and a carefully shaped moustache, giving him an air of creativity. She didn't recognize him, but on first impression he looked as if he might be in a band of some sort – not that that would qualify him for the role. She glanced towards Azeez, whose expression told her that he knew exactly who the man was.

'Welcome to *Britain Bakes*,' said Mo, a bouncy young comedian. 'Joining Amanda today is our guest judge, food journalist and author of *The Sweet Stuff*, Angus de Winter!'

Angus nodded, twisting the right tip of his moustache.

'Our first challenge of the competition,' said Mo, 'is the Baker's Dozen Challenge. You will be given the task of making *not thirteen* but *twelve* identical drizzle cakes.'

'You have just two hours to complete your bakes,' finished Katie, his wholesome counterpart.

'Three . . . two . . . one . . .'

'Bake!'

It was a long time since she had used an oven that was brand new, the door shiny and the numbers clear to read. She needed to make friends with it. As she clicked it on, it lit up like the lights at the theatre, smelling newly of plastic. The recipe she was using belonged to Rose, but in recent months had been modified to create something a little more experimental. In her opinion, you could never have too much of the drizzle part. There was nothing more delicious than the combination of a crisp sugar crust concealing a sharp, sodden sponge.

'What have we got here?' said Amanda, so that she almost dropped an eggshell into the sponge mixture. She looked up to see her smiling at a terrifying proximity. It all felt so real without the safety of a TV screen between them.

'I'm making rhubarb and custard drizzle cakes,' she said, lining each of the twelve holes in the mini loaf tin. 'It's a modified version of my niece's lemon drizzle.'

'Two of my favourite things,' said Angus de Winter, his eyebrows leaping with enthusiasm.

'And are you confident . . .' said Amanda, her gaze serene and yet interrogating, 'that the rhubarb will deliver that zing, in the same way that citrus does?'

She felt a creeping sense of self-doubt as the words spun in her mind. Perhaps she should have followed her own advice and kept it simple, sticking to the traditional lemon flavour which was, quite frankly, unbeatable.

'I hope so.'

'And I see you're using imperial scales?' Amanda added. 'I don't think we've ever had a contestant do that before.'

'I've only ever baked with these,' said Jenny, as she added three tablespoons of custard powder to the batter before whisking it together, suppressing the urge to lick the whisk. 'I'd be lost without them.'

Dividing the mixture between each loaf, she spread it into the corners with a spatula.

'Going in,' she said, expecting no one to hear. Within seconds a camera appeared by her side, capturing her as she opened the oven door and slid the loaves on to the middle shelf.

'What's next?' said the lady behind the camera, adjusting the lens.

Her mind whirred.

'Now it's time to make the drizzle,' she said, chopping a handful of pink rhubarb to reveal their zesty green centres. 'Of course you can't squeeze rhubarb as you would a lemon, so I've got to stew it.'

'Where do you end up if you steal a rhubarb?' said Mo, appearing out of nowhere, his face alive with mischief.

'Custardy!' he said, igniting a sea of giggles from nearby bakers.

'Very good,' she said, her knees clicking as she crouched by the oven.

She rested her forehead on the warm handle and gazed in at her loaves, which were swollen but pale, not quite done.

'Thirty minutes, bakers,' called Katie from the back of the room, 'that's thirty minutes!'

The energy in the room changed, as if they had become codebreakers given just minutes to save the world.

'Coming out!' called Azeez, ducking behind his workstation. The cameras followed him and there was some sort of discussion as he put his ear to the cakes. After a couple of seconds he turned around, signalling what she could only interpret as his neck on a guillotine.

'Are you all right?' she mouthed.

He shook his head, miming a thumbs down, before turning back to the camera.

Her nose alerted her to the familiar smell of a vanilla sponge that was sufficiently cooked.

'Coming out!' she called, as the camera appeared again. She slid the tin of twelve reassuringly golden domes on to the worktop, prodding each one lightly with her finger.

'Is this how you were expecting them to look?' said the lady.

Jenny nodded. 'I'm just going to insert a skewer into the middle of them to see if it comes out clean,' she said.

To her delight, the skewer came out shiny each time.

'Well, this is as planned,' she said, pricking the cakes with a cocktail stick and dousing them in rhubarb juice so that it sank slowly into them like water into sand.

'Bakers, please put your bakes on the end of your work-tops,' called Katie.

She transferred her drizzle cakes on to a stand in twelve quick pinches, before coming up for air. Looking around the room, the other bakers looked equally dishev-elled, mopping their brows with their aprons, flour in their hair.

'Congratulations on completing your very first chal-lenge,' said a man in a black T-shirt. 'Please follow Carys to the green room whilst the team tidy up your kitchens and we get some pretties.'

'Pretties?' she whispered to Carys as they walked out of the barn in single file, as if they'd just finished an exam.

'They're basically close-ups of your cakes,' she smiled, as they trudged across the lawn. Jenny felt an urge to rush back in there and check on them, as if she had been pulled away too soon.

'I've royally screwed that up,' said Azeez, slumping on

to the green room sofa like a puppet cut loose from his strings. 'My sponges didn't cook evenly; some were over-done and others still raw.'

'It's hard when you're used to your oven at home,' she said, 'but it's early days, there's another bake to go.'

'I really don't want to be the first out,' he said, his face dropping. 'Did yours go okay?'

'I think so,' she said.

They stood by their workstations as Amanda and Angus made their way around the room at a painful pace. She strained to listen to their verdicts as days were made and ruined, her heart sinking for Angela as her lemon and lime drizzles were described as dense. Sorcha's gooseberry and elderflower ones, however, were met with high praise. As they walked towards Azeez, her shoulders tensed. She was as worried about him going home as she was for herself.

'So, green cardamom and orange,' said Amanda, lifting a forkful towards her mouth.

After an excruciating pause, she added, 'They're a little dry.'

He nodded keenly as if to show that he was taking the feedback on board, and pity curdled in Jenny's stomach.

'Great flavours though, the green cardamom is perfectly balanced with the orange,' added Angus.

She tried to catch his eye but he was too relieved to notice, and before she knew it, the judges were heading directly towards her. She wrung her hands together below the counter, biting the inside of her cheek.

'How did it go?' said Angus, gesturing towards her bakes.

'Okay, I think,' she said, as they sliced into one. It held

together well and she could see the pink stained sponge where the rhubarb had soaked through. She tried to read their expressions as they chewed, looking for a raised eyebrow or shared glance.

Amanda broke the silence first by placing her fork back on to the plate with a clatter.

'Very neat, but I have to be honest, I was worried when you said that you were using rhubarb for your drizzle. It really doesn't cut through the way that citrus fruits do, and personally I find that it's best left in crumbles.'

She gulped, desperately trying to keep a straight face for the cameras.

'But you've proven me wrong. It's quite delicious.'

Her heart lurched.

'The sponge has a lovely, light consistency to it. The vanilla custard is just about coming through and the rhubarb gives it that wonderful moisture. A great bake,' said Angus, holding her gaze to show that he meant it.

'Thank you,' she said, taking a deep exhale as they walked away. Azeez flashed her a small thumbs up at waist height and she thought of Bernard and longed to tell him the news. One down, one to go.

Chocolate and Orange Battenburg

There were approximately three seconds each day when Jenny's secret was not fluttering in her chest or twisting in her gut, and it was in the blissful space between sleep and consciousness. First thing in the morning, the light that flooded through her curtains was closely followed by the heavy dawning of her terrible mistake. She spent the rest of the day trying to escape it by pretending it wasn't there, in the futile hope that it might go away. Instead, it invaded her thoughts as she tried to concentrate at college, it hovered on the sidelines of every conversation and it was all she thought about when she was alone.

'Why do you always save the marzipan 'til last?' said Sandra, watching as Jenny carefully stripped the slice of Battenburg of its marzipan coat, which sat in the palm of her hand as they walked home from college.

'It's the best bit,' said Jenny, biting into the soft, pink sponge, a sadness lodged in the back of her throat.

'You know that if you ate it that slowly at my house,' said Sandra, shielding her mouth with her hand, 'you wouldn't stand a chance. By the time you got to the marzipan, someone would've eaten it.'

She feigned a polite, unconvincing sort of smile, so that they continued in silence.

'Is everything all right?' said Sandra, dusting the crumbs from her hands.

'Yes, fine,' said Jenny. 'I think all that typing has tired me out . . .'

Sandra chipped a pebble with the toe of her shoe so that it rolled into the gutter. 'Me too,' she said.

As they walked past the park, Jenny dragged her palm along the iron railings.

'I've actually got to go this way today,' she said, slowing to a halt at the gates. 'I've got a few errands to run for Aunt Ethel.'

'I can come?' said Sandra. 'How long will it take?'

'Honestly, don't worry. It's nothing exciting.'

'All right,' said Sandra with a nod, 'I'll see you in the morning.'

Jenny watched as Sandra continued down the street, her shadow a giant in the afternoon sun.

'Thanks for the Battenburg!' she called over her shoulder.

Jenny walked further into the park, nibbling at the inside of her cheek as she navigated her way to the bench. It was the quietest bench in the park, shaded by beech trees and removed from the path. The underarms of her dress felt damp with sweat, a feeling she always had before seeing him, but this time the thrill was so tangled with fear that she couldn't tell the two apart.

As she waited, her eyes flitted between anything that moved: a rustling branch, a paper bag, a mother pushing a pram. When he turned the corner, she spotted him in an instant: the confident strut of his walk, his dark eyes as he narrowed them in the afternoon sun, the cigarette hanging nonchalantly from his lips. She looked down at her hands, pushing her cuticles into the crescent moon of her nail beds.

'Fancy seeing you here,' he said, the dimple appearing in his left cheek as he planted himself next to her, threading his arm behind

174

her on the bench as if he owned it. 'You couldn't wait until Saturday to see me?'

'No . . .' she said, looking down at the ground through the wooden slats of the bench, her heart racing.

'There's something I think you should know, and it's not something I wanted to say in the shop,' she said.

'If it's that you love me, I'd already guessed,' he said, shrugging his brows.

'It's come as quite a shock . . .'

He withdrew his arm from behind her and dropped his cigarette, squashing it into the dirt with the toe of his boot.

'What is it?'

'It's that I'm . . .' she carved thin grooves into the bench with her nails, 'I'm expecting a baby.'

It was the first time she had said the words out loud, so that they felt unfamiliar, as if she were telling a lie.

He looked out across the park, his hand bristling across his chin and then through his hair. If it weren't for his knees — which began bobbing up and down — she would wonder if he had heard her.

'Who knows?' he said, his words like pins, puncturing the silence.

'No one knows,' she said, 'you're the only person I've told.'

He leant forward over his knees, clasping his hands together as he stared down at the ground. His silence was unnerving, unpredictable, so that she felt as if she were standing too close to an unexploded firework.

'What exactly do you want from me?' he said.

She flinched, heat flooding her cheeks. She wanted him to say that it was going to be all right, that he loved her, that it wasn't the best situation but that he would speak to his wife, and then to her father, and that somehow they would make it work. She could hide the bump until a wedding was organized, and then they would do something small, private. How foolish she had been to hold even the faintest hope.

'I don't know,' she said. 'I thought you weren't very happy . . . in your marriage.'

'You didn't seriously think that I would leave Margaret for you, did you?' he said, an ugly smirk spreading across his face, betrayed by the panic in his eyes. 'I mean, how do I know it's even mine?'

She felt as if a bucket of ice-cold water had been thrown over her.

He looked away again across the park, as if there was something more interesting in the distance. It seemed to her that he was buying time, gathering ammunition.

'You're the only person I've ever been with, Ray,' she said, her voice unsteady as she felt herself unravelling. 'I don't know how you can say that . . .'

'Let's be honest, Jennifer,' he said, using her name like an insult, 'you weren't shy in opening your legs for me. For all I know, it could be anyone's.'

She wanted to pound her fists against him, to shake him, to smash away this veneer in the hope that beneath it was the Ray she recognized, the Ray she had fallen in love with. All at once she was overcome with the fury of being entirely misunderstood, and yet his words undermined her with their sharp, shameful truth. She had given herself to him too soon.

'It's your fault,' she said, grabbing his arm on an impulse.

'Don't make a scene,' he said, his jaw clenched as he snatched it back. 'You're behaving like a child.'

'But you said it would be all right! That this wouldn't happen! And now you're speaking to me like I'm a complete stranger and it's going to –'

He grabbed her shoulders with both hands, the force of him shocking her into silence.

'Now you listen to me,' he hissed, his lips thin with anger. 'You will not say anything about this to anyone, and if you have to, under no circumstances will you mention my name. You will hand your notice in at my mother's shop before you ruin her reputation along with your own, and you can consider this the last time we speak.'

He held her for a second before loosening his grip, and as he did so she jumped to her feet, her cheeks stained with tears.

'I hate you!' she said, before she turned on her heel, and ran.

Jenny followed Azeez into the barn, the pressure of the afternoon ahead pulsing through her veins as the crew busied themselves with last-minute rituals. It felt as if she were backstage at the theatre, just seconds away from the curtains coming up.

She pulled her apron over her head under the bright studio lights whilst Azeez leant on her worktop, rocking her scales like a seesaw. 'I don't know how you get the right accuracy with these,' he said.

'You sound like my Bernard,' she rolled her eyes. 'I probably don't, but it's hard to shake a lifetime's habit when you've been alive as long as I have.'

'If I make it through this week, I'll show you how to use the digital ones – it will literally change your life,' he said, stacking the weights into his palm. 'That could be your cookbook name . . . Jenny goes metric?'

She smiled, concealing a sharp twinge in her chest as she remembered the three recipes she had carefully written out in the cassock-blue book, many years ago.

Angela let out a peal of laughter and almost immediately apologized for it, as the barn grew silent.

'Afternoon, bakers,' said Katie, as she walked to her

spot at the front of the room, Amanda, Angus and Mo in tow. The atmosphere turned serious within a matter of seconds.

'Welcome to the Baker's Delight Challenge,' said Mo. 'You have three hours to show off your very best skills on the theme of . . . Battenburg cake.'

'Three . . . two . . . one . . .'

'Bake!'

She looked at the array of ingredients stacked up on her worktop: jars of ground almonds, flour, a bowl of fresh apricots. There were so many components to this that she stalled, losing her thread. Referring to her notes, she started at the end: the candied orange peel.

'What have you got for us today then, Jenny?' said Angus, his eyes scanning her ingredients.

'I'm making a chocolate and orange Battenburg cake,' she said, as she removed thin spirals of orange skin with a knife, tiny citrus jets bursting from its waxy surface. 'It's my grandmother's recipe, but I'm doing chocolate and orange sponge, sandwiched together with apricot jam and covered in a chocolate marzipan with candied orange peel on top.'

'Sounds delicious,' he said, rubbing his hands together, 'and does this bake have any particular significance for you?'

'Well, Battenburg was my childhood friend Sandra's favourite,' she said, smiling as she remembered how quickly she used to eat it. 'I often brought her a slice to college, many years ago.'

'Why have you chosen to make it with apricot jam rather than, say, something orangey or a chocolate buttercream?' said Amanda.

178

'I really wanted the orange-y flavour to come through and I read that Jaffa cakes are flavoured with apricot rather than orange,' she said, desperate for Amanda's seal of approval. 'It's less bitter.'

'I see. Well, I look forward to tasting it,' she said, gliding towards Sorcha in a swan-like fashion and leaving Jenny with a tinge of doubt that she should've just made her life easier with chocolate buttercream instead.

Next up, an orange and a chocolate sponge. She didn't use a Battenburg tin as some of the others were doing, but instead followed her grandmother's instructions and baked both sponges together with just a piece of greaseproof paper folded in the middle to separate them. It required very precise measurements, but if it was good enough for her grandmother, it was good enough for her.

'Going in,' she said, waiting for a camera but noticing that they were gathered around Angela, who appeared to be making a rainbow-coloured Battenburg, her mixing bowls like paint pots. It was a feast for the eyes but she suspected she might have prioritized aesthetic over flavour, since the primary ingredient appeared to be food colouring.

'What have we got here?' said Mo, eyeing up her tins.

'I'm just putting my sponges into the oven,' she said as she navigated the door with a tea towel and slid them on to the shelf. 'Time is the enemy; I've still got to make an apricot jam.'

'Did you manage to keep to time in practice?'

'No,' she said, pulling a face, 'I was ten minutes over, but I've changed the order of things to hopefully speed it up.'

'I believe in you, Jenny,' he said, giving her a high five with a spatula.

'Thanks, Mo,' she said, removing the small kernel from the centre of an apricot.

'Bakers, you have just one hour left!' called Katie, causing a wave of anxious exchanges, as *'oh no,' 'oh hell,' 'I've got so much to do'* echoed around the barn, everyone's movements changing pace. Three hours was a long time in the real world but she was beginning to learn that in the *Britain Bakes* barn, time took on a whole new meaning.

'How are you getting on?' she said to Azeez, who was scowling into the cold light of the fridge, his hand on his hip.

He sighed, scratching his head, his hair sticking up in exasperated tufts.

'I'm just waiting for the chocolate to set on these coffee beans for my garnish; they're taking their sweet time.'

There was something about the seriousness with which he said this sentence that, combined with his expression, gave her a sudden flash of perspective. Clasping her hand to her mouth, her shoulders began to shake.

'Jenny,' he said, turning to her in shock, 'are you laughing at me?'

She couldn't answer, her hysteria catching on so that they ended up giggling into the fridge like a couple of schoolchildren.

'What's going on here?' said a camera hovering next to them.

'We've got some troublesome coffee beans,' said Azeez, catching his breath. 'I don't actually know why we're laughing so much; it's all Jenny, she's a bad influence.'

Before she could explain herself, her attention was snatched by the persistent beeping of her timer. The sponges. She hot-footed it back to her oven, the camera chasing her.

'Here we are,' she said, opening the oven door and lifting them on to the worktop, rich waves of cocoa warming her cheeks as she pulled back the greaseproof paper.

'They've shrunk away from the edge which – fingers crossed – means they're cooked.'

Once the sponges had cooled, she cut them into four long pieces and stacked them on top of each other in a checkerboard pattern, gluing them together with the apricot jam.

'Five minutes, bakers, that's five minutes!' called Katie.

Putting her sponges in the middle of the marzipan she had made, she wrapped them up like a baby in a blanket, smoothing the edges with her fingers so that there were no bumps or creases. Transferring it on to a board, she cut off each end to reveal a neat cross-section of brown and cream contrasting squares.

'Thirty seconds,' said Mo.

Ideally the candied peel would have been left a number of days but she didn't have that luxury, so she picked it up in pinches and arranged it down the centre of the Battenburg, the edible equivalent of a mohican.

'Time is up! Please step away from your Baker's Delights,' said Katie, chiming a spoon against a saucepan.

Jenny took a step back, overcome with relief. As they filed out of the barn and took a seat on the steps outside, savouring a blast of sweet spring air, she grew aware of how tired her body felt, her joints heavy, her mind depleted. She was so consumed in the barn that she barely thought or felt anything, but as soon as she stopped, reality hit, knocking her off her feet.

'Yours looked great,' said Azeez. 'Were you pleased with it?'

'Thank you. I think so, I just hope the flavours come through. How was your espresso martini Battenburg?'

'It went all right,' he said, screwing his nose up as if he'd tasted something he didn't like. 'The squares weren't quite even enough for my liking.'

'You know what?' she said. 'I've never actually had an espresso martini.'

'Really? It's just a very delicious coffee cocktail, I'll have to introduce you –'

'Right, nearly there, guys, if you could head back into the barn for me,' called Carys, flicking her fringe out of her eyes.

They headed back inside, an apprehensive silence taking hold as one by one they carried their Baker's Delights up to the front of the room. Each comment about an 'uneven checkerboard' or a 'flavourless sponge', whilst directed at another baker, made her feel increasingly insecure about her own. Had she made sure there was enough orange zest in the sponge? Was apricot jam a mistake? Should she have chosen more exciting colours?

Eventually, the moment of truth. She picked up her Battenburg and carried it up to the judges, placing it in front of them as if she were presenting her heart on a plate.

They twisted the board, scrutinizing it before picking up the knife and slicing through it.

'Nice equal squares,' said Angus, before taking a forkful.

It was painful to watch. She considered the three hours

that it had taken to make and how quickly it was devoured, the aesthetic destroyed as the candied peel scattered across the plate.

'I don't like this,' said Amanda, narrowing her eyes.

She felt the floor drop from beneath her feet.

'I love it.'

She exhaled sharply, clutching her neck as the floor returned.

'I'm getting orange, I'm getting chocolate and I'm getting almond. It's a lovely combination and the apricot jam really works. However . . .' she raised an eyebrow, 'one last test.'

She picked up a piece of the candied peel and tapped it against the plate.

'That's just about a pass,' she said, her smile slightly skewed. 'It's crisp enough to make a noise.'

'Oh, thank you,' said Jenny, retrieving her bake and heading back to her workstation, giddy with praise.

'Thank you, bakers,' said Katie. 'Now for the moment you have all been waiting for. Tomorrow, two bakers will compete for the coveted *golden whisk* . . . but who will it be?'

'Remember,' added Mo, 'the judges will choose the two *strongest* bakers to go head to head in the Blind Bake Challenge. The winner will be awarded the golden whisk, which means immunity from next week's elimination.'

He paused, stretching the silence like dough.

'Judges, please make your decision.'

A muted conversation ensued between Amanda and Angus, their hands cupped over their mouths as they whispered. Jenny looked around at the sea of wide eyes and raised shoulders, and then down at her shoes, taking deep breaths.

'Angus, Amanda,' said Katie, putting an end to their discussion. 'Will you please reveal the names of the two bakers that you think have been the strongest this week.'

Angus tidied his bun and cleared his throat, stretching the silence even further.

'Paul,' he said, nodding towards him, 'and Jenny.'

She froze, the moment a heady blur of applause and bright lights.

'Me?' she said soundlessly, putting her hand to her mouth.

'You smashed it!' said Azeez, signalling a double thumbs up.

Before long, the crew flooded the room, each focusing on their own little cog in this huge machine as they tidied away cakes and ferried around equipment.

'Thank you, guys, great work on a brilliant day one,' said Andy, appearing from behind the curtain on the gallery side of the barn. 'Remember, identical outfits again tomorrow.'

There was a chorus of chatter as everyone began to relax and she stood in the midst of it all, stunned.

'Keep your aprons on! We need to get master interviews with you all before you jump on the bus back to the hotel,' he said, straining to compete with the noise.

'Nice one!' said Carys, bounding towards her. 'How did you find it?'

'It's just incredible,' she replied, as Carys led her outside for her interview. 'The whole thing was surreal, I've never experienced anything like it . . .'

'You did great,' she said, leading her towards a gentleman

with a camera perched on his shoulder like a parrot. 'I'll see you bright and early for round three.'

Jenny said goodbye and tidied her hair, savouring the birdsong and the rustle of the trees in the cool dusk breeze. It was a welcome escape from the chaos inside the barn.

'How does it feel,' he said, squinting through the lens, 'being chosen to compete for the golden whisk in week one?'

'I can't believe it,' she said, shaking her head as it dawned on her all over again, '. . . fingers crossed I pull it out of the bag tomorrow, because I've got a taste for it now.'

18

Pineapple Upside Down Cake

Jenny didn't like surprises, or audiences for that matter, but today she was faced with both. Her fellow bakers watched on keenly from the sidelines as she stood behind her workstation, waiting for the Blind Bake to be revealed. She took a small amount of comfort from the fact that Paul was used to rescuing people from burning buildings, and yet he looked equally nervous, his hands behind his back as he stared up at the rafters.

She studied the tea towel in front of her which concealed her fate, analysing every bump and corner as if it were a present. Her worst nightmare was that underneath it might be something that she had never even heard of.

'Today, the judges are turning baking on its head with a retro classic,' said Mo, gesturing towards the cloche on a pedestal at the front of the room. 'Angus, do you want to do the honours?'

He nodded, stepping forward and in a dramatic sweep of his arm, removing it.

'It's a pineapple upside down cake!' he said, as she

strained to see. 'Remember; you can take a closer look, but you can't touch.'

'Your ingredients are underneath the tea towel in front of you, but in the Blind Bake Challenge, you have *no recipe*,' said Katie, her tone serious. 'You have seventy-five minutes to complete your pineapple upside down cakes.'

'Judges,' said Mo, 'this challenge is judged blind, so if you would please step outside . . .

'Three . . . two . . . one . . .'

'Bake!'

Jenny snatched away the tea towel, her eyes immediately drawn to the fresh pineapple where she had expected to see tinned. What on earth was she supposed to do with that?

'I imagine you've made a few of these in your time, Jenny?' said Mo, appearing to her left as she switched on her oven, a mischievous glint in his eye.

Her Aunt Ethel had made an upside down cake once and only once after her father had complained of an itchy mouth. It had since lost its place on the menu and she hadn't minded, agreeing that pineapple in sponge was an odd mix.

'As a matter of fact, I haven't,' she replied, her hand tracing her lips as her eyes flicked between the example and the ingredients. Without a time or temperature, she guessed at gas mark four.

'I know what one is, though, which is something.'

Without a moment to spare, she had no choice but to get going, and before she knew it, the pair of them were frantically chopping pineapple, stirring caramel and cracking eggs.

'Going in!' said Paul, reminding her that she didn't have long.

Tipping the sponge mixture on top of the pineapple rings and spreading it evenly with a spatula, she glanced back at the example and wondered how long it might need in the oven. At this point, she only had thirty minutes anyway.

'Going in,' she called, as a camera appeared by her side.

'I have no idea how long that needs,' she said, fanning herself with an oven glove, 'so I'm just going to have to keep an eye on it.'

With that, she sat down next to the oven, willing her bake to hurry and watching as it defied her. In the corner of her eye she spotted Paul drizzling caramel on to the back of a glass bowl to make a sugar cage, so that she considered crawling towards the exit whilst no one was watching.

'How's it going?' asked a producer, joining her on the floor.

'I'm a bit worried,' she said, squinting through the heat. 'I've got ten minutes left and I can't tell if this is cooked or not. The sponge looks done but the pineapple needs to be cooked through and I can't see it, of course, with it being upside down.'

Paul was now turning out his pineapple upside down cake and delicately balancing his sugar cage over the top of it, prompting her to retrieve hers from the oven, leaving it to settle on the side.

'You've got three minutes,' said Mo, his eyes wide.

'Right,' she said, pursing her lips. 'Let's do it, then.'

This was it, the moment of truth. Never had the bottom

189

of a cake mattered quite so much. The cameras gathered around as she flipped the whole thing over, pausing to give it a firm tap before removing the tin as if she were making a sandcastle.

Her face fell.

'Oh no,' she gasped, looking between Mo and the yellow mess on the plate. 'I forgot to line the tin . . .'

Mo leant over it as if it were a small animal in trouble, whilst she frantically attempted to revive it, pulling steaming pieces of pineapple from the ruins.

'Your time is up!' called Katie. 'Please bring your Blind Bakes up to the front.'

She looked towards Azeez, who was watching through his fingers.

One half looked passable, but the other was uneven where she had chiselled the remaining pineapple from the bottom of the tin and balanced it on top of the cake in a desperate attempt to salvage it.

Reluctantly, she carried it towards the front of the room and placed it behind the picture of herself smiling, a stark contrast to how she currently felt. She glanced at the example which was perched cruelly on a pedestal at the centre of the table, and then at Paul's which looked like something from the cover of a food magazine. Hers was a bad tribute act, his the real deal. She thought of her father and his itchy mouth. Nothing relating to Aunt Ethel ever came to any good.

Jenny pushed open their squeaky gate and walked towards the front door, which opened before she had even got her key out of her bag.

'Welcome back, darling,' said Bernard, taking her bags with his left hand, an oven glove on his right.

It had only been a couple of days and yet it took her a few seconds to reacquaint herself with him.

'Well I never,' she said, flooded with a warm sense of familiarity, 'Bernard Quinn wearing an oven glove?'

'Indeed,' he said, planting a kiss on her cheek. 'How did it go?'

Wholesome smells of jacket potato crept down the hallway as she wriggled out of her coat and exchanged her shoes for slippers.

'Shall we have supper and I'll tell you all about it?'

She followed her nose all the way to the kitchen, where the table was laid with their very best silver and a bright vase of tulips stood proudly at its centre next to a bowl of salad and some leftover quiche.

'Thank you for this,' she said, sitting in her chair. 'The tulips are beautiful – are they yours?'

'They are,' he said, retrieving the potatoes from the oven and transferring them on to dinner plates. 'They've all burst out in the last few days.'

She watched as he steadily cut them in half as if he were performing a surgery, before slotting a particularly large rectangle of butter into each, which melted into delicious, golden pools.

'I'm impressed,' she said, as she sprinkled it with pepper.

'Well, I was left good instructions,' he said, his mouth forming an oval shape as he simultaneously tried to chew his food and cool it down.

'Go on then,' he said, taking a sip of water. 'How was it?'

'I don't even know where to begin,' she said, stabbing a

tomato with her fork. 'My rhubarb and custard drizzle was a success. Amanda said she was worried that I hadn't used a citrus fruit and I started to doubt myself, but in the end she was pleasantly surprised.'

'Well done, darling,' he said, mashing his butter into the potato, 'I thought that one would be a winner. And what about the Battenburg?'

'That went even better,' she said, watching as his mashing slowed and he looked up. 'They liked it so much that I was one of the two bakers chosen to compete for the golden whisk . . .'

His cutlery clattered against his plate as he clapped his hands, a smile encompassing his whole face. 'Bravo!'

A forkful of food hovered by her mouth before she retracted it, her face falling.

'Oh no, what?'

'Well, that was a total disaster. It was a pineapple upside down cake . . .'

'I'm not keen on those. They used to give your father an itchy mouth, didn't they?'

'Yes. And I completely messed it up by forgetting to line the tin, so half of it got stuck in the bottom,' she said, before resuming her eating. 'Such a silly, silly mistake.'

'I'm sorry,' he said, his eyes round, captivated. 'So go on then, what happened?'

'Well,' she said, neatly folding a piece of lettuce with her knife, 'Paul – who I was up against – he won the golden whisk, so he's immune from elimination next week.'

He nodded tentatively.

'And I lived to survive another week.'

'Yes! I knew you'd do it, darling!' he said, reaching across to squeeze her shoulder. 'So who went home?'

'A young farmer called Fergus . . . It was a close call, but his Battenburg was a very odd shape,' she said, her face growing serious at the thought.

'Well, what a result,' he said, still revelling in the fact that she had made it through. 'What's next week?'

'Biscuit week,' she said with a gulp.

Key Lime Brandy Snaps

As she cleared their plates, she felt the presence of her secret in the pit of her stomach, in the back of her throat, in her hot palms. It was becoming increasingly difficult to hide, even under her looser dresses and cardigans. Just this morning she had studied her profile in the mirror, her body becoming less familiar with each passing week. The swell of her chest, her thickening waist, the tea-coloured line that had mysteriously appeared up the centre of her stomach like a seam. She wondered how much longer she could pretend.

'I've made one of your favourites for pudding,' she said, forcing enthusiasm into her voice.

'Lucky me,' said her father, raising his brows. 'The question is, which one?'

She retrieved a plate of neatly rolled brandy snaps, plump like cigars and filled with the cream she had saved from the top of the milk, placing them on the table. Their sickly smell was unusually potent, so that rather than enticing her as typically it would, tonight it made her nauseous.

His face creased into a smile.

'Brandy snaps,' he said, reaching for one and balancing it between his lips in his best impression of Winston Churchill.

Usually she would laugh, but she couldn't meet his eyes, her conscience forcing her to avoid them so that she appeared quiet, distracted. Every day she vowed to tell him and every day she failed, wanting to sustain his belief that she was a daughter to be proud of.

She crushed the brandy snap between her teeth, forcing herself to eat it as the thoughts in her mind grew loud, overwhelming her other senses. She returned it to her plate, unable to finish it.

'Are you all right, Jen?' he said.

She nodded, her smile taut as if it were pinned at the corners.

'You have it,' she said, pushing her plate towards him.

He didn't take it.

'It's not like you, to leave something sweet.'

As she met his eyes, she felt herself becoming unpicked. The pressure of her secret reared up inside her like a great wave so that she covered her face with her hands.

'What's wrong?'

She dropped her head, listening to the scrape of his chair against the floor as he faltered, unsure of how to respond.

'Has something happened?' he said, his tone now urgent.

Salty tears streamed down her face, stinging her cheeks.

'It's all my fault,' she said, the words bolting. 'I've done something terrible.'

'Now, now,' he said, pressing his lips into a sorry line, 'what terrible thing could you possibly have done?'

His concern only amplified her guilt. She felt her chest heave, a sob lurching from the core of her.

He stood up and crouched beside her, pulling a handkerchief from his sleeve.

'You can tell me,' he said, placing it in her hand, 'whatever it is.'

'I'm —' she said, the words erupting from her, 'I'm having a baby.'

It was the second time she had said those words out loud, and yet she still felt as if they did not belong to her.

The look on his face in that moment was something she knew would haunt her forever, as she watched his heart break in his eyes. She longed for him to say something, to be angry, but instead her words were followed by silence. Resentment ripped through her: for Ray, for the life inside her, for herself.

The corners of his mouth turned down so that he looked different, unbearable.

'I'm sorry,' he said, his chin trembling. 'I know it's not been perfect, but I thought I had done all right without your mother.'

She reached for his arm, her heart twisting.

'You have, Daddy,' she said, 'you have.'

He dropped his head.

'No,' he said. 'I've failed you both.'

Jenny heated together the butter, demerara sugar and golden syrup in the bottom of a pan, glad to be back in the safe surroundings of her little kitchen. The slick chaos of the barn had been replaced by an afternoon play on the radio, and the only thing that appeared next to her was a large cup of tea. She picked up her timer from the windowsill, an old friend. It was nothing special, just a small Bakelite square with a dial, but whilst it had yellowed over the years and the numbers had worn away, its comforting tick was the soundtrack to some of her most contented afternoons. Twisting the once-red arrow, she began her mission to perfect her Baker's Dozen, Mo's voice in her head as he announced *not thirteen* but *twelve* brandy snaps.

She dragged the wooden spoon along the bottom of the pan, hovering her ear above it to listen for gritty granules of sugar, so that it throbbed in the heat. Instead, she heard the distant hacks of Bernard's cough, which drew closer as he neared the kitchen.

'Are you all right, darling?' she said, alarm rising in her chest as he rested one hand on the doorframe, the other a fist over his mouth as he heaved and barked like a cold engine.

He nodded, stooping over her to reach for his inhaler on the top shelf of the cupboard.

'That's a nasty cough,' she said, her concern heightening with each great wheezing puff. 'Do you think we should go to the doctor's?'

He clicked the lid on his inhaler and put it back in the cupboard.

'I'll be all right,' he said, his voice rasping, 'it's just a common cough.'

She looked at him, noticing that his eyes were weepy, dull.

'You don't look well,' she said, a shadow falling across her heart, 'or sound it. I'm going to worry if we don't get you checked over.'

'Don't worry, it will pass.' He popped a lozenge into his cheek. 'What are you making? Do you want me to ask you some questions?'

'Bernard,' she said, crossing her arms, 'I'm not sure I should be going away this week, if you still feel like this.'

'I'm fine,' he said, in a tone that suggested she was fussing unnecessarily. 'If it gets any worse I'll go, but you don't need to worry about me.'

She paused, sighed.

'All right,' she said, resuming her stirring with some reluctance, '. . . I'm making key lime brandy snaps.'

Bernard hummed in approval, tapping the worktop with his swollen fingers. She couldn't pinpoint the moment when his hands had grown old, his once shapely fingers now ruddy and inflamed, and she reached out to stroke them.

'How do you make them into tubes?'

'Well,' she said, pulling the pan off the hob for a moment before adding flour, ground ginger, lime zest and juice, 'you wrap them around the handle of a wooden spoon.'

'Clever,' he said, interrupted by the phone, 'back in a second.'

The kitchen was cloaked in a brume of rich toffee as she spooned the mixture into puddles on a baking tray and posted them into the oven. As she took one set out, she swiftly replaced it with another, gently folding each around the handle of an oiled wooden spoon whilst it was still pliable.

Next, she filled the cloth piping bag with lime zest and cream, wringing the top between her hands so that it peeped out of the nozzle. She piped a dot on to the end of her finger like toothpaste on a brush and popped it into her mouth. She would add some lime curd to the final thing, she thought, to really sharpen the cream.

'Rose and Jeremy send their love and congratulations,' said Bernard as he returned to inspect her progress, his voice heavy, crackling. 'They just called to find out how you got on . . . also, Rose has been promoted to partner at her law firm.'

'How lovely,' she said, filling each end of a brandy snap. 'And that's just brilliant. Well done Rose, she's got it all.'

'She has. Margot would have been so proud.'

As she picked up the next one, she understood – for the first time – just a glimpse of how it might feel to have lived a life of making people proud, of walking confidently into a room as a lawyer, a mother, a success.

Chocolate Teacakes

She lay on her bed, watching the life inside her push against the wall of her stomach, a part of her and yet exercising its own free will. A fleeting movement shot across the side of her bump like an eye under an eyelid. She pressed on it lightly and it retreated as if it were playing a game, determined not to be found. Her secret had become her greatest ally, a source of company and comfort in her isolation. Stroking it in circular motions, she admired its perfect roundness. With each day that passed, she felt heavier with the weight of carrying two hearts.

Easing herself on to her tired feet, she made her way to the kitchen and reached for the biscuit tin. Using her bump as leverage to prise off the lid, she was met with the metallic reflection of her own face. Forcing the lid back on, she searched for alternatives. A slice of bread? An apple? Neither would do.

She pulled on her duffle coat, pushing the toggles through the loops but leaving the bottom two undone so that it skimmed shapelessly over her bump. With three months to go it was almost impossible to disguise, but she had to at least try — just in case she saw someone that she knew.

'Where are you going?' said her father, making her jump.

'Just to the shops.'

'I can go? What do you need?'

'I'll go, I need some fresh air. I haven't left the house all week . . .'

He hesitated, his face lined with worry.

'Wait a moment,' he said, disappearing upstairs.

It had been a month since she had told him her secret, and they had only spoken in stilted exchanges, as if they were each a reminder to the other of the hurt, the shame.

When he returned, she noticed he was clutching something in his hand.

'I think you should wear this, if you're going out in public,' he said, holding a dainty gold band in his palm, which she recognized as her mother's.

She paused before taking the ring and pushing it over her swollen knuckles.

'Thank you,' she said, her voice flat. 'I won't be long.'

He pulled out a chair, gesturing for her to sit down.

'I've spoken to Aunt Ethel,' he said.

She nodded, bristling at the thought of her reaction, certain that she would bask in her failure.

'She said there are places you can go.' He looked at the table, at the floor, at her mother's ring. 'Homes for girls in your situation. You can go and have it and no one will ever know.'

'And what about the baby?'

'They will be adopted by a married couple who have the means to raise them and give them a happy, loving home.'

'Like a naughty girls' home?' she said, twisting the ring around her finger.

'They're not called that.'

'How long do you go for?'

'You go for six weeks before the . . . arrival, and six weeks after.'

She looked away as she processed his words.

'Aunt Ethel has made contact with one; she thinks it's best for you and best for the . . .' he paused, his voice wooden, '. . . the baby. And I think she's right.'

They sat for a moment in an uncomfortable silence.

'But we managed,' she said, 'just the two of us.'

He ran his hand through his hair.

'It's different, Jen,' he said with a sigh. 'Your mother and I were married when we had you. You want that one day too, don't you?'

She nodded.

'I've thought about what your mother would do, I've asked her in my prayers,' he said, his eyes desperate. 'The truth is, I just want to do the right thing, and I worry that your future will be . . . difficult, if you've got another man's child.'

She swallowed, her throat dry.

'I know it feels like the end of the world at the moment,' he said, searching her face, 'but you are so young and my hope is that you will look back on this one day, when you have a family of your own, and it will all make sense.'

She picked up her satchel from the floor.

'If you go to one of these homes, no one ever needs to know.'

'I'm sure you're right,' she said, the words a betrayal to her heart. 'I'll be back shortly.'

Closing the front door behind her, she pulled up her hood. Outside the trees were quickly becoming silhouettes, as leaves were stripped from their branches, whirling and diving like confetti; burnt sienna and gold. Autumn was usually her favourite time of year, the season of colder days and darker nights, sugar-coated by fires, pavements that crunched underfoot and shiny, auburn conkers. This year, she felt as if her pockets were full of stones.

The streets grew busier the closer she got to town. Trapped in the heat of her duffle coat, a bead of sweat ran down her chest and she felt the burning stare of passers-by as she pulled up her left sleeve so that they might assume a different story. Her eyes darted between the faces of strangers as she searched for Ray, or worse, Sandra, who thought she had left college on doctor's orders due to ill health. It was strange how when you were terrified of seeing someone, everybody looked like them, developing their stature, their walk, their laugh.

A bell chimed as she entered the newsagent's, drawing unwanted attention. She moved quietly in an attempt to remain discreet, although she was sure that the shopkeeper was glaring straight at the centre of her coat. Wasting no time, she headed straight over to the silver and red striped foil of the Tunnock's Teacakes that she had been inexplicably craving. Picking one up, she held it in the palm of her hand before placing it by the till. Adding another three, she reached into her purse and pushed the coins towards the gentleman, who looked at her as if she had inconvenienced him. He exhaled a curling cloud of smoke before handing back her change and she pushed the treats into her pockets, making a swift exit.

As she walked through town, her feet moving with a brisk sense of urgency, she felt as keen to get home as she had been to leave. Turning a corner on to a quiet street, she pulled one from her pocket, peeled back the foil and bit through the chocolate with a snap. The marshmallow stuck to her lips and coated her teeth, transporting her to a happier place. Still enjoying the first one, she started to unwrap a second, taking a bite as if it were as vital to her as oxygen.

She felt a flutter.

'Hello, little friend,' she said, dabbing at her mouth with the back of her sleeve, 'somebody's got my sweet tooth.'

*

Jenny walked towards the barn, clutching her umbrella as the rain drummed against the plastic, droplets racing down the sides like mice.

'How are you feeling?' said Azeez, stooping under so that neither of them could quite fit, their height difference making it impossible to accommodate the both of them.

'Wet,' she said, as a raindrop fell from the end of her nose, 'and terrified.'

They sped up, the rain gaining momentum.

'Your brandy snaps were perfect, and your gingerbread church got you into the Blind Bake Challenge for the *second* week in a row . . .' he said, gripping her arm as they carefully navigated the stone steps. 'You've absolutely got this.'

'Thank you,' she said, as they entered the bright lights of the barn.

'Break a leg,' he said under his breath, as he joined the other bakers at the side.

Like a ritual, Jenny and Angela headed towards their workstations, looped their aprons over their heads and tied them behind their backs. Moments later, Amanda took her position at the front of the barn, followed by this week's guest judge: Camilla Wainwright. Jenny had recognized Camilla instantly as the founder of a prestigious cookery school and author of many cookbooks – none of which she actually owned. In person, she was well-spoken and had a depth of voice which gave her an air of great authority. The idea of presenting a woman of Camilla's talent with anything she had baked felt – at best – humiliating.

'Jenny, Angela,' said Katie, 'welcome to the Blind Bake Challenge.'

She looked from the lumpen tea towel on her workstation, to the cloche at the centre of the room, willing it to be something familiar, an old friend.

'Camilla,' said Katie, 'will you do the honours?'

'I will,' she said, stepping forward and removing the cloche so that they both grew a couple of inches taller, as they strained to see what looked like a plate of chocolate game show buzzers, one neatly cut in half to reveal the layers.

'My favourite: chocolate teacakes,' said Mo. 'Your ingredients are underneath the tea towel in front of you, but in the Blind Bake Challenge, you have *no recipe*. You have two hours to make six identical teacakes. Judges, any tips?'

Amanda's eyes narrowed. 'Think very carefully about your timings.'

Jenny peeled back the tea towel to reveal the usual suspects: eggs, sugar, flour and chocolate.

'Ever made chocolate teacakes, Jenny?' said a man squinting into the lens of a camera.

'For the second week in a row, I'm ashamed to say that I haven't. I know exactly what they taste like though; I'm well acquainted with the Tunnock's variety.'

With that, she set about rubbing together the ingredients for the biscuit base, adding a splash of milk to help her press it into a dough. Next she rolled it into a sheet, punching six identical circles into it with a biscuit cutter.

'How's it going?' said a camera, appearing next to her.

'Well, they look like biscuits so that's something,' she said, heading towards the fridge. 'I'm going to cool them whilst I do the meringue, as I don't want them to spread out too much in the oven.'

The camera quickly retreated, moving swiftly towards

Angela who was scraping runny white meringue into the bin, beads of sweat clinging to her brow.

'It's okay,' said Katie, her voice hopelessly optimistic, 'you've got time.'

Angela didn't look at all comforted as she wetted a tea towel and tied it around her head like a bandana, preparing to start again. In fact, she looked as if she were in a gruelling tennis tournament, and the chocolate teacake was about to take the second set.

'I'm going to leave these on the worktop to cool,' Jenny said to the camera, whilst quickly painting the inside of the silicone moulds with chocolate. 'One lesson I learnt in practice is that refrigerated chocolate loses its shine.'

'Bakers, you have one hour left, that's one hour left!'

'Going in,' Jenny called, her heart racing as she transferred her biscuits to the oven. 'I have no idea how long to do these for. I'll just have to keep an eye.'

She whisked together the egg whites, sugar, vanilla and golden syrup over a pan of simmering water until it began to transform into a toothpaste-white mixture, the sugar creating a nitid sheen.

'I'm looking for stiff peaks so it will hold when I pipe it,' she said, creating little waves with her whisk so that the very tips collapsed forward like a child's drawing of the ocean.

'Sweet heavens above!' she heard Angela say, the back of her dress dark with sweat.

She scanned her own deconstructed teacakes, holding off putting them together for fear of disaster.

'Thirty minutes, bakers!' called Katie.

It was now or never. She piped the Italian meringue into

the six chocolate-lined domes like dollops of shaving foam, lightly pressing the biscuits on top before sealing them with chocolate. Stepping back, her shoulders slowly lowered themselves from just below her ears. All she could do now was wait.

'Angela and Jenny, you have five minutes. That's five minutes,' said Katie, as the cameras dashed between them, catching the moment of truth.

Mo stood next to Angela, unblinking as he watched her slowly remove the mould with a gasp. A liquid meringue flooded from the seam where the dome met the biscuit, so that each teacake transformed into a melted snowman wearing a chocolate bowler hat. Jenny winced. There was no fixing that.

She heard a snigger from the side of the room and looked over to the other bakers, who were watching on, transfixed. Azeez had his hand over his mouth in dismay, but behind him Sorcha appeared to be stifling hysterical giggles.

'Jenny,' said Katie, diverting her attention back to the task in hand, 'you've got two minutes.'

She nodded.

'Here we go . . .'

The room grew quiet as she flipped the silicone mould on to a plate, holding her breath in the knowledge that she had absolutely no control over what was about to happen. In the manner of a surgeon, she gently pulled back the rubber corners to reveal a shiny chocolate shell.

'Looking good,' said Katie, as she put the first teacake on to a plate, 'just five more to go.'

As she peeled each one from the mould and it remained intact, her great relief developed an aftertaste of guilt, as in the corner of her eye she noticed a runner handing a tissue to Mo, who handed it to Angela. Her laughter, which usually filled the barn, left a hollow silence so that all that could be heard was rain pattering against the roof.

'Jenny, Angela, time is up!' announced Katie, louder than anticipated given that she was standing just a foot away. 'Please bring your chocolate teacakes up to the front of the room and place them behind your pictures.'

'Bakers,' said Mo, gesturing towards the group, 'please join Jenny and Angela for the results.'

Jenny and Angela processed to the front as if they were presenting offerings at a harvest festival, whilst the other bakers muddled into a crescent position, shifting their weight between their feet and wringing their hands in the pockets of their aprons.

The judges entered, examining their offerings with their eyes. At the centre of the table were the picture-perfect examples. To the left were Jenny's, which certainly resembled them but with the charm of something home-made, and to their right were poor Angela's, like clowns at a beauty pageant.

'Oh dear,' said Camilla, picking up one of Angela's teacakes which left a trail of white drips, 'someone has had a disaster with the Italian meringue. I would hazard a guess that the eggs were under-beaten.'

Jenny caught sight of Sorcha, sure that she was smirking, and then she looked towards Angela, a disappointed slope to her shoulders. She felt a rush of great empathy as her best efforts were dashed.

'Mmm,' said Camilla as she took a bite of hers, dabbing meringue from her lips, 'these are almost spot on, well done.'

Jenny felt a wave of relief.

'Just be careful that you keep things uniform,' said Amanda. 'There is a slight variation in the thickness of the chocolate.'

She made a mental note, allowing herself for a fraction of a second to imagine winning biscuit week, before expelling it from her mind.

'Now for the moment of truth,' said Mo, as he handed Camilla the golden whisk. 'Which of these two bakes was your favourite?'

Silence ensued.

'It has to be this one,' she said, pointing to Jenny's.

'Oh!' she gasped, a tremble taking over her chin as Azeez put his arm around her, giving her a firm squeeze. A brim of salty tears formed in her eyes, so that when she blinked they spilled down her cheeks. She dabbed at them with her apron, feeling pats on her back from the hands of her new friends.

Camilla walked towards her with the golden whisk and her heart thundered.

'Well deserved,' she said.

Jenny traced it with her fingers, surprised by the weight of it, the shininess.

'And now for the difficult part,' said Mo, wearing a stern expression, which didn't come naturally to him. 'Paul, as the winner of last week's golden whisk, you are immune from elimination. However, time is up for one of your fellow bakers.'

Paul pressed his lips into a modest smile, the others twitching with suspense.

'Judges, which baker are you sending home?'

There was a long pause.

'Martin,' said Camilla, as she looked towards the vicar.

He smiled graciously, as everyone gravitated towards him with outstretched arms. A little further along, Angela had her hand over her mouth, her eyes wide with shock.

'It's okay,' he said, as he returned hugs and well wishes. 'It's my time to go, I was lucky to be here in the first place.'

Jenny recognized his words and felt a hot indignance rising in her chest.

'You weren't lucky, Martin,' she said, as she planted a kiss in the air by his cheek, 'you made your own luck.'

'Thank you,' he replied, pausing for a moment as if her words really meant something.

On her way out of the barn, she placed the golden whisk in the glass jar at the front of her worktop, so that her kitchen wore it like a medal.

'I knew you'd do it,' said Azeez, giddy in the knowledge that they had lived to survive another week. 'Shall we go for a celebratory espresso martini? There's a bar near the station, so technically it's on the way home.'

She glanced at her watch. 'That would be lovely,' she said, 'but just the one; I mustn't be too late home to Bernard.'

'Congratulations,' said Carys, bounding over and squeezing her. 'Can I grab you for a quick interview outside?'

'Of course,' she said, 'Azeez, I'll meet you back in the green room.'

The sun was falling in the sky as she made her way through the orchard and across the lawn towards the camera, inhaling as much of the fresh evening air as she could fit into her lungs. As she drew closer, she noticed that Angela was still doing her interview, blotting her tears with the back of her hand.

'I'm just embarrassed really,' she heard her say to the camera.

Jenny slowed down, hovering with concern.

'I really messed it up.'

The producer gave her a tentative tap on the arm before she headed back towards the green room, her steps heavy and her arms limp by her sides.

'Angela,' said Jenny, speeding up to intercept her, 'don't be too hard on yourself. Remember my pineapple upside down cake last week? It was a total disaster, and that was a far simpler thing to bake than chocolate teacakes.'

'Thank you, Jenny. I just feel like I made a real fool of myself,' she gulped, '. . . and between us, I saw Sorcha laughing at me.'

Jenny reached into her pocket, pulling out one of Bernard's handkerchiefs, embroidered with his initials.

'That says far more about her than it does about you,' she said, pressing it into her hand, 'and you were chosen to do it because you were in the top two, so between us, I might be inclined to think it's jealousy.'

Angela nodded, the corners of her mouth flickering upwards as she looked at the handkerchief.

'Who's BJQ?'

'My husband, Bernard.'

Angela smiled, dabbing at her cheeks. 'I don't feel I can blow my nose on it now.'

'Oh, he wouldn't mind,' she said, knowing it to be true,

'and by the way, I rather liked your teacakes. They reminded me of snowmen.'

'Snowmen in the Sahara,' Angela replied, the light coming back into her face.

'A little, perhaps,' she agreed, causing Angela to throw her head back as she laughed.

'Thank you,' she said, 'I needed that. And well done, you deserved to win.'

'Jenny!' called Carys, waving her arms around frantically. 'You need to do your interview before we lose light.'

'Coming!' said Jenny, giving Angela a hug. 'See you next week.'

As they parted ways and she trudged across the lawn towards the interview spot, she felt the embers of connection, of having lifted someone else's spirits.

'Just here please, Jenny,' said the man with the camera, as she reached into her pocket, applying a quick coat of lipstick.

'How does it feel, winning the golden whisk?'

'It's hard to put into words. Never did I think I'd win biscuit week; I was just hoping to stay in . . .' She hesitated, allowing herself to be honest, 'I've never truly believed that I was good enough to be here, but today, I felt good enough.'

'And of the three things you baked this week, which are you proudest of?'

'I'm proudest of my Baker's Delight,' she said, with great certainty. 'It was modelled on the church where I married my husband, Bernard. We've been married fifty-nine, nearly sixty years, so it's a special one.'

'Brilliant, thank you, Jenny. One last thing, would you like to call Bernard on camera and tell him the good news?'

'Go on then,' she said.

He handed her a phone and she dialled their number.

'If you hold it out in front of you and press the speaker button,' he said, watching as she did it, 'that's it.'

The pauses grew longer between each ring as she anticipated him answering, rearranging sentences in her mind as she tried to work out the best way to deliver her news. Even something as simple as speaking to her husband suddenly felt complicated under the gaze of the camera. Eventually, she was asked by a robot to please leave a message after the tone.

'That's odd,' she said, giving the phone a closer inspection, 'maybe he's in the garden.'

'Shall we try one more time?' he said, and she agreed, her expectation diminishing with each ring until again they were met with an automated voice.

'Never mind,' she said, as she handed it back, 'he'll be trying to get something finished in the garden; he never hears the phone from outside.'

'No worries. Well done again, Jenny,' he said, as he slung the camera down by his side like a briefcase.

She walked back towards the green room, carrying with her an acute sense of longing, a longing to share her news with the person that she loved most.

Retrieving her phone and turning it on, she slowly typed a message, each letter a musical note so that it sounded like a badly tuned piano. DEAR BERNIE, GOING FOR QUICK DRINK, WON'T BE TOO LATE LOVE JENNY X. She decided she would save the good news to tell him in person and pressed send, watching her message disappear into the abyss with a *swish*, before turning it off.

As she looked up at the darkening sky, she missed him madly. She had once read somewhere that the tragedy of monogamy was that you never fell in love again, but how wrong it was. Over the years, she had fallen in love with Bernard over and over and over.

21

Espresso Martini

'Two espresso martinis,' said the waiter, raising his voice above the chorus of chatter as he pushed two drinks towards them across the dimly lit bar.

She was perched on a stool, her feet suspended high above the ground, certain in the knowledge that she had never been anywhere quite like this in her entire life. It was bustling with cosmopolitan people having interesting conversations over intricate drinks: glasses with salted rims, crystal cut tumblers stuffed with mint leaves and flaming spirits which were quickly extinguished, reminding her of Christmas puddings. In the background she could hear music but it had no words, an electronic heartbeat perpetually pulsing, reaching neither a verse nor a chorus. The waiters wore plimsolls with their white shirts, sported perfectly manicured beards and were shaking, pouring and garnishing drinks as if it were a circus act, juggling utensils between them in a well-rehearsed dance.

'Well, look at this,' she said, observing the biscuit-coloured foam which had levelled into a perfect line, reminding her of stout.

Azeez returned a smile, the light flickering in the irises of his eyes.

'To *Britain Bakes*,' he said, looking around to check that no one had heard him as he raised his glass, 'and to winning the golden whisk.'

'And to new friends,' she added, meeting his glass with a careful chink.

She took a sip, holding the stem as she felt the foam tickle her top lip. It was ice-cold and deliciously smooth, with a two-second delay before a potent kick hit the back of her throat and blazed a trail all the way down to her stomach.

'What do you think?' he said, the corner of his mouth curling in anticipation of her verdict. 'Nice?'

She paused, her face serious.

'I like it,' she concluded, dabbing her top lip with a napkin. 'It's strong, isn't it?'

'You adapt to it surprisingly quickly,' he said.

She glanced around at the clientele. 'I'm definitely upping the average age in here.'

'And the average talent,' he said, leaning further into the bar and dimming his voice to an excitable whisper. 'What they don't know is that you're the champion of biscuit week.'

She took another sip of the rich, mahogany drink.

'So how are you finding it? The show, I mean.'

'It's terrifying, thrilling, more pressure than I think I've ever felt over something that was once just a pleasure, but it's joyous too . . .' she said, lowering her glass to the

218

bar, '. . . having something of my own, something to be proud of.'

Azeez smiled. 'I think that gingerbread church was your best bake yet.'

'Thank you,' she said. 'Your gingerbread Colosseum was quite something to behold.'

'I think what I learnt there, is that Rome wasn't built in a day,' he said with a wink, 'and it sure as hell wasn't built in three hours.'

She laughed and swallowed at the same time, so that she spluttered.

'It really is quite an experience,' she said, her brow suddenly pinched. 'My biggest worry now is bread week, if I make it that far.'

'Why's that?'

'I've never enjoyed making bread. I follow the recipe and it always turns out dense, inedible.'

He narrowed his eyes. 'Do you knock it back, after it's proved?'

'Yes,' she nodded, 'always.'

'That might be it, then,' he said. 'I used to do that too. I find it just pushes all the air out again, and it's the air that keeps it light. Shaping it is usually enough.'

'Really?' she said, leaning back before steadying herself, forgetting that there was no back rest. 'I'll try that. How are you finding everything alongside your studies?'

'The university have been very understanding so I've got an extension on my deadlines,' he said, emitting a deep sigh, '. . . less so my relationship.'

'Ashley?'

'Yeah . . . I don't really have any time to see him at the

moment and he's annoyed because I keep cancelling on our friends. It's so hard seeing them and keeping the secret, plus I need every spare minute to practise.'

'I imagine he's missing you,' she said, 'but at least it's only for six weeks.'

'I know, but it's more than that. I just feel like I'm changing a bit.' He looked down, crossing his legs. 'I don't know what to do, because my priority at the moment is the show – it has to be – and I think he takes that as a rejection of our relationship. I thought it was him changing at first, but he thinks it's me. I've come to the conclusion that he's probably right.'

She twirled a stirrer in the foam, making small, glossy waves.

'My dear, remind me how old you are, if you don't mind me asking?'

'Twenty-three.'

'It's not a bad thing, you know, that you're changing. New experiences change us all, and whilst it can slow down with age, it never stops . . . I'm seventy-seven and I'm still changing. We are, after all, just a sum total of all of our experiences, walking around in a pair of shoes . . .'

'In what way are you changing?' he said.

She thought about this for a moment.

'I don't know where to start,' she said, taking another sip. 'This whole experience, being away from home, making friends with people that I'd never usually meet, it's a new world for me. It's the first time I've been alone with myself, independent if you like, in almost sixty years . . . it's bringing back all these memories.'

'What sort of memories?'

'Memories of who I was before I met Bernard, I suppose.'

'That's interesting,' he said, tracing the stem of the glass with his fingers. 'I guess you're rediscovering yourself as an individual . . .'

'Something like that.'

'So how have you managed sixty years of two people changing?'

'Well, that's a very good question.' She readjusted herself on her small perch, wishing she was on a chair with her feet tucked under a table.

'I'm no expert and I certainly haven't done everything right over the years, but the strongest couples I know have grown together, supporting their partner's changes rather than harnessing or fearing them. It's a bit like growing roses – you don't get to choose exactly which way the stems unfurl, but if you help them climb you get the pleasure of watching them flourish.'

'I love that,' he said. 'It's so nice to speak to someone that's not my age about relationship stuff. I can't really discuss it with my parents with me being, you know, gay.'

He sipped his drink which had almost disappeared, leaving behind a pattern on the glass like seafoam on the shore.

'Do they know?'

'Yes, they know, and they're accepting. It's just a bit uncomfortable; they're quite traditional and I wouldn't choose to discuss it with them.'

'Well, I think you're brilliant.'

'Thanks,' he said, 'but I didn't really have a choice, did I? It was either that or be miserable forever. I couldn't live a lie.'

She thought about this as she watched the waiter run a wedge of lime around the edge of a glass. 'You know, a lot of people do. Sometimes there is nothing more terrifying than facing judgement, disapproval –'

'Another drink, sir?' said the waiter, before throwing something shiny into the air and catching it behind his back.

'One for the road?' said Azeez, the twinkle returning to his eyes.

'Go on then,' she said, finishing the remains of her martini, a rush of warmth flooding her cheeks.

'You were saying . . . Do you wish you'd done things differently?'

'There are certain things . . .' she said, a flash of confidence igniting inside her, '. . . that I wish I could change.'

'What sort of things?' he said, his interest piqued.

Her secret was an unruly dog, pulling ahead of her on a leash. She held the reins but was losing control.

'You know how you said, just now, that you didn't have a choice? That you couldn't live a lie?'

'Yes,' he said, his voice soft, invested.

She took a deep breath, letting go of the leash.

'Well, I have a secret too,' she reduced her voice to a whisper, 'except I was never as brave as you.'

Her words surprised her, lingering for a second before diffusing into the bustle of the bar. She felt safe here, anonymous, her friendship with Azeez so removed from her life with Bernard; their cups of tea, his neatly gardened borders, her brimming cake tins.

'How do you mean?'

A strange lightness took hold of her limbs, making her feel momentarily indestructible.

'I've kept something from Bernard,' she said, her voice quick, as if by telling her secret she was ridding herself of it. 'I've kept it from him for almost sixty years.'

Azeez's face remained still, his eyes unblinking.

'And is it something you wish you'd told him?'

'Well, I couldn't have told him, not at the time,' she said, checking that no one was listening. 'We wouldn't be together now if I had . . .'

He considered this for a moment, waiting for her to continue, but she didn't.

'Whatever it is, and you don't have to tell me, but why can't you tell him all these years later? I know I've never met Bernard, but from all that you've said about him, he sounds to me like a kind man, the sort of man who would understand . . .'

'He's the kindest man I know,' she said, her words like needles, unpicking her. She thought of her father, of how in spite of his love and kindness, their relationship had never quite returned to the way it was before.

'Didn't you keep the show a secret from him too, at first?'

'Yes,' she said, her vision now soft around the edges, as if she'd forgotten her glasses.

'And how did he take that? Does he support you in doing the show?'

'He was hurt but he forgave me. He supports me more than I support myself,' she shook her head, 'but it's completely different.'

'Here we go,' said the waiter, pushing their drinks towards them and dropping a coffee bean into the top of each so that the foam sizzled.

Azeez looked at her, his eyes awash with concern. 'How is it different?'

She pictured dear Bernard waiting for her at home, her conscience writhing in her chest.

'I couldn't bear –' The words stalled in the back of her throat as she stared into her lap. 'He's eighty-two. It would undermine everything he's believed to be true for the last sixty years. It could upend our life together, our marriage . . . he would be utterly devastated.'

Her admission hung between them as her eyes welled with tears, sobered by a sudden sense of having said too much.

'He doesn't deserve it,' she said, in a broken whisper.

Azeez reached out to comfort her, his hand on her arm.

'You say –' He paused, taking a moment to consider his words. 'I don't know the situation . . . but when you say he doesn't *deserve* it, don't you think that what he *deserves* is . . . the truth?'

She fell silent, retreating back into the safety of herself as she chased some loose grains of sugar around the bar with her finger.

'And you never know,' he added, a glimmer of hope in his voice, 'his reaction might not be quite as you've imagined it to be. My parents' wasn't.'

She nodded, his words causing great shifts inside her. Perhaps in protecting Bernard from the truth, she had forced him to live a lie. Perhaps it was time to do the very thing she'd vowed never to do.

The taxi trickled down the dark lane, her body juddering as the wheels navigated the cobbles beneath. She felt nauseous, her mouth bitter with the lingering aftertaste of coffee as she replayed the conversation in her mind. It was that time of the evening when the neighbours' curtains were drawn but aglow with quiet activity, and she pictured Bernard in his chair, reading his newspaper in blissful ignorance. She allowed herself for a moment to imagine his reaction – the hurt in his eyes as his world crumbled – before banishing it from her mind. He *deserved* the truth, in spite of her fears. Her long-buried secret now simmered just beneath the surface.

'Just here, please,' she said, gripping on to the back of the headrest as if it controlled the brakes. The driver jumped out, opened the door and hauled her bags from the boot, and she handed him a note from her purse.

She walked up the path towards the front door, feet unsteady, chest pounding, her hand damp as it squeezed the handle of her suitcase. They couldn't live a lie any longer, she had to do this now.

She paused, noticing that Bernard had left the curtains in the front room open and the lights off. Twisting her key in the door, she wiggled it where it always caught.

'Yoo-hoo!' she called, inhaling the unique smell of home; the must of their bodies, their washing powder, last night's supper. It was a smell which she only noticed when she had been away for long enough. She flicked on the lights. He didn't reply.

She dropped her bags and walked towards the kitchen.

'Bernard?' she said, but the room was still, silent except for the steady hum of the fridge.

She pushed open the living room door, sure that he wasn't in there because it was dark and she couldn't hear the mumblings of the television, the rustle of the news-paper, his snore.

'Bernard?!' she called again, a little louder this time.

Pressing her face against the glass of the back door, she scanned the dark flower beds for movement, her heart skipping at every rustle. He wasn't there. She returned to the kitchen and opened the fridge. The portion of shepherd's pie which she had left for his supper was untouched, her cooking instructions beside it. It was late, he wasn't supposed to be out tonight, there was nothing on the calendar.

She rushed up the stairs, her head spinning as she pushed open the bedroom door, the study door, the bathroom door, greeted each time by a Bernard-less void. She took a deep breath, her mind frantic as she tried to fathom where on earth he could be, sure that this was life's way of punishing her.

She froze. The shed.

Racing back down the stairs, she flung open the back door and marched towards it. She creaked open the door and switched on the light, a naked bulb hanging from the ceiling. It was dim and damp and cluttered with tools, and her heart dropped; he was nowhere to be seen. Her eyes were drawn to a tissue on the workbench, stained with what looked like oil. Picking it up, she studied it closely. It wasn't oil. She held it tightly, her heart propelling her back inside where she began to notice drops of it on the floor. First one, then two, then a trail towards the bin. She pressed her foot against the pedal so that the lid sprang open. It was full of tissues that had blotted an alarming amount of what was definitely blood. It was no longer a shocking red but a deep brown. This had all happened hours ago, when she was miles away, ignorant. When he had needed her most, she was absent.

It was then that she recognized the footsteps outside. They weren't Bernard's steady strides, but Ann's neat heels clipping the path as she walked. She ran to the front door, Ann's shadow nearing the glass. *The light's on, she must be back from Rose's,* she heard her say as she grabbed the handle, swinging it open.

'Ann!' she said, her face pinched with worry. 'Bernard is –'

'Hello, dear,' said Ann, her manner unusually withdrawn, a pale-looking Fred behind her and a little to the left.

'Jenny,' she paused, her mouth small, serious. 'I don't want to panic you, but Bernard is in hospital.'

She felt somehow separate from what was unfolding, her head thick with fog.

'Is he all right?' she said, trying to read their faces. 'What's happened?'

'He's had a nasty fall,' said Ann, in a forced tone of calm. 'He called us earlier and we've been in A and E with him all afternoon . . .'

The words *nasty fall* and *A and E* hit her with great force, her head whirring, her heart pounding.

'He's in good hands,' countered Fred, in an attempt to reassure her. 'He fell in the shed and knocked his head on a corner. He thinks it was because of his cough, feeling dizzy . . .'

'I shouldn't have left him,' she said in a mutter, the ground shifting beneath her. 'I knew it – his cough – I shouldn't have left him.'

Ann looked at Fred, her lips pressed into a sympathetic line.

'Where is he now?' said Jenny, her mind so full of questions that they fought to be voiced. 'What did the doctor say?'

'He's had some stitches above his right eye,' said Ann, signalling where on her face, '. . . but they've kept him in because of something else.'

'Something else?' said Jenny, her eyes flicking between them.

'The thing is, it's almost sort of a good thing he had a fall,' said Ann, avoiding her gaze, 'because they heard him coughing and they think that he's got pneumonia.'

'Pneumonia?!'

She felt a hard pebble in the back of her throat. How could she have let this happen?

'They said he's more susceptible because of his asthma,' said Ann, stepping inside and pulling her into an unlikely embrace, her edges small, sharp. 'And of course, his age. But he's in the right place, he's being well looked after.'

Jenny wiped a tear with her sleeve, her make-up gathering in the lines under her eyes, on her cheeks. She felt suddenly as if she were watching someone bake in her kitchen, so that she had a desperate urge to take over, to regain control. She couldn't listen any longer, she needed to go to the hospital herself.

'I need to see him,' she said, doing up the buttons on her coat. 'I can go straight away.'

Ann looked at Fred, and then back to Jenny.

'It's very late, dear,' she said, 'they won't let you in if it's outside of visiting hours. He was going to sleep when we left him . . .'

'We can pick you up in the morning – first thing?' said

Fred, patting her arm with clumsy hands. 'We'll drop you at the hospital, bring you home, whatever you need.'

Jenny must have looked alarmed, because Ann continued.

'I gave the nurse your home phone number; he said they would contact you if there's an emergency.' She rummaged in her handbag, retrieving a child's drawing with some writing on the back of it. 'This is the ward, and their phone number.'

Jenny took it from her, read it, held it tight in her palm.

'Is there no way . . .' she faltered. 'Surely as his wife . . .'

'It'll be gone eleven o'clock by the time we get there,' said Ann. 'They were asking people to leave for the night as we left . . .'

'Right,' she said, fighting against her every instinct, 'all right. And thank you, for being there for him.'

After she had said goodnight and closed the door, she leant against it and sobbed. She pictured him struggling as he dialled their number instead of her own, floored by the fact that she had been completely oblivious, probably worrying about a gingerbread church or a chocolate tea-cake. She would never be able to comprehend the strange borrowed time that you experience before bad news hits; the minutes, hours, sometimes days where you reside in a bubble of ignorance, a place where small things still matter, before it is pierced by the needle of perspective. The idea that she might have been baking, or worse, celebrating whilst Bernard was in A and E filled her with shame, as if she should have some sort of sixth sense that meant if something happened to him, somewhere in her heart an alarm would sound.

That night as she lay in bed, restless, exhausted and alone, she questioned how, just hours before, she had even considered shattering the very foundations upon which their life together had been built. Her instinct had been right all along. He was too old, too precious, for any time he had left to be destroyed by the pain of her deceit. She could never do it to him, not now.

22

Cheese and Onion Pie

To those with no context, it was a beautiful house. It had a Victorian grandeur about it, set back from the road down a tree-lined driveway which made it feel secluded from the rest of society, much like its inhabitants. Perhaps it was the steep pitched roof or the narrow windows, but something about it felt cold, almost eerie. She couldn't quite put her finger on it, but she had always believed it to be true that buildings absorb much of what they witness.

As she hauled her bag up the stone steps to the front door, she fought to suppress the image of her father's face as she had bade him goodbye, carrying the grandchild he would never meet, his eyes webbed with fine red veins. They had barely spoken about the secret, perhaps in the hope that nothing would change, that it would disappear as silently as it had arrived. The unspoken lingered like an unacknowledged guest, refusing to let them be alone together in the way that they used to be. She had made his worst nightmare a reality and she wasn't sure if it could ever be fixed.

She felt a sharp kick as if the baby were hurrying her. Taking hold of the shiny brass knocker, she struck it three times. As she waited, she tidied her hair and adjusted her coat, undoing a toggle so that it hung loose around her middle.

'Hello,' said a woman wearing an inconvenienced expression, as if she had just interrupted her family Christmas. 'Miss Jennifer Eaton?'

'Yes,' she replied, sure that she had emphasized the Miss, spitting it from her lips like an insult.

'Follow me,' she said, turning on her heel and letting go of the door so that it swung towards Jenny. She stretched out her hand just in time and pushed it open, stepping into a sparse but elegant hallway, devoid of pictures, shoes or coats.

'I haven't got all day,' snapped the woman who was now a small, square figure, marching towards a door.

She picked up her bag and tried to catch up, her swollen stomach restricting her lungs as the two fought for space.

'This is where you will eat,' the woman said, striding through a dining hall of hard tiled floors lined with long wooden tables. The ceilings were high and the echo of their footsteps hung in the air which had a stillness to it, reminding her of church.

'This is the kitchen,' she said, pushing open the door on to a stale-smelling room which looked as if it belonged to a bygone era. There were no jars or ingredients or recipes cluttering the worktops. Instead it was cold, sterile, unlike any kitchen she'd ever known.

'And the laundry room is here.'

She peered around the corner, pausing for a moment as she spotted the first sign that someone actually lived here. A row of terry nappies, stained and damp, hung from the airer, prompting within her the realization that her secret might soon require nappies, clothes, a bonnet.

'Do try and keep up,' muttered the woman as she turned a corner and disappeared up a staircase that smelt overwhelmingly of polish.

Jenny followed behind her, her feet heavy and her cheeks flushed as she wrestled with her suitcase.

'It's so clean,' she said, catching her breath as she ran her palm along the cool wood of the banister.

'That will be your job. You will clean between the hours of seven and noon.'

She nodded, stopping for a moment to rest her bag on the stair so that relief rushed into her hand.

'And what about in the afternoons?'

'You rest and prepare a layette for your baby box,' the woman said.

'Baby box?'

Her footsteps grew heavy with irritation. 'You fill it with bonnets, booties, nappies for the parents.'

The word felt tender as if it were a bruise which the woman had poked, and then it made her think of her own father and how devastatingly lonely she felt without him, as if in the absence of his love, she didn't exist.

The woman stopped abruptly. 'This is the first floor,' she said, gesturing down the landing, her hands noticeably thick.

Jenny's eyes followed the pristine floorboards searching for any other signs of life – a pram, a blanket, a person – but she noticed only a distant wail echoing through the rafters.

'Is that the wind?'

'That's the nursery,' the woman said. 'This floor is for the new mothers.'

Jenny followed her up another flight, a bead of sweat running down her back under the thick wool of her coat.

'You'll sleep in here,' she said, arriving at another corridor and pushing open a heavy wooden door. 'Your bed is in the far left corner.'

With that she disappeared down the landing, leaving Jenny in front of an audience of seven pairs of eyes, all of which appeared to be studying her meticulously. She froze in the doorway as if someone had unexpectedly pulled back the curtains and she had found herself on stage in some horrifying mix-up.

'Afternoon,' she mouthed silently, before dashing to her corner, her eyes fixed to the floor so as to attract as little attention as possible. She placed her suitcase down with a thud, lowering herself on to an unfriendly-looking bed with cast-iron bars and tightly tucked sheets.

To her relief, the quiet chatter resumed as the girls continued with their activities; some knitting, others reading, a small group in the corner playing a game of cards. She had never seen so many expectant women all in one place and longed to be invisible just so she could sit and observe each of them at length. Instead, she stole carefully timed glances at the fullness of their bumps and the way that they held them, mesmerized by how free they were in their own bodies. In here, she realized, their secrets were no longer masked in winter coats, or lied about with borrowed rings.

'I'm Mary, nice to meet you,' said a voice from the bed next to her, so that she quickly diverted her gaze.

Mary shuffled towards the edge of her bed so that her slender feet hung over the edge, her skin so pale that Jenny could see the green pattern of her veins. Her frame was childlike and her bump sat proud at its centre, so large in comparison that Jenny wondered how she managed to stand up, let alone clean for five hours each day.

'Nice to meet you, Mary. I'm Jenny,' she replied, attempting to focus on her face so that Mary didn't think she was staring. Her lips were a deep red against her fair complexion and her clear blue eyes sat above heavy grey circles.

'I know. I'm enormous.'

'I wasn't thinking that,' she said, her tone suggesting otherwise.

'Liar,' said Mary, reaching her feet towards the floor and sliding off the bed. 'I'm only joking.'

A wicked twinkle flashed across her eyes as she jumped the gap and positioned herself next to Jenny, the frame of the bed creaking as she crossed her legs.

'When are you due?' she asked, clasping her hands on top of her bump.

'Mid-January,' said Jenny. 'How about you?'

'Early February,' she said, studying Jenny through narrowed eyes. 'So how has someone like you ended up in a place like this?'

Jenny twisted a lock of hair around her finger, conscious of how quickly Mary had made an assessment of her. Did she come across as naive, or prim, or shy? She had never been a rule breaker and for as long as she could remember it was in her nature to please; her teachers described her as a pleasure to teach and a keen learner. And yet, here she was, having done something so shameful that she questioned whether she knew herself at all.

Mary reached out her hand and placed it on Jenny's bump, so that she flinched.

'Sorry,' she said, retracting it. 'Did that hurt?'

'Not at all,' Jenny replied. 'It's just that no one has ever touched it before.'

Mary nodded and Jenny knew that she understood.

'So the father isn't around?'

'No,' she said, faltering on the edge of divulging her secret. Perhaps it was because they were in a similar boat, or maybe because in spite of her child-like looks Mary had a worldliness about her, but Jenny decided to continue.

'I work, well, worked, in a clothes shop that his mother owns.'

She looked down, pulling at a splinter of hard skin in the corner of her fingernail.

Mary's eyes narrowed. 'Does he know?'

'I told him, yes,' she replied, twisting at the skin like a loose tooth, 'but he's married with a baby. He wanted nothing to do with me when he found out.'

'I'm sorry,' said Mary, gently rubbing her arm in a small gesture of solidarity. 'Did you love him?'

'I thought I did,' she replied, peeling off the skin and leaving a sore pink strip down the side of her nail. 'I regret ever meeting him now. I should never have done it, any of it.'

'Does his mother know?'

'Mrs Smith?! No,' she said, aghast, 'she could never know. She thinks I left on doctor's orders . . . I've had to leave my secretarial course too; even my best friend thinks I'm unwell. I've been locked up in the house for weeks.'

'I see,' Mary said, changing the subject. 'Do you think it's a girl or a boy?'

'A boy,' she said, the words leaving her lips with such conviction that she surprised herself, 'called James.'

'Oh, is it now?' Mary said with a grin. 'And what makes you so sure about that?'

'I have absolutely no idea,' she replied, and they giggled, which in turn made their bumps bounce up and down in such a ridiculous fashion that they giggled even more.

'It hurts to laugh,' she said, catching her breath as she stroked her bump, relishing the freedom of being able to do so publicly. It dawned on her that this was the first time she had experienced this strange sensation, having not laughed for so many months.

'What about you — are you with the father?'

For a fraction of a second, a shadow fell across Mary's face.

'No, I'm not,' she said, unfolding her legs as she pushed herself back towards her own bed, marking the end of the conversation. 'I'll let you unpack your things in peace.'

Jenny turned to her suitcase, contemplating how someone could *incite such openness and yet suddenly become so closed. She fiddled with the buckles, heaving it open like a book so that it released the distinctive smell of home-cooked meals, as if the spirit of home had packed itself as a reminder to her of all that she had left behind. Beneath the neatly folded nighties and large knitted cardigans, her eyes were drawn to something that she didn't remember packing. As she pushed aside the clothes surrounding it, she noticed that it was wrapped in greaseproof paper.*

'What's that?' said Mary, sitting tall as if she were looking over the neighbour's fence.

She picked it up cautiously, her face softening in recognition as she rustled back the layers.

'My father must have made it,' she said, tapping her finger against the crisp, golden pastry. 'It's his cheese and onion pie.'

She admired the full dome, noticing that the crust was pinched in the shape of his fingers. She pictured him rolling out the dough, slicing the onions and grating the cheese, and in doing so communicating everything that he had wanted to say but hadn't been able to put into words. If love was an action then it was sealed within this pastry case. She inhaled the savoury tang, noticing that in the middle was a shape which had crumbled out of place. She tilted her head, smiling as she made out the letter 'J'.

J for Jennifer, she thought, but also for James.

'Hello?' said the intercom, as she leant towards it, clutching a bag she had packed for Bernard.

'Hello. I'm here to see Bernard Quinn. I'm his wife, Jennifer.'

There was a short pause, followed by the click of a lock. She pushed the heavy door and walked down a starkly lit corridor, her feet sticking to the linoleum floor. The air was tinged with the stale combination of illness and mass cooking, and every so often a bed would rush past on wheels so that she caught a glimpse of jaundiced skin, closed eyes, tubes. She wished she hadn't searched *'octogenarian with pneumonia and asthma'* in the early hours of the morning, the internet confirming all of her worst fears.

She spotted Bernard before he saw her, through the glass in the door to his room. Even though she had spent last night tormenting herself, she felt entirely unprepared for the reality of how broken he looked. His eyes were shut and he had a plastic mask over his nose and mouth, which – even though it was there to help him – looked so invasive strapped to his precious face. He was her strength, her constant, and yet in an instant the most permanent love she had ever known felt impermanent, as vulnerable as fruit on a branch.

'Bernie,' she said softly, pushing the door with caution, 'it's only me.'

To her relief his eyes blinked open and he fumbled with the mask, removing it with shaky hands.

'Hello, darling,' he said, his voice a croak through lack of use, as he turned his head towards her.

'Oh Bernard!' she gasped, unable to hide her horror at the right-hand side of his face.

It was swollen, his skin dappled with a tender greenish hue which turned to a deep purple around his eye. Above his eyebrow was a large white plaster, attached to his face with a sort of human-friendly masking tape, and as he looked at her she noticed his eyes were glazed, distant, but worst of all, sad.

'What happened?' she said, a sharp pain in the back of

her throat as she fought to suppress it, determined to be strong for him.

'I was making you a new pastry board, a bigger one,' he said, his breathing laboured as if he had a great weight on his chest, 'and I started coughing . . .'

She took his hand and stroked his arm, his skin soft and slack like an overripened peach.

'. . . before I knew it . . . I'd gone dizzy . . . hit my head.'

His face twisted in pain as he coughed, the sound abrasive, distressing, so that he put his mask on for a couple of breaths. She could feel the presence of a mutual thought, an unspoken one, one which neither of them would ever voice. Falls of this variety happen to old people. Somehow, without being able to pinpoint a specific moment, he had grown old.

'You should've called me,' she said, the words out of her mouth before she could stop them.

'Absolutely not,' he said, his features gaunt and grey. 'What could you have done?'

'I could have come home!' she said, her voice unsteady. She focused on his left eye, unable to look at his swollen right.

'I know . . . and that is exactly why I didn't call you.'

The silence that followed was underpinned by stubbornness, so that she knew they would never agree.

Picking his bag up off the floor, she placed it in her lap. It was a canvas drawstring rucksack which fastened with a worn leather strap. In another life it had been Bernard's work bag, and she used to fill it with his favourite sandwiches (cheese and pickle), a piece of fruit, and a generous portion of whichever sweet treat she had baked that week.

Today it looked faded and threadbare, a reminder of the years that had since passed. She pulled it open, unpacking his things.

'I've brought you fresh pyjamas, underwear, slippers . . .' she said, putting the neatly ironed pile on his bedside table, '. . . the newspaper, a pencil for the crossword and a packet of Liquorice Allsorts.'

If she had looked up, she would have seen a glint of light flash across his eyes like a shooting star.

'Thank you,' he said.

There was a rustle as she wrestled out a large circular object wrapped in shiny foil, reminiscent of a UFO. It looked as if it would never have fitted in his bag and yet, somehow, it had.

'I was worried you might not be eating properly,' she said, placing it in his lap, '. . . and I couldn't sleep, so I made you this.'

He peeled back the foil with tremulous hands, revealing a perfectly plump, golden pie with a neatly pinched crust.

'It's cheese and onion,' she said, remembering her father's many years ago, 'comfort food.'

At that moment, through the slats in the blinds, a robin caught her attention as he fluttered past outside, dipping and bobbing in the wind, a glee to his chirp.

'Do you know him?' said Bernard, his voice like gravel, as the robin landed on a bush by the window, chittering his finest tune.

'Funnily enough,' she said, wondering if the memory had summoned him, 'I think I do.'

She watched as he hopped off into a bush.

'B . . .' said Bernard, his finger tracing the browned, twisted letter on top of the pie '. . . for *Britain Bakes* champion?'

She rolled her eyes affectionately, relieved that he could muster a joke.

'For *Bernard*,' she said, biting the inside of her lip, '. . . or *bloody get better soon*.'

His laugh quickly developed into a cough, tainting the moment with guilt.

'Thank you,' he said, steadying his breath. 'I'm missing your cooking.'

She swallowed, clasping her hands in her lap and dropping her head.

'Well, you won't have to miss it any more,' she said, a sinkhole opening inside her. 'I'm not going back to *Britain Bakes*. I'm staying here, with you, where I should have been all along.'

The silence that followed amplified the hum of the strip lights, his crestfallen expression saying more than words ever could.

'I knew it, deep down, that I should never have entered,' she continued, a pain swelling in her throat as she tried to justify herself, 'and what ha–'

'You absolutely mustn't quit,' he said, his hand on his ribcage as if it hurt to speak.

'Of course I must. You've got pneumonia, I need to be here to look after you . . .' She shook her head, ashamed. 'I wasn't there when you needed me most and I won't make that mistake twice.'

He reached for the plastic cup by his bedside, taking a slow sip of water, his hand unsteady so that it ran from the corners of his mouth and down his chin.

'This is your moment, Jenny,' he said, dabbing his mouth with the sleeve of his pyjamas, his chest heaving and wheezing. 'You have a gift and I've known it for years . . . but now other people are seeing it . . . you have to follow your star.'

'But none of that matters, Bernard!' she said, a knot tightening in her heart. 'None of it. What really matters to me, is you.'

'And *I* will be very upset if you quit.'

She held her head in her hands.

'I'm well looked after here . . . and when I get out, if I ever have another accident, I promise I'll call you.'

'That's no good,' she said, silently considering that he might never get out at all. 'We don't yet know how long you will be in here for, or how serious this might be. And even if you were at home, I don't have my phone in the barn. What if something happened in the middle of a challenge and I found out hours later? I won't risk it.'

'Jenny,' he said, holding her hand as tight as his limited strength would allow. 'We could all live in fear of the worst-case scenario, but it wouldn't be a lot of fun . . .'

She fell silent, searching for a way around his words.

'Try to be led by hope, rather than fear,' he said, his face softening into a smile. 'I sound like I'm in for a terrible time if everything unfolds as you're imagining it.'

'You are,' she said, the faintest glint of humour in her voice.

They sat for a moment in their individual thoughts.

'Go on then,' he said, 'how did it go?'

'How did what go?'

'Biscuit week.'

'Oh.' She sighed. 'I won the golden whisk.'

His eyes brightened and he looked at her, astonished.

'I know,' she said, unable to resist a smile.

He lifted her hand in a frail attempt at a cheer, before lowering it back to the bed.

'That's brilliant,' he said. 'How can you *possibly* consider leaving?'

She shrugged, pressing her lips together, her stomach curdling with the conflict of it all.

'I want you to promise me something,' he said, his voice rasping.

'And what's that?'

'I want you to promise me that you won't give up.'

She shook her head.

'I can't do that,' she said, staring down at the blue speckled floor.

'Why?' he said.

'Because I've already dropped out.'

Eton Mess and Coffee Walnut Choux Buns

Strength, she soon realized, came in numbers. As she walked up the high street, her bump now too pronounced to disguise in a duffel coat, the disapproving looks felt slightly less personal in a group. They had ventured into town for the afternoon and were swinging shopping bags by their sides, filled with cloth nappies, balls of wool and chocolate éclairs from the local bakery.

'Walk behind with me,' said Mary, dragging her feet as she looped her arm through Jenny's, hugging it close to her warm body.

'You're slowing me down,' Jenny said. 'I'm not sure if it's your bump, or your little legs,' and Mary gave her a sharp pinch through her coat.

'Ouch!'

'Serves you right.'

Mary was the first friend that Jenny had ever had who was smaller than her, and whilst they had known each other only a month, it felt as if they had always been friends. The foundations of friendship are so often built on shared experience, and as their secrets grew, so did their fondness for one another. In many ways they were chalk and cheese, Mary from a family whom she mentioned only in glimpses and always with a tone of resentment due to her strained relationship with her stepfather, whom her mother defended at all costs, and Jenny from a loving home, with a father she adored completely. Mary was a walking contradiction — fearless and yet vulnerable, rebellious and yet scared, confident and yet insecure — and Jenny felt an overwhelming compulsion to take care of her.

'I just can't wait to get this baby out, Jen,' she said, her breathing heavy as the slope of the high street grew steeper. 'I'm uncomfortable all of the time, it's like torture.'

'I know,' Jenny said, squeezing her arm. 'I don't think it will be long.'

'Careful what you wish for,' said a girl called Sylvia, pausing to light up a cigarette. 'You've got to give birth to it.'

'Thanks for that,' said Mary, narrowing her eyes. 'So have you.'

'My sister said we should be practising the *Grantly Dick-Read* method,' said Sylvia.

'The what?' said Mary, nudging Jenny in the ribs as if to say here she goes.

'Grantly Dick-Read. It's all about learning to breathe when you give birth.'

'I can already breathe,' said Mary.

'Not like that, stupid. It's to do with relaxing; apparently it helps with the pain.'

'Let's not bicker,' said Jenny. 'We've all got to do it at some point . . . Where do we go to learn that, Sylvia?'

'I think they do classes at the hospital.' She took another puff on her cigarette. 'But that sort of stuff isn't for the likes of us.'

Mary looked up, her mouth curling into a smirk.

'What?' said Jenny, brushing her chin with her sleeve. 'Have I got éclair on my face?'

'No,' Mary laughed, 'you're just so sensible, you'd make a very good mother.'

Jenny looked down at her feet which were obstructed by her

stomach, flattered for a moment by Mary's words before they dispersed, leaving a heavy silence.

'Sorry,' said Mary, under her breath, 'I didn't mean it to –'

'It's okay,' she said. 'I think I would too.'

She ground to a halt.

'What's wrong?' said Mary, almost tripping since their arms were linked.

'I've forgotten something,' she said. 'I'll only be a minute, I'll catch you up.'

Before Mary could object, she freed her arm and scurried towards the newsagent's.

It was still and quiet, and she headed straight for the stationery shelf. There, nestled between the pencils and the envelopes, sat a little notebook, cassock blue for a boy. She picked it up, stroking its soft cover and pushing against its spine as she flicked through it, creating a gentle breeze. Looking around to ensure no one was watching, she raised it to her nose, inhaling the promise of pristine pages. It was perfect.

They spent the rest of the afternoon in the recreation room, her favourite part of the day. It mainly involved simply passing the time, but was a welcome relief from her mornings spent mopping floors and polishing staircases. She picked up her knitting needles, the beginnings of the left front of a tiny matinee jacket hanging from them in the softest white wool. Flicking through her pattern book, she admired the pictures of babies in wool bonnets with ribbons tied under their chins, crocheted coats with neat little buttons and sweet round collars. She would make sure that James looked just as beautiful. He would have the carrying coat, the matinee jackets, the vests, the modesties, just like the babies in the pictures. As she continued with a buttonhole on the seventy-fifth row, her needles tapped together in a steady rhythm, the repetitiveness comforting. Often, when she was in a knitting induced daydream, he *would kick as if he knew and she would tell him:* Hold on in there, you can't arrive until your layettes are done.

'*Why does yours look so lovely and mine is a mess?*' said Mary, *feeding her a mouthful of chocolate éclair. She studied Jenny's box — wrapped in pale blue patterned paper — and pulled from it a pair of soft booties the colour of custard, threaded with shiny white ribbon.*

'*Maybe because you're always playing cards,*' Jenny said, her *mouth full of fresh cream.*

'*They're so tiny,*' Mary said, putting one on the end of each finger *and walking them across the table.*

'*I do hope you haven't got chocolate on your fingers,*' Jenny said, *but Mary appeared not to have heard.*

'*Look at this.*' She prised a delicate crocheted shawl from the *bottom of the box and held it up to the window so that the other girls gathered around to admire it.*

'*That's fit for a royal baby,*' said Jean, a reserved girl who listened *to the others from behind her knitting, rarely getting involved.*

Sylvia reached out and took the shawl from Mary, wrapping it around her head like a scarf and using the window as a mirror.

'*Thank you,*' said Mary, sensing Jenny's discomfort and snatching *it back.*

'*Is anyone going to put anything special in their box?*' said Sylvia. '*A trinket for their baby when they turn eighteen?*'

'*Like what?*' said Mary, folding her arms on top of her bump.

'*I've got a silver crucifix that my mother gave me,*' said a voice *from the corner.* '*I might put that in.*'

'*Are we allowed to put a photograph in?*' came another.

'*I doubt it,*' replied Sylvia, and the girls fell into a reflective silence *so that all that could be heard was the tapping of knitting needles and the swish of playing cards being shuffled against the table.*

'What about you, Jen?' said Mary, always keen to avoid any moments of introspection.

'I did actually have one idea,' she said, pushing her knitting further down the needle.

'Go on.'

'A recipe book.'

'A recipe book?' Sylvia looked confused.

'I have a couple of family recipes and I'd like to pass them on. I thought I could write them out in a notebook for him; maybe one day he'll make them.'

Mary nodded, but Sylvia didn't appear convinced.

'There's something of love in food, isn't there?' Jenny said. 'If he sees I've written him recipes, he'll know that I care.'

'Have you ever thought about keeping him?' said Sylvia, picking at her nails.

'Of course, but I don't really have a choice. How could I? He'd have no father, I'd have no husband. My father thinks he deserves a family, like I had.'

'I disagree,' said Mary, dealing a round of cards. 'If you want him, you're all the family he needs.'

'I couldn't support him on my own.'

'Why are you not keeping yours then, Mary?' said Sylvia. 'If that's what you think?'

'Because it's different,' she said, pausing in the middle of arranging her hand to stare Sylvia straight in the eye. 'I don't want this baby.'

'Shall I help you make a shawl?' said Jenny, tapping Mary's leg with her foot.

'No thanks,' she said, storming towards the bedroom and leaving an uncomfortable silence in her wake. 'I'm going for a nap.'

The door slammed shut behind her, and Jenny felt an ache for her friend, for the pain that she buried inside herself.

She placed her knitting to the side and picked up her baby box, resting it on her lap. One by one, she proceeded to put everything back in again, folding the shawl into a neat square and pushing her fingers into the sleeve of a tiny jacket, before buttoning it up and straightening out the collar. She felt for a moment the excitement of how it might feel to dress him, to manoeuvre his chunky arms through the sleeves, to guide his soft feet into booties, to tie the ribbons on his mittens, and then she wanted to scream. She wanted to scream because it wouldn't be her.

It was early evening and day one of patisserie week was drawing to a close, Jenny noted, as she sat in the back of Ann and Fred's car. Bernard was in the front, and she stole glimpses of the deep line of stitches above his eye in the wing mirror, thanking her lucky stars that after six long days and nights, they were heading home.

'Careful, Fred!' said Ann, grabbing the back of his headrest with claw-like hands as he took on a speed bump with a little too much enthusiasm. 'We're trying to get home from the hospital, not end up back in there.'

'Sorry, folks,' he said, bobbing in his seat, 'didn't see that coming.'

'Jenny,' said Ann, pulling open the bag which was squashed between them, 'I've made you this so you don't need to think about supper.'

Jenny peered in, the glass dish a window on to grey worms of mince and lumpy mashed potato, condensation clinging to the film stretched over the top of it: Ann's cottage pie.

'Thank you, Ann, that's very thoughtful,' she said, reminding herself of how kindly it was meant, even if it was devoid of all seasoning. 'You've both been a real god-send over this last week.'

Whilst Ann shared stories about everyone she had ever met – or not met but heard of – that had had pneumonia, Jenny's mind wandered to thoughts of the barn. She wondered how they had all got on, what they had baked, if there had been any triumphs or disasters. Patisserie week was notoriously challenging, and she felt a sharp twinge in her chest at the thought of having missed it, which was quickly extinguished by guilt. The main thing, she reminded herself, was that Bernard was coming home with her. How could she want for more than that?

She pulled her phone out of her handbag and turned it on.

Her stomach lurched; she had a message from Azeez. He was the first person she had called after dropping out, and initially he had thought she was joking. But upon hearing about Bernard, his shock turned immediately to concern. He was entirely supportive of her decision, though she could hear in his voice that he was struck with disappointment.

She opened the message. It was a picture of him and Carys at her workstation, their faces beaming, her cast-iron kitchen scales sparking a quiet yearning, like a corkscrew twisting into her. Below the picture he had written a message:

Hi Jenny, how is Bernard? Missed you A LOT today but I've done you proud. It's me vs Sorcha in the Blind Bake tomorrow (controversial since she 'accidentally' knocked over Angela's Baker's Delight whilst making room for her own in the fridge!!) Any tips? Azeez xxx

She gasped, a Catherine wheel of joy whizzing inside her, quickly snuffed by Ann's studying eyes. She gathered herself, adopting a serious demeanour as she steadily tapped out a reply.

YIPPEE! WELL DONE! MY TIP IS TO FOLLOW YOUR INSTINCTS AND MOST OF ALL ENJOY. HOPE ANGELA OKAY, SEND HER MY LOVE. BERNARD IMPROVED, WE ARE HEADING BACK FROM HOSPITAL NOW. MISSING YOU AND GOOD LUCK. JENNY X

She looked out of the window at the sun-drenched streets, imagining him winning the golden whisk, the thrill of it countered by the thought of not being there to celebrate with him. She turned off her phone, pushing it back into her bag as the car pulled up outside their house.

'Thanks for everything,' said Bernard, as Fred turned off the engine.

'No problem at all,' said Fred, 'and if there's anything we can do, you know where we are.'

'That's very kind,' said Jenny.

'Don't forget the cottage pie,' Ann reminded her.

Jenny picked up their bags in one hand, linking his arm with the other, and they made their way up the path towards the front door. His walk was less steady than before, so that it felt as if he were made of paper.

'Home sweet home,' he said, between heavy breaths.

As they drew closer, Jenny noticed that something was awry.

'That's odd,' she said, a crease appearing above her nose as she clocked a light glowing through the glass. 'I'm sure I didn't leave the light on . . .'

Pulling her keys out of her handbag, she was about to

put them in the lock when the door swung open, making her jump.

'Rose!' she said, her mind whirring. 'What on earth are you doing here?'

'Oh, Uncle Bernie!' said Rose, tilting her head as she studied his bruised face. 'You poor thing . . . that looks so painful.'

'Is everything all right?' said Jenny, stepping inside. 'Shouldn't you be at work?'

'All fine,' said Rose, gently removing Bernard's coat from his stooped shoulders. 'I've taken some time away from the office.'

'Really?' she said, as they slowly made their way towards the kitchen. 'Where are you going?'

'Well – if it's all right – I'm staying here.'

Jenny looked at Bernard as she tried to work out what was going on, but he didn't appear to be even remotely concerned. Jeremy and Rose had seemed so happy when she last saw them . . . it couldn't be, could it?

'Oh dear,' she said, her tone tentative, '. . . what's happened?'

'I'll explain,' said Rose, clicking on the kettle. 'Who would like an Earl Grey?'

'Yes, please,' they said, in accidental unison.

Jenny helped Bernard into a chair whilst Rose poured the tea, struggling her way around their unfamiliar kitchen, opening and closing the wrong cupboards. Eventually she joined them at the table, her face serious as she tucked her hair behind her ears.

'I have a proposition,' she said, clasping her hands in front of her like a newsreader.

The knot in Jenny's stomach tightened in anticipation of what she might have to say. For a moment, she thought she caught a shared glance between Bernard and Rose, but she couldn't be sure.

'I would like to look after Uncle Bernie for the next couple of weeks whilst he recovers,' Rose said, taking a sip of tea, 'so that you can return to *Britain Bakes*.'

Jenny looked from Rose to Bernard, her eyes wide, her lips parted. Bernard gave a nod of appreciation towards Rose, so that she assumed they must have talked about it already.

'That's so kind,' she said, breaking the silence, 'but I can't let you do that. You've got Poppy, Max, not to mention a new job . . .'

'You can,' said Rose, her voice firm as Bernard nodded in agreement, 'and you must. Jeremy is more than capable of looking after Poppy and Max, and it's only for a couple of days a week. I can work remotely, they've signed it off.'

Jenny took a deep breath as the rollercoaster of the last week caught up with her.

'I so appreciate the offer . . .' she said, overcome by the reality of her decision all over again, 'but it's too late.'

Rose shook her head, as if she knew better.

'It is, I've missed patisserie week,' Jenny said, a great weight inside her. 'It's one of the hardest weeks, it wouldn't be fair on the others. They wouldn't let me go back now, even if I wanted to –'

'You can!' said Bernard, interrupting with startling enthusiasm. 'I gave Rose Carys's email and she's spoken to her. She said that because you won the golden whisk last week, you're immune this week anyway, so you wouldn't have gone home. You're allowed to return for week four.'

Rose nodded, her smile loaded, willing her to accept the offer.

Jenny blinked, a chink of light creeping in, before her eyes settled on the bruised face of her beloved Bernard.

'It's not just that,' she said, tapping her heart. 'I don't know if I can, *in here*.'

Rose looked towards Bernard, as if they were silently making a plan through eye contact only.

'I tell you what,' said Bernard, a flicker of disappointment at the corners of his mouth. 'Why don't you take this evening to think about it? Perhaps you could bake one of the things that you didn't get a chance to this week.'

She contemplated this for a moment, enticed by the distraction of a bake, before taking mental stock of the ingredients in her cupboards.

'I suppose I could make my Baker's Dozen,' she said. 'Eton mess and coffee walnut choux buns?'

'Yes, please,' said Rose, winking towards Bernard.

'All right,' said Jenny, 'challenge accepted.'

It wasn't until more than two hours later that Rose returned to find that one half of the kitchen looked like a baking apocalypse, a witness to either disaster or genius. The sink was piled high with baking trays, whisks and mixing bowls, the worktop covered in smashed meringue and abandoned pans.

'How did it go?' she said tentatively.

'Good, I think,' said Jenny, wiping some flour from her cheek, 'but I haven't tasted them yet.'

The Eton mess choux buns were covered in a raspberry pink icing and dipped in crushed meringue so that they looked almost like snowballs. Next to them were their coffee counterparts, covered in crisp craquelin, fractured like dry earth and finished with a gold dusted walnut.

'I honestly don't think that I've ever seen anything quite like it,' said Rose, as she studied them intently.

'Then I think we'd better try them,' said Jenny, 'to see if the flavours are any good.'

With that, she carried the plate into the living room and placed it on the coffee table in front of Bernard, whose face was hidden behind the newspaper.

'Help yourself, both of you,' she said. 'The pink ones have a raspberry filling and are coated in crushed meringue, and the brown ones have a coffee filling.'

'Goodness,' said Bernard. He put his paper to the side and picked up one in each hand. 'I might have both if that's all right . . . I've got some making up to do.'

Jenny sank her teeth through the light pastry pocket and into the rich, raspberry filling which oozed out of the sides so that she had to lick her fingers. There was a chorus of ums and ahs as they smacked their lips, taking a breath and then going back for more like creatures possessed.

'Wow,' said Bernard, his cheeks taut like a hamster. 'You've baked some amazing things in your time, darling, but these are incredible.'

'Are they crisp on the outside and light in the middle?' she said.

'They are,' said Rose, her hand shielding her mouth, 'and all identical.'

'Which is your favourite?'

'Eton and walnut,' came the collective response, their answers overlapping.

'I'd take that as both,' said Bernard, shooting her a knowing wink.

As they dusted off their hands and patted their stomachs, Jenny wondered what the judges might have said to her, had she been there.

'Can we take a minute, please, to just appreciate how far you've come,' said Rose, perching her last pink mouthful on the side of her plate. 'You've always been brilliant, but this isn't just a chocolate log or a piece of tiffin . . .' She gestured towards the plate, 'It's tea at the Ritz!'

Jenny smiled, concealing the great tug of war inside herself.

Jenny looked out across the garden and into the moving darkness, a quiet orchestra of leaves clinging stubbornly to their branches as the wind tore through them. The rubber gloves shrank against her skin to form tight wrinkles as she scrubbed a plate as if she were trying to remove the pattern. She balanced it on the draining board before capsizing the washing-up bowl, watching as the water spiralled down the plug hole, the soapy remains crawling back up as if they were trying to escape their fate.

'Bernard's gone to bed,' said Rose, appearing in the doorway. 'I don't think he's finding it easy getting up those stairs, but he's all right if he takes his time. Can I help with the washing up?'

'That's very kind,' she said, 'but no need. I've about finished.'

Rose leant on the worktop, loitering, so that Jenny could

tell she was wrestling with something on the tip of her tongue.

'Have you had a chance to think?' she said, her blue eyes following Jenny around the kitchen as she put the utensils back in their rightful places.

'A little,' she replied, drying a saucepan with the tea towel.

'And?'

'What you've proposed is one of the kindest things anyone has ever offered to do for me,' said Jenny, shutting the cupboard door, before picking up a whisk from the draining board, 'and to be honest, there is a part of me that would love to go back . . .'

Rose nodded. 'But?'

'But what happened last week with Bernard, it reminded me that time is precious,' she paused as she searched for the words, '. . . and how little of it we might have left together.'

The painful truth of her admission squeezed in her chest.

'I understand that,' said Rose. 'Can I share something with you?'

'Yes, of course,' said Jenny, putting the whisk into the utensils jar.

'I love Poppy and Max more than I can put into words, and if I could, I would be there for every minute of their growing up; I wouldn't miss a second of it. I know that a day comes which silently marks the last bedtime story or the last milk tooth, and most of the time it passes by without you even noticing it. So you're right, time is *so* precious.'

Jenny felt a hot wave of emotion brim in her eyes, so

that she focused on drying the plate in her hand, disguising it.

'But I also know that it's important to give yourself the time and the love that you give to others. For me, that's my career, and nurturing that part of myself does not compromise the love I have for them.'

Jenny put the plate in the cupboard, turning to look at her.

'What I mean is, it's not always an *either or*. It's not your own ambitions *or* Bernard. You don't have to choose between them. I truly believe that both are of great value.'

Jenny remained quiet, relief forcing its way up through the worry like a winter snowdrop.

'Not only that, but if you're fulfilled in yourself, I think often you can be a better person to those around you.'

'It's not an either or,' Jenny repeated, a weight lifting from her shoulders as she said the words aloud. 'You've always been so wise, Rose, even as a little girl.'

Rose moved towards her, pulling her into a tight embrace so that she could smell her shampoo.

'I promise you,' said Rose, drawing back to look her in the eye, 'that I will take the greatest care of Uncle Bernard.'

'I know you will,' she nodded, wiping a tear from her cheek, before emitting an almighty sigh.

'Well,' she said, shaking her head as she hung the tea towel back over the oven door, 'of all the weeks to return to *Britain Bakes* . . . I'm returning for bread week.'

Cottage Loaf

It happened on the eleventh of January. She pulled back the tea towel to see a pale dome, smooth and round like her bump. Turning the bowl on to the floured table, she pressed her finger into its soft flesh, leaving a dip which grew back slightly like a wet sponge. She stretched the dough, folding it inwards over and over to rid it of air, the smell of yeast so overwhelming she could taste it. It felt slack beneath her palms as she pummelled it into submission, a dull ache in the arch of her back.

Tearing off a quarter of the dough, she began shaping the two pieces into rounds, pulling the top taut and tucking it tightly underneath itself as if it were a bedsheet. She pressed the smaller loaf on top of the larger one, pushing two floured fingers through the centre of both until she reached the hard surface of the table. Using a knife, she patterned the top with eight sharp slits before leaving it to prove a little longer. As it grew, it reminded her of a child's interpretation of the Queen's coronation crown.

She bent down to put the loaf into the oven, noticing a trickle of warmth run down the inside of her leg so that she searched her skirt. The wetness wasn't visible but she could feel it against her skin.

Closing the oven door, she dashed down the hall towards the toilet, crossing Mary who was kneeling by the stairs next to a bucket with a brush in her hand, looking as if she might never get up.

'Where are you going in such a hurry?' she said, sitting back on to her heels.

Jenny drew her legs tightly together, studying the sharp bristles on the brush in Mary's hand.

'Are you all right?'

'I think so,' she said, lowering her voice. 'The matron asked me to make a cottage loaf and when I went to put it in the oven, something happened.'

'What sort of thing?' said Mary, her eyes narrowing as she lowered the brush to the floor.

'I don't know, it's as if I've had an accident.'

Mary hauled herself up using the banister as a crutch.

'Do you need to borrow some knickers?'

'I . . . it didn't feel like that, it felt different.'

'What do you —' Mary grabbed her arm. 'Do you think it's the baby?'

She looked down at her bump which was now low and heavy.

'It might be.'

'What do you think you're doing?' said the matron, marching towards them.

'I —' said Jenny, her heart sinking.

The matron's eyes dropped as she glared at the dark rose growing on her skirt.

'Go and get yourself a nappy,' she said, 'and then straight to the front door.'

Mary leapt up, taking her arm.

'It doesn't take two of you,' the matron said, tapping the bucket of water with her foot. 'The floors won't clean themselves.'

Before long, Jenny was bundled into a taxi wearing a nappy underneath her skirt, her hand clasping the small of her back which continued to ache. She looked out of the window as they drove through the streets, shapes blurring into straight lines, the red brick of the houses fading into the brown of the pavements, blackbirds reduced to smudges against the afternoon sky. She pressed her hand against the cold glass which separated her from the outside, and she felt entirely alone. She wanted her father, she wanted her mother. She wanted to ask her what was happening, what she should do? She wanted to hold the hand that first held hers and squeeze it tight, crushing it with love and fear.

When she arrived at the maternity hospital, she was greeted by a nurse wearing the forbidding expression which had grown all too familiar over the last nine months. Sylvia had warned her about the shave, enema and hot bath routine that was compulsory before birth, but that didn't lessen the shock of it as she endured the cold, merciless hands of the nurses, withdrawing into herself as she willed it to be over. Afterwards she was led to a small room and instructed to change into the starched hospital gown which was folded on the end of the bed. She did as she was told, struggling with the ties so that she was left humiliatingly exposed, the back gaping open as she lay on the bed.

Minutes turned to hours as she waited to be seen, punctuated by waves of torturous pain which started in her back and gradually encompassed her entire being. She clenched her jaw, a deep moan escaping through her teeth. Occasionally she would hear the echo of a guttural scream from the other side of the wall, and she listened in shock, waiting for it to happen to her. Forcing her nails into the mattress, a hot fury overtook her as she thought of Ray and how little consequence he had faced.

'Help!' she called into the empty room, blinking tears from her eyes as the waves gathered momentum so that she felt as if she had completely relinquished control to this relentless force.

'I'm in here,' she wailed, certain that she had been forgotten about, 'somebody, help me, please help me . . .'

'That's quite enough,' said a clipped voice, marching towards her in a plastic apron. 'There is no need to cause a scene, Miss Eaton, I imagine you've done quite enough of that already.'

Before she could digest her words another wave hit, the pain so acute that her legs began to shake.

'Let's take a look,' said the midwife, pushing them apart as another nurse entered.

'That happened quickly,' she said, as they prodded and poked her with hard instruments, their disgust apparent in their steely faces and sharp movements. Jenny felt more alone than she had done in the hours before.

It was in her deepest suffering that the midwife held a small, shiny trumpet against her stomach, pressing her ear against it to discover the p-tm p-tm p-tm of his heartbeat, a ray of hope through the darkness. She wasn't alone at all, for she had someone she needed to meet.

'Is he coming?' she gasped, her eyes screwed tightly shut.

'Not yet,' came the terse reply, as both nurses left the room.

She filled her lungs as the spaces between the pain began to close, her heart racing as she released her breath, writhing in determination. You're going to be all right, she said to him, I'm trying my best, I promise.

Overtaken by a sudden need to push, she engaged the very core of herself, discovering a strength in her exhaustion that she didn't know she possessed. Nurses flooded the room but she couldn't see them, not really. Her perception of what was going on involved just a sheer determination to meet him and a white-hot burning between her legs.

'Almost there,' said the midwife.

She mustered one last, gut-wrenching push, making a sound

unlike any she had made before, a howling, rasping scream that came from the very pit of her soul like a wolf to the moon. She screamed for all that she had been silent about for so long, for the life that she had created and the shame she had been made to feel.

'It's a boy,' said the midwife, and she nodded, because she knew.

'It's James,' she said, as he was placed on her chest.

She traced the delicate shape of his ears, the curve of his tiny nose, his pursed lips. It was as if before this moment she had been blind and as she settled her eyes on this tiny being, the sheer beauty of the world flooded into her like morning light through the trees. Beneath the blood, his head was covered in a helmet of dark fluff, and as he looked at her and she at him, she felt as if she were holding her entire heart. His gaze was not like that of a newborn but of an old man, placid and wise as if he had always existed. Everything about him was familiar, and as she stroked his wet cheek with the back of her finger, she knew her world had changed forever. She was no longer just Jennifer Eaton; she was his mother.

'Let's get him washed and weighed,' said the midwife, easing him out of her grip.

She resisted, clutching him to her chest.

'He's coming back,' she said, engaging a little more force, 'we just need to clean him up.'

As the midwife took him from her, her arms felt limp and empty and her eyes followed him out of the room so that once again she was alone. It was then that she sobbed. She sobbed because she loved him so very much, and because she never wanted to let go of him again.

Jenny's return to *Britain Bakes* brought with it an unexpected heatwave. She sat on the stone steps, warming her palms on them as if they were the top of an Aga. Her eyes narrowed as she looked at the barn in the bright glare of the morning sun. How on earth had she ended up in the Blind Bake Challenge for bread week? Perhaps we are just like eggs, sugar, butter and flour, she thought to herself, capable of being transformed into almost anything.

'I should've been more careful what I wished for,' said Azeez, as he edged into the shade, his nervous energy palpable as he rolled his sleeves up and then back down again, and restyled his hair. 'I was *desperate* for you to return to the show, and now I'm up against you.'

'I can promise that you have nothing to worry about,' she said, shaking her head. 'I mean, you might have had, if it was cake week, but it's not.'

He laughed, an infectious sort of a laugh so that she couldn't help but join in, the tension loosening in her shoulders.

'I don't know about that,' he said. 'You claim to be bad at bread, but your hot cross buns and your plaited loaf got you into the top two . . .'

'That was a combination of beginner's luck and the advice you gave me,' she said, her eyes following the crew as they dashed between jobs, carrying mixing bowls, bags of flour, tripods.

'Bakers, please head back into the barn for the Blind Bake Challenge,' called Carys, holding a small battery powered fan in her right hand so that her fringe defied gravity.

Azeez helped Jenny to her feet and they followed Sorcha, Paul and Angela into the barn. The three of them took their seats at the side of the room, whilst Jenny and Azeez returned to their workstations and tied their aprons behind their backs. Jenny noticed that everyone except for

266

Sorcha had wished them luck, and she appeared entirely uninterested as she picked her nails, which looked extraordinarily long for a baker.

Amanda entered the barn alongside this week's guest judge: Luca Loretti. He was a celebrity chef and bread connoisseur, his chiselled jaw and cheeky demeanour garnering him quite a large following. Jenny had once caught the beginning of his bread show on the television, but he had made an inappropriate comment whilst shaping a baguette and Bernard hadn't looked impressed. She noticed that Sorcha was no longer studying her nails, her attention focused entirely on him.

'Afternoon, Jazeez, and welcome to the Blind Bake Challenge,' said Mo, their nickname causing a ripple of laughter from the spectators.

'This week, the stakes are even higher,' continued Katie, her face stern and her words exaggerated, 'because the winner will be immune in next week's semi-final, making them the first baker to be *guaranteed* a place in the *Britain Bakes* final.'

A charged silence swept the room and Jenny was sure the drum of her heart could be heard through her chest. Competing with Azeez went against every instinct, it felt entirely wrong, and so she resolved to think of it as her versus bread.

'Luca, would you like to do the honours?'

Luca stepped forward, his bicep fighting with the seam of his shirt as he removed the cloche to reveal what looked like a squashed snowman.

'It's a cottage loaf,' he said and Jenny stared in disbelief, the events of sixty years ago vivid in her mind.

'You have two and a half hours to make your loaves,' said Mo, as Azeez looked at her like a rabbit in the headlights.

'Three . . . two . . . one . . .'

'Bake!'

Jenny removed the tea towel and folded it over her arm. Underneath it sat very few ingredients: bread flour, lard, yeast and salt.

'A cottage loaf?' mouthed Azeez. He went to have a closer look at the example, his eyes puzzled. 'Have you heard of one before?'

She nodded. 'They're old-fashioned things.'

'And no bread mixer?' he said, rolling up his sleeves as he got started. 'This is going to be hard work.'

Pulling her cast-iron kitchen scales into the centre of her worktop, her memory took hold as she weighed out the ingredients, momentarily disappearing behind a cloud of flour. *Just one more loaf,* she told herself, *and then never again.*

Jenny walked up to the front of the room, her blouse clinging to her back as she inhaled warm clouds of freshly baked bread, igniting a Pavlovian response as she imagined spreading it with thick lashings of salty butter, the elastic centre soft between her teeth. Nestling the loaf behind her photograph, she glanced at Azeez's. His was more crusty and gourd-like as it burst from the slits he had made, the eccentric counterpart to her own modest attempt.

Paul, Sorcha and Angela joined them as the judges entered, Sorcha visibly more relaxed than the others as the controversial winner of last week's golden whisk.

'We're looking for something well bonded, with a golden, crusty exterior and a good rise,' said Amanda, her eyes flicking between the two loaves. 'Today's heat will have made this particularly challenging, because the weather can cause bread to rise too fast and be prone to collapsing.'

They nodded at slightly different intervals, fidgeting in anticipation.

'Let's start with this one,' said Luca, picking up Azeez's entire loaf and knocking against the bottom of it, as if communicating with it in code.

'Can you hear that?' he said, his ear hovering next to it. 'That's lovely and hollow which means the water has evaporated – just how it should be.'

He carved through it so that the top splintered, shattering into golden shards, before taking a piece and holding it up to point out the pockets of air.

'Good crust,' he said, his hand shielding his mouth as he chewed, 'and a light, fluffy centre.'

'It's impressive,' concluded Amanda as she returned it to the plate with a crescent shaped gap, so that Jenny's stomach fluttered for Azeez. Her excitement quickly sobered as the judges walked towards her own.

Amanda cut two slices, handing one to Luca, and the pair of them took a bite. The silence that followed was drawn-out, excruciating.

'This one is good . . . but it could've done with longer in the oven,' said Amanda. 'It's ever so slightly gummy in the middle, but not bad.'

Jenny bit her bottom lip, holding her breath.

'It has a nice full flavour though,' added Luca.

She exhaled, relieved that it wasn't a total disaster. Thanks to Azeez's advice, she hadn't been entirely defeated by bread. It was edible, 'good' even, and that was progress.

'Now for the moment of truth,' said Mo, as he handed Luca the golden whisk, his speech slowing. 'Judges, which of these cottage loaves was your favourite?'

'They were both a good effort, but it's got to be . . .' said Luca, hovering between the two of them in a cruel dance, '. . . this one.'

He stood behind Azeez's loaf, and she turned to look at him – a waxwork of surprise.

'Yes!' she said, squeezing him with every last drop of her remaining energy, as Luca placed the golden whisk in his hand. He stared at it as if it were alive, speechless, and Angela, Paul and Sorcha gathered round, Sorcha doing her best impression of looking pleased for him.

'Congratulations to our first finalist!' said Mo, and she clapped and clapped and clapped, until her hands throbbed.

'Another successful week,' said a man with a camera on his shoulder.

'Indeed,' she said, the afternoon sun beating down on her. 'I was certain I wouldn't survive bread week, but here I am.'

'And how do you feel about Angela leaving?'

Angela's severely underbaked 'hot cross bun faces' flashed through her mind, their novelty expressions making them look as if they had taken the whole thing extremely personally.

'Angela will be greatly missed. She's a lovely lady and an . . . imaginative baker. It won't be the same without her, she is such fun,' she said, 'but Azeez winning the golden whisk goes some way to softening the blow. He really deserves it and I'm thrilled that he's in the final.'

He signalled for her to move slightly to the left, before giving her a thumbs up.

'And have you ever made a cottage loaf before, or was today your first time?'

'I have actually made a cottage loaf before,' she said, looking down at the cracked earth, the parched grass, 'about six decades ago.'

'And how did it compare?'

'I don't know,' she hesitated, 'I never actually had a slice.'

25

Blackcurrant & Elderflower and
Apple & Cinnamon Doughnuts

A young man entered the ward clutching a bouquet of flowers and a handful of post, both looking and trying not to look at the same time as he scanned the beds, bewildered lines etched into his forehead. His face changed, softening into a beam as he walked towards her. She returned a vacant smile, disguising the panic that rose in her chest as she searched for any indication of who he might be. Why was he so pleased to see her?

'There you are,' he said, stopping at the bed next to her and planting a kiss on the woman's cheek. 'Peggy, she's perfect.'

Peggy's face lit up, her skin bare so that she looked almost childlike, dimples appearing in her cheeks as she wrapped her arms around him.

'Such beautiful flowers, pink for our girl,' she said, closing her eyes as she buried her nose into them. 'Did they let you see her?'

'I looked in through the nursery window,' he said, stroking her shoulder. 'The nurse held her up, she's beautiful.'

Moments later, another two gentlemen entered the ward and joined their respective wives with a joy so alien to her that it hurt to watch. Together they opened their cards, cooing over the well wishes of friends and family as they struggled to fit them on to their bedside tables.

'Is your husband coming this evening?' said Peggy. 'He's only got half an hour, he needs to hurry.'

The attention of the other couples snapped towards her so that she grew conscious of her solitude, her bedside cabinet empty except for a glass of water. She reached for it, taking a sip, rotating it between her palms.

'He's not, unfortunately,' she said, watching the way the light flickered on its surface, '. . . he's in the Navy, away at sea, couldn't get back in time.'

'Oh, that is a shame; hopefully he'll be back soon to meet his bouncing baby boy.'

'I hope so,' she said, noticing that the upturned corners of their mouths contradicted the look of pity in their eyes.

She was as eager to be invisible as they were not to see her, overcome with relief when they turned their backs and continued their conversations. Rolling on to her side, she closed her eyes so that they might think she was asleep, pulling the sheet over her ear to deaden their voices. Her body felt unbearably tender, as if she were no more than just a vessel from which James had been ripped, and as she lay there she longed to be back with Mary, where she didn't have to pretend.

She woke to the wheels of a trolley being pushed through the ward, a rhythm of squeaks and clunks which grew louder as they neared her bed. Blinking open her eyes, she positioned herself upright, holding her breath as she navigated her soreness. In her pretending she must have slept, since all of the fathers had left.

The nurse placed James at the end of her bed in his box, and from it came a cry as he forced the air from his lungs in powerful bursts so that she felt a desperate need to make him stop. She reached for him *and held him to her chest, helping him feed as his tiny hands settled on her skin. He quickly fell into a contented silence as she stroked the hair on his temples which covered his skin like a peach. After months of being a burden she suddenly felt so needed. She studied the perfect dip of his cupid's bow and the way it moved when he suckled, the soft dimples in the backs of his hands, his down-like hair, a warmth running through her as she drank him in. When he was finished, she kissed the top of his head, breathing in his sweet musk as he wrapped his fingers around hers so that she thought she might burst.*

'Hello, dear,' said a deep croak of a voice.

She looked up to see the cleaning lady leaning over her with a halo of grey curls.

'Hello,' she said, noticing that between her cigarette-stained fingers she was clutching a paper bag, patterned with blotches where fat had seeped through.

'I hope you don't mind me disturbing you,' she said, hovering next to her, 'but I just wanted to say that your baby is beautiful.'

Jenny hesitated, her throat tightening.

'He reminds me of my son, many years ago. He had a lovely head of hair, just like that.'

'Thank you,' she said, 'he's called James.'

'It'll take him anywhere, a name like that,' the lady said, falling silent as she fought, it seemed, with the words on her lips.

'I noticed that you haven't had any visitors, so I brought you these.' She placed the bag on her bedside cabinet, patting it lightly. 'It's just a couple of jam doughnuts.'

'How kind,' said Jenny. 'I have a sweet tooth, you must've known.'

The lady glanced at her watch.

'I'd better get home,' she said, smiling at James. 'Enjoy him. They don't stay like that for long.'

*

275

*When the babies had been taken back to the nursery for the night
and the ward was dark, she soaked her pillow with tears. For seventeen years, time had served only as a reminder of when she needed to
be somewhere, or a gauge by which to prepare a meal or bake a cake.
Overnight it had transformed into the most precious commodity and
she would do anything, anything at all, to make it stop. They don't
stay like this for long. She pictured his first gummy smile, his first
precarious step, his first word. Would it be mummy? She couldn't
bear to think.*

*Slipping her feet out of the bed and on to the cold floor, she tiptoed
her way down the corridor in search of the nursery, holding her
breath. Pressing her hands against the glass, she peered in, her eyes
scanning the rows of cots, searching the tiny faces that peeped out
from under their blankets. There he was, second in from the left. She
recognized the curve of his cheek, his head of dark hair. He looked
peaceful, angelic, naive to the situation she had brought him into,
punishment for her sin. Every minute that passed was a minute less
with him. She only had six weeks.*

Jenny was first on the minibus. She sat a couple of rows
back from the driver in a quiet spot where she had a
detailed view of the back of his head, which was shiny and
freckled, a raw pink island on its very top where she
assumed he must've bumped it. As the fresh blanket of
morning dew lifted and the sun warmed the earth, the birds
appeared to be giving the dawn chorus a bit of something
extra. She tuned into one particular voice, a blackbird perhaps, which sang with such vigour that it sounded as if it
might burst into a thousand feathers. She imagined the
same happening to her – baking until she exploded into a
cloud of icing sugar. What a way to go.

'Sorry I'm late,' said Azeez, glancing at his phone before pushing it deep into his pocket and collapsing into the seat next to her. Sorcha and Paul followed, nodding their good mornings as the engine roared into life. The bus felt different, empty, a reminder that it was just the four of them left.

'Why are you so smiley?' said Azeez, rubbing his sleep-swollen eyes.

'I was just imagining bursting into a cloud of icing sugar,' she said, hesitating as she heard the sentence out loud. '. . . It doesn't matter.'

'I think it's a good job that it's the semi-final and we're nearly at the end,' he said, a tickle of amusement in his voice. 'We've all lost the plot.'

They raced down the motorway in a contemplative silence, their eyes glazed as they ran through their recipes like the lines of a play, kneading and frying in their minds.

'What flavours are you doing again, for the doughnuts?' he said, his head tilted back over the headrest, eyes closed.

'A dozen blackcurrant jam doughnuts with elderflower sugar, and a dozen apple doughnuts with cinnamon sugar.'

'That's actually just made my mouth water and it's not even six a.m.'

'What about you?'

'Mango creme and yuzu, and chai spiced rings.'

'They sound delicious,' she said as they turned the corner, crunching on to the gravel driveway for what was potentially the last time. 'I don't know that I've ever seen a yuzu . . .'

'Really?' he said, blinking open his eyes. 'It's like the love child of a lemon and a lime.'

She giggled, able to imagine it perfectly.

As they wound down the track towards their fate, she thought of all the places that held a secret meaning: the church spire on the horizon above Kittlesham, a sign of home whenever she had been away, the twisted oak tree that Poppy renamed *The Uncle Bernie Tree* because it meant that they were near their house, and now the grand gates of the *Britain Bakes* manor. They had come to represent the thrill of possibility at a time in her life when she thought there was none.

'Whatever happens today,' she said, 'I will remember this for the rest of my life.'

He smiled. 'Me too.'

The dough clung to her hands like chewing gum and she pressed it into the worktop, scraping it off her fingers as it stuck to everything it touched. This week's guest judge was Frida Malik, a former *Britain Bakes* champion, and Jenny felt awestruck as she approached.

'Is this a family recipe?' said Frida, peering beyond the mess at her notes.

She had the most expressive eyes that Jenny had ever seen, and her manner was just as warm and down-to-earth as it had appeared on the television.

'Not on this occasion, no,' she said, taking short breaths as she continued to knead the dough. 'It's one of my own. My mother's recipe for doughnuts didn't include yeast; it was self-raising flour, margarine and a saucepan of fat which didn't quite fit the bill on this occasion.'

'That sounds like a true wartime doughnut,' said Amanda,

appearing next to her. 'Have you flavoured the elderflower sugar yourself?'

'I have. We have a lovely elder tree at the bottom of our garden so I put a couple of elderflower heads into a jar with the sugar a little while ago, so hopefully it's infused.'

Frida picked up the jar and held it under her nose, her eyes lighting up, before she passed it to Amanda so that she could do the same.

'Blackcurrant is a very strong flavour,' said Amanda, returning the jar to the worktop. 'Are you confident that the elderflower will come through?'

'I hope so . . .' she said, her words trailing off with her confidence.

With that, Jenny focused on her recipe so that her world shrank to the size of a doughnut production line for the next couple of hours, each ball of dough bobbing around the scalding tank of oil like a hook-a-duck at the fair.

'Bakers, you have thirty minutes left,' called Mo, 'dough *nut* fall behind!'

One by one she rolled them in the elderflower sugar and set them aside to cool, funnelling the jam into syringes so that she felt for a moment as if she were a nurse. In the corner of her eye, she noticed Mo dashing towards Paul, who appeared to have dropped a bowl of sugar and was collecting it up as if it were his grandmother's ashes.

'There is nothing more disappointing than biting into a doughnut, only to discover that it contains a morsel of jam,' she said to the camera, inflating one with blackcurrant so that it looked as if it might burst at the seams. 'If nothing else, these won't be short of filling.'

She removed the syringe and slotted in its place an edible flower, repeating this twenty-four times before arranging her doughnuts on to a glass cake stand in two tiers.

'Jenny, they're beautiful,' said Katie, putting the palms of her hands together in delight as she approached.

'Thank you. I've done my best so what will be will be,' she said, pushing the cake stand towards the end of the worktop, her mind wandering to thoughts of telling Bernard of her success, the title of '*Britain Bakes* finalist', the sense of having achieved. A moment later, she stamped out her dreams like glowing ashes, smothering them before they turned to disappointments. She wanted to stay more than she would ever admit.

Jenny stood in the car park, clutching a paper bag with two of yesterday's doughnuts in it, one of each flavour.

'Do you want me to wait with you?' called Carys who was laden with bags, her arms piled high with mixing bowls, a walkie talkie balanced on top which she was steadying with her chin.

'I'll be fine, thank you,' she said, a small hope sparking inside her every time a car slowed at the gates. 'I'm sure Bernard will be here any minute.'

She glanced at her watch, her phone, the darkening sky. He was eleven minutes late, twelve now, and he was always punctual – especially where she was concerned. She sighed, perching on the edge of her suitcase. He was also eighty-two years old, recovering from pneumonia and had recently sustained a head injury. A knot of frustration tightened in her chest as she scolded herself for allowing him to pick her up, even if he had insisted. She twisted a lock of hair around her finger, pulling it tight as she pictured him racing along the motorway, swerving, rolling. She checked her phone again.

'Darling!'

She looked up, jumping to her feet as he pulled up beside her.

'Sorry I'm a few minutes late,' he said, stepping out to relieve her of her bags.

'I've got them,' she said, heaving them into the boot. 'I was just starting to worry.'

She lowered herself into the passenger seat, inhaling a combination of plastic tinged with synthetic cherry from the faded air freshener which hung from the rear-view mirror.

'Sorry, darling,' he said, his smile fading, 'have you been waiting long?'

'Just ten minutes, but you know what I'm like – I thought the worst had happened.'

'The worst?' he said, navigating his long limbs into the driving seat. 'I've never been involved in an accident in my life and I don't intend to have one now.'

He pulled his seat belt across his chest and fastened it with a clunk before slapping his hands on his knees and turning to face her.

'So,' he said, 'go on then.'

She looked into her lap, smoothing out the creases in her skirt.

'How did it go?'

'Well,' she said, 'there was a twist.'

'A twist?'

'The bottom two, instead of the top two, did the Blind Bake . . .'

She could see him working it out, his face contorting in thought.

'So only the winner went through to the final . . .' she said.

'. . . and the loser went home?' he finished.

She nodded.

'Clever,' he said, 'so . . . were you in the Blind Bake?'

She took a deep breath as the moment closed in on her.

He reached for her hand, gripping it tightly.

'I wasn't,' she said, a smile flickering across her face as her words became real. 'I'm in the final, Bernie.'

She heard the click of his seat belt as he leant over, squeezing her so tightly in his arms that she could barely breathe.

'You did it!' he said into her neck. 'You bloody did it!'

With that, he turned to the steering wheel and honked the horn in three sharp bursts.

'Bernie!' she said, covering her mouth as her shoulders began to shake, laughter and tears merging to form a weightless hysteria.

'I knew it!' he said, his face a picture of sheer delight.

She caught her breath as her eyes met his, her emotions tangled in a delirious knot.

'Are we having one, then?' he said, reaching for the paper bag.

'Don't you want to wait until after your supper?'

'Absolutely not,' he said, mischief dancing in his eyes.

'No?' she said, raising her eyebrows. 'Me neither.'

They sat in the car park, side by side, watching the sun

fall out of the sky as they sank their teeth through the deep-fried crust and into the soft white dough, eventually reaching a burst of jam which dripped down their chins in mouth-watering dollops. They licked their sugar-coated lips, making quiet hums of appreciation as they angled their hands for the next bite.

'Happiness is,' she said as she savoured the moment, one of thousands of little moments which together formed a lifetime.

'You're very clever,' he said, winding down the window to brush the sugar from his hands. 'But then again, I've always known that.'

26

Treacle Tart

Cradling his head in her left hand, she used her right to swish the water over his soft, round tummy, his limbs jerking and kicking in spontaneous bursts. He slapped his palm against the surface of the bath so that droplets showered her dress.

'Is that nice?' she whispered, smiling as his eyes flared with wonder, flickers of expressions crossing his face like evening shadows. She tried to memorize these moments completely, stashing away every detail so that they would never fade.

Immersing him slightly deeper, she wet the top of his head, his wisps of hair clinging to him in dark threads. His face changed, crumpling in horror so that he grew red and wrinkly in a matter of seconds. She scooped him into her arms, wrapping him in a towel as he emitted a scream which left a throbbing impression in her ear.

'I'm sorry,' she said, rubbing his back as she rocked him, kissing his damp cheek. He gasped for breath before letting out another cry, his face scrunched tightly to reveal angry pink gums.

'Come on now,' she said, drying his hair so that it stuck up in sweet tufts as if he had just hatched. She settled his head against her skin, his breaths calming as he nuzzled into her, the antidote to his tears. Laying him on the towel, she showered him in talc as if it were icing sugar, patting it into the creases around his legs and arms, his eyes shiny with the remains of his tears. Threading his arms through the sleeves of his nightie, she sat him up, leaning him forwards as she tried to fasten the buttons at the back with one hand. He was unsteady, his balance relying entirely on her, his face earnest like a wizened old man.

'Nearly done,' she said, slipping him into his baby bag and buttoning up the bottom edge, looking at her embroidered initials. One day he might notice them, maybe he'd ask about them, a trail of crumbs to whom he truly belonged. It was a futile hope, she knew that. His face was changing again, the faint muscles where his eyebrows would grow knitting together in warning. She picked him up, diverting his cry as she settled him on her shoulder, rocking him gently as she returned him to the nursery.

The cots were lined up in rows, his now second from the door and moving closer with each departure. She held the blue label which was tied to it, rubbing the paper between her finger and thumb. It read Eaton, James. Date of birth: 11th January. Weight at birth: 8lb 3oz. There was something about reading his name, the way it looked on paper, that filled her with a sense of belonging; of him to her and of her to him. She soothed him gently in her arms, watching as his eyelids grew heavier with each blink, feeling his warm weight against her body and knowing that he would forever be her most beautiful creation. Beautiful not only because of his velvet skin and his button nose, but because of the innocence and hope that he encased. He was a miracle of unfurled life, of memories not yet made.

Once he was asleep, she reluctantly relinquished him to his cot and tiptoed from the room, pausing as she heard a cry from Mary's little Sarah, who had been born two weeks after James.

'There, there,' she said, scooping her up and kissing her forehead which smelt sweetly of milk. She rocked her gently, her tiny features illuminated by the light of the moon.

'Back to bed immediately,' said the matron, making her jump as she marched across the nursery towards her. 'She's not your baby.'

She lowered Sarah back into her cot, gently rubbing her tummy as she tucked her up, before making a swift exit.

Slipping her tired body into bed, she reached over to her bedside cabinet, pulling from it her diary and a pencil. Folding it open, she struck through the day with a menacing cross, tracing the lines over and over so that the paper thinned and the air smelt of lead.

'Can I get in?' whispered Mary.

She nodded, moving up to make room as they pulled the sheet over their heads, making a sort of tent with their knees.

'I pinched this from the kitchen,' Mary said, putting a sliver of something on to the palm of her hand.

It was sticky and smelt deliriously good. As she took a bite, the texture was softly crystallized, like the top of a jar of honey. The pastry beneath crumbled, balancing the cloying sweetness as it moulded together on the roof of her mouth.

'Mmm,' she said, taking another bite, 'treacle tart?'

'Correct,' said Mary, crumbs clinging to her lips. 'What are you writing? The recipe book?'

She finished the last bite, quietly dusting her hands out of the side of the bed.

'No, not tonight. I've been crossing the days off since James was born,' she said, joining her back under the warmth of the covers.

Mary said nothing, reaching for her hand and gripping it tightly.

'I'd rather stay here for the rest of my life than say goodbye to him,' she said, pulling her hand away, to cover her face.

'I know,' said Mary, rubbing her shoulder.

'Do you feel the same about Sarah?' Jenny said, blinking open her eyes which felt tight in their sockets.

Mary paused.

'I do,' she said, her hair falling across her face. 'I never expected to love her.'

'Not at all?'

'No,' she said, 'I didn't choose to have her . . .'

Jenny hesitated for a moment, decoding her words which landed like arrows.

'I thought I would hate her. I was scared she would look like him.'

'I'm sorry,' said Jenny, pulling her close, 'I had no idea.'

They held each other tight in the darkness, cocooned from the outside world.

'How many days do you have left?' said Mary, picking up her diary and flicking through the leaden crosses.

'One,' she replied.

They barely spoke a word that morning, their spirits heavy with a shared but silent grief.

'He looks beautiful,' said Mary, as Jenny carefully tied a ribbon under his chin, framing his plump cheeks with the knitted bonnet she had been saving for best.

'Thank you,' she said. 'Would you mind holding him whilst I check that he has everything?'

Mary picked him up, kissing his cheek and rubbing his nose against hers. He looked like the front of the pattern book, dressed from head to toe in clothes Jenny had made: mittens, a matinee jacket, booties to match.

She carefully lifted the lid of the box, imagining being the one to receive it as she ran her eyes over the neatly folded layettes in yellow, blue and white, enough to last him for the next couple of months at least. Beneath them were three dozen nappies and two crocheted shawls: a simple one for everyday and a smart one for best. She picked up her blue recipe book, thumbing through it as she skimmed over the Black Forest Gateau, Grandma Audrey's Chocolate Crispy Cakes and her father's Tiffin, written in her very best handwriting. Kissing the cover, she placed it carefully on top of the clothes, hesitating for a moment before closing the lid. Through this she would be with him always.

'Hurry, Jennifer, your taxi's outside,' said the matron, her face lined with agitation as she burst into the room and pressed an envelope into her hand. 'These are important, do not lose them. They're your papers.'

She nodded, pushing them into her bag.

'I would strongly recommend that you two cut ties after today, and leave this most unfortunate incident in the past,' she said, before turning on her heel.

Jenny headed out to the taxi carrying her suitcase in one hand and the box in the other, Mary following with James. The front door slammed heavily behind them as if it were pleased to see her go, and they crunched down the gravel driveway without exchanging a word, a pressure building inside them. The moment they had been dreading had become a reality: time had run out.

'I'll take this,' said the driver, relieving her of the suitcase and opening the car door. She wondered, for a brief moment, whether he knew what was happening, if he made this journey often.

She looked at Mary, her plain dress skimming over her swollen stomach, dark circles under her eyes. James was cradled in her arms, wonderstruck by the tree above his head, staring in perfect ignorance.

'Goodbye, then,' said Mary, clinging to them both and not letting go, her ribcage heaving and unsteady. 'I don't know how I'll cope in here without you.'

'You will,' replied Jenny, her voice catching as she wrestled with composure. 'You will for Sarah. I'll miss you so much.'

At the last possible moment they drew apart, and Jenny climbed into the car.

'Good luck, little one,' said Mary, her eyes stained pink as she kissed James's head, lowering him on to Jenny's lap. She held the door open with one hand and searched her pocket with the other.

'This is for you. I asked Sylvia to take it,' she said, pressing something into Jenny's palm. It was a photograph of James in his cot, his bright eyes open, his hair dark, his tiny fingers curled around the edge of his shawl.

'Oh, Mary,' she said, studying it. 'I'll keep this forever, thank you.'

The engine roared into life, prompting Mary to shut the door behind her, her eyes wide, desperate. As they pulled away, she remained on the driveway, one arm holding the lower part of her ribcage and the other waving frantically, tears streaming down her cheeks. Jenny watched as she grew smaller and smaller, until they turned a corner, and she was gone, never to be seen again.

Jenny turned to look at Bernard, whose nose was jutting out from under the duvet like a fin above the ocean. Her ears had involuntarily decided to focus on his breathing, its heaviness, the irregularity of it. Sometimes an entire ten seconds would pass between exhale and inhale, forcing her to lean over, her eyes searching for the twitch of a pulse in his neck. It would come and she would sink back into her pillow feeling relieved and neurotic and awake. Her body was in bed but her mind was in the middle of the *Britain Bakes* final, winning the competition in a heady euphoria and then tragically losing it in a complete disaster. Her skin was damp, every position uncomfortable, the tick of the clock growing louder and louder.

Slipping her feet out from under the duvet, she put on her slippers and knotted her dressing gown around her waist, tiptoeing down the stairs and into the kitchen. She closed the door firmly behind her. It was warm and dark, the appliances humming, the oven flashing 03:07 so that the numbers were etched into her vision when she looked away. She clicked on a lamp, half-opened the blinds and looked out across the garden which was eerily still.

Turning on the oven, she retrieved a ball of pastry from the fridge, a couple of lemons from the fruit bowl and a heavy tin of Lyle's golden syrup from the cupboard. On the worktop were the notes for her final Baker's Delight which looked like the jottings of a mad professor: workings out, scrawled amendments, intersections of bakes. Any day now, she needed to submit the final ingredient list for her biggest challenge yet.

She walked over to the calendar which hung from the wall next to the fridge, displaying the month of June with a fitting portrait of her baking, as interpreted by Poppy in an array of abstract shapes, glitter flying from her bowl, her teeth bared. In truth, she related to this manic, kitchen-dwelling creature more than ever at this unsociable hour. Her eyes scanned the dates, *Britain Bakes filming at home* scrawled in today's box. Below it, in green capital letters, read the words *BRITAIN BAKES FINAL*, small dashes bursting from it like confetti. It looked terrifyingly real written down, out of place amongst the dental appointments, the bowls matches and the cups of tea. It was life on paper, the extraordinary rubbing shoulders with the ordinary, the long-awaited holiday nestled between someone coming over to fix the boiler, and a doctor's appointment. In there too were the blank boxes, the dates that don't require words because the numbers alone are carved into the core of who you have become.

She levered the lid off the syrup with the handle of a teaspoon and poured it into a saucepan, watching it hit the surface in frantic squiggles, growing faster as it thinned. It reminded her of holding a spoon high above her porridge, watching it cut through the oats to create a golden well at its centre so that if you looked carefully enough, you could see the pattern on the bowl.

Leaving it to warm, she halved a lemon, spearing it on to the point of the glass squeezer and twisting it so that it lost structure with each turn, the pulp catching as the juice ran into the outer ring like a moat, before adding it to the syrup.

The next part was a little trickier to do quietly. She plugged the food processor into the wall, tearing slices of bread into it as if she were feeding the ducks. Holding her breath she pulsed the machine, wincing as each blast cut through the silence like a pneumatic drill, holding her hand over the chimney in the hope that it might muffle the sound. She paused, unclipping the cylinder and shaking it, observing the crumbs with an air of disapproval. Too big. She reattached it, pulsing again.

Taking her shortcrust cases, she divided the thick amber mixture between them, watching as they levelled into jewel-like pools. Using the leftover pastry from the fridge, she rolled it flat and sliced it into delicate lengths, laying them across the tarts at measured intervals, weaving the perpendicular strips between them, over and under, over and under. Her fingers trembled with the precision of it as she created twelve lattice tops, her mind lost somewhere beneath the folds.

As she slid them into the oven she pulled up a chair next to it, meeting the face of her dark reflection in the oven door: her silver hair, her tired eyes, the lines in her skin which had formed from laughter, from tears, from living.

'Since it's such a lovely day, I think let's get you out in the garden,' said Carys, lifting a tripod in one hand and a sand-bag in the other. The crew followed behind her in a blur of bags, poles and coffee cups.

'Morning, Jenny, big week this week,' said the sound operator, nodding towards her as he passed. 'Morning, Bernard.'

'This won't be as long as last time, I promise,' said Carys, clicking her pen. 'It's really just a quick interview with Bernard, about you being in the final.'

'Can I get anyone a tea? Coffee? Treacle tart?' called Jenny from the doorway, watching on as filming equipment filled the garden and lights were constructed above the flower beds.

'Yes, please,' rang the chorus of replies.

'Coffee, milk, three sugars.'

'Black coffee for me, please.'

'Coffee, splash of milk.'

'. . . I'll just do a tray,' she concluded, heading back inside.

She pulled up a stool and reached for the cafetiere which lived in the cupboard above the extractor fan through lack of use, alongside a SodaStream and several forgotten Tupperware. Lifting it down, she filled it with fresh coffee grounds, the rich aroma tickling at her nostrils.

She waited for the kettle to boil and watched from the window as they clipped a microphone to the inside of Bernard's collar, getting him to stand to the left, and then to the right a little. Several familiar faces fussed around him, one with a microphone on a stick which looked rather like a badger hovering just above his head, another crouched down with a huge silver disc angled towards his face. He looked nervous, but in a way that only she would notice; a little quieter than usual, his smile slightly withdrawn, his sentences punctuated with polite laughter. It was a surreal picture and she felt nostalgic as she watched on, as if she were looking back on the moment as a memory, even whilst it was happening.

'So,' said Carys, looking down at her phone and scrolling through it with her thumb, 'if you could repeat the question in the answer for me that would be great, because my questions will be cut out.'

He nodded, his shoulders stiff.

'Let's get going then,' she said, turning to the crew. 'Are we good?'

The woman behind the camera held her thumb up in the air.

'All right,' she said, 'and do feel free to relax, Bernard, as if you and I are just having a conversation. There are no right or wrong answers, it's chilled.'

'I'll do my best,' he said.

'How has it been, watching Jenny's journey through the competition so far?'

'Jenny's journey through the competition so far has been nothing short of inspiring to witness. She kept her application a secret at first, even from me, I think because she didn't believe she would get very far . . . and now she's in the final.'

He smiled as something crossed his mind, taking his hands out of his pockets and clasping them together in front of him.

'Last night in the early hours, I had a dream that someone was breaking into my shed – well, I thought it was a dream, but I could have sworn I heard a drill. Anyway, this morning I realized it was Jenny using the blender, practising her baking in the dead of night.'

There was a rumble of laughter amongst the crew, and she smiled as she filled the cafetiere with hot water, watching the grinds float to the top.

'And this isn't unusual,' he said. 'She set her heart on this, and she hasn't stopped. The staff at the local supermarket think we're running a bakery, and I'm not surprised because I've been buying them out of flour and sugar for months.'

'Brilliant,' said Carys, 'and did you ever think she would make it to the final?'

He took a deep breath, giving her question some thought.

'Did I ever think Jenny would make it to the final? Yes, I didn't doubt it.'

'Ahh,' said Carys, 'and do you think she could win?'

She slowly pushed the plunger, feeling the resistance of the water against her palm.

'We've been married almost sixty years now, and to be honest, I believe that this lady can do anything she wants,' he said. 'Whatever happens, she's already a winner in my eyes, because I know what it's taken to get this far. Old age can make us feel like we need to live a smaller life, but Jenny has shown that our dreams have a place at every stage of our journey . . . that they can be achieved *because* of our age, and not in spite of it.'

She gulped, pressing her lips together.

'But I'll be glad to have her back,' he said. 'I've missed her, you see.'

Just as she picked up the tray, she was interrupted by the sharp ring of the doorbell, her stomach replicating the plunging motion of the cafetiere. She paused for a moment, in the hope that whoever it was would go away. Another ring. The crew glanced over towards the window, the sound operator wearing an agitated frown.

'Sorry,' she mimed, putting down the tray, 'just a second.'

She dashed to the door, making out a slight figure through the glass. Of course. Who else?

'Hello,' said Ann, her heels together on the doorstep, her toes turned out. 'I feel as if I haven't seen you in quite some time – is everything okay? Is Bernard well?'

'Yes, he's much improved,' said Jenny, a strained smile emerging. 'We must get something in the diary. Fred all right?'

'He's just at home. I wondered if you had my baking dish, the one the cottage pie was in?'

'Oh. Yes,' she said, 'I'm a little busy at the moment but I can drop it round over the next few –'

She watched as Ann's attention followed something behind her. Looking over her shoulder, she spotted Carys unzipping a rucksack in the hallway.

'Who is that?' said Ann, her arms now tightly folded.

Jenny looked from Ann to Carys, and back to Ann.

'Let me explain,' she said, 'come in . . .'

Ann stepped inside in one neat movement, as Jenny closed the door behind her.

'Carys,' she said, 'this is my good friend and neighbour, Ann.'

'Oh –' said Carys, unsure of whether to introduce herself or hide. 'Hi, Ann.'

'So, Ann . . .' she said, looking to Carys for help, 'doesn't know.'

'Know what?' said Ann.

'Right,' said Carys, 'we'll just have to get her to sign an NDA. She's a friend, so don't worry too much.'

'What on earth is an NDA? Will someone please tell me what is going on?'

'I've not been entirely honest over the last couple of months,' said Jenny, blood rushing to her cheeks. 'I'm a contestant on *Britain Bakes*.'

Ann's lips zipped tightly together and she grew a little taller, glaring towards Jenny.

'This is Carys, she's one of the producers,' she said, as Carys held out her hand.

Ann tentatively returned her handshake, observing Carys as if she were an alien creature.

'And I'm in the final.'

Ann wasn't a lady often silenced but this information rendered her mute, her eyes like saucers.

'I knew it!' she shrieked, before throwing her arms around Jenny in the most uncharacteristic outburst that she had ever witnessed. She looked towards Carys, who was watching the situation unfold, mouth slightly ajar.

'That day of Bernard's accident . . . he wouldn't let us call you! You arrived back so late! I thought either you'd started to lose your marbles, or you were up to something.'

'I'm sorry I didn't mention it sooner. I'm not supposed to say anything until it's announced in the press; nobody knows, just family.'

Jenny looked back towards Ann, who was now pulling a peculiar expression, her chin gravitating down towards her collarbone.

'Ann?' she said, grabbing her arm. 'Are you all right?'

With that, Ann let out a disturbing splutter, ripping a tissue from her handbag and covering her face with it.

'Oh, Ann,' said Jenny, wrapping her arm around her small, sharp frame, 'don't cry.'

'I can't believe it,' she said, blowing her nose with a disproportionate honk.

'Sorry to interrupt,' said Carys, holding out a clipboard. 'Ann, would you mind signing this to say that you won't tell anybody until we give you the go ahead?'

'Of course,' she said, dabbing her snivels with the rag of tissue.

'Also, would you be up for doing an interview for the show, as Jenny's friend? We'll just ask you a couple of questions about her, it's nothing scary.'

'Oh goodness,' she said, tucking her blouse into her skirt, 'with pleasure.'

With that, she followed Carys into the garden, Jenny in tow with a tray of coffee which was descended upon immediately by the crew.

'Ann?' said Bernard, panic flashing across his face.

'Don't worry,' she replied, 'Jenny's told me . . . you must be so proud.'

'Thank goodness,' he said, his face relaxing into a beam. 'I am.'

Jenny reached out and put her arm through his, watching as the crew fussed around Ann, who looked particularly tiny in the middle of them all. In spite of her shock, she stood proud, her chest puffed out like a bird, fresh from its bath.

'You said earlier, Ann, that you suspected something was going on? Can you just elaborate on what it's been like, witnessing Jenny prepare for this competition?'

'Well, Jenny has always been quite the domestic goddess,' she said, her words rushed. 'My husband Fred is always eager to come over and sample whatever she has been baking, usually in rather large quantities . . . I hold her solely responsible for his expanding waistline.'

Jenny bit her lip, sharing a smile with Bernard as they watched.

'She used to make, well, classic home bakes. Fruit loaves, shortbreads, that sort of thing, but over the last couple of months it's gone to whole new levels. We've been lucky enough to come over for a cup of tea, only to be greeted by all kinds of elaborate treats.'

'And what are your thoughts on her having made it all the way to the final?'

Ann looked towards Jenny, shaking her head so slightly that it looked like a twitch, her gaze returning to the camera.

'I'm utterly thrilled for her,' she said, clasping her hands tightly together. 'We are behind her all the way.'

A Picnic Through Time

Jenny sat on the steps with Azeez and Sorcha, watching the crew dash in and out of the barn as she twisted her wedding ring around her finger, up to her swollen knuckle and back down again. Every now and then she shuddered involuntarily, a combination of the chill breeze and exhaustion.

'Can you hear that?' said Azeez, grabbing her arm.

They listened, exchanging the sort of glances usually associated with seeing a ghost. In the distance they could hear the rumblings of a crowd, growing louder and quieter with the direction of the wind.

'That's definitely them, I can hear my mum's laugh,' said Azeez, covering his face with his apron.

'How do I look?' said Sorcha, blinking at them through thick lashes, her lips shiny with gloss.

'Great,' said Azeez, nudging Jenny's leg. 'Whatever happens today, we've been lucky enough to make it to the *Britain Bakes* final.'

'Especially Jenny,' said Sorcha, disarming them both.

'Why Jenny?' said Azeez, his eyebrows contorting.

'After missing patisserie week.'

Jenny felt her face flush, exposed by Sorcha's words which were spoken so casually.

'I wouldn't say a personal crisis was particularly *lucky*,' said Azeez, 'and she'd won the golden whisk, so it made no difference anyway.'

Sorcha blinked uncomfortably, with no retort.

Azeez turned to Jenny. 'Why is it so much more scary knowing that our relatives are here?'

'We will be so busy, we won't even notice . . .' she said, with a grain of conviction, as she searched for the frequency of Bernard's voice. Her heart was now thumping so intensely that she could barely hear anything outside of her own being.

'Sorcha, Azeez, Jenny!' called Carys, making large sweeping gestures with her hands towards the door of the barn. 'In you go.'

Azeez extended an arm around her shoulder, pulling her close. 'You've got this,' he said.

They walked down the steps and towards the barn in a nervous huddle, tightening their aprons with double knots.

As she stood behind her workstation for the final time, she placed a hand on her cast-iron scales as if she were swearing an oath. Amanda entered the room looking sublime in a shocking pink suit, tailored to perfection with the matt shine of raw silk. Behind her followed guest judge Tony Conway, her polar opposite. His cheekiness countered her sophistication and despite being a Michelin star chef, he had the manner of a pub landlord. He had a bald head and a pedestrian face, the sort which would be particularly forgettable if it weren't for his thick-rimmed blue spectacles, which gave him an eccentricity that only the famous could pull off.

'Welcome, finalists,' announced Mo. 'This is your *last ever* Baker's Delight Challenge.'

He paused, giving his words a chance to sink in. She felt the presence of a camera to her right as she pressed her lips together, nowhere to hide.

'This week you have *five hours* to make your ultimate picnic: a hamper filled with your very best bakes. The judges have specified that these must showcase at least four different baking skills,' added Katie, looking towards Amanda and Tony who remained as still as waxworks.

'Three . . . two . . . one . . .'

'Bake!'

Smoothing her hand over the list of instructions on her worktop, she watched as the letters and numbers merged to form the visual equivalent of white noise, her brain whirring like a tired engine in desperate need of a jump start.

Mo, Katie, Amanda and Tony approached, settling opposite her.

'Good morning, Jenny,' said Tony, folding his arms on top of his stomach. 'What have you got for us today?'

'I'm making A Picnic Through Time,' she said, 'an ode to the family recipes that have got me to where I am today.'

'What a lovely sentiment,' said Amanda. 'So what will it involve?'

Jenny rolled the corner of the instructions between her fingertip and the worktop, softening the paper so that it curled.

'Twelve Black Forest éclairs, twelve treacle and cardamom tarts – inspired by an old friend of mine who once brought me a slice to cheer me up.' She paused, before continuing, 'Twelve pieces of my father's tiffin made with homemade biscuit, dried fruit and dark chocolate, and my grandmother's tea loaf, an ode to the simple and reliable.'

'All sweet,' said Tony, rubbing his chin. 'Where did you get the idea of combining Black Forest with éclairs?'

'Black Forest gateau is my signature birthday cake,' she said, 'it's very dear to me.'

She pictured the blue cover of his recipe book. It was the first recipe she had written for him and she wondered if he had ever made it, if he had known – as he mixed the batter – just a fraction of the love that she had felt for him.

'And because I missed patisserie week, I thought it would be a good chance to make choux pastry.'

'I'll look forward to tasting it,' said Tony.

'One thing I will say,' said Amanda, attempting to make eye contact, 'is that these bakes all sound well within your comfort zone. How are you going to make sure that you don't play it too safe?'

'Well,' said Jenny, meeting her gaze for less than two seconds before returning to the recipes, 'I'm going to make the hamper out of gingerbread.'

The judges looked at each other, whilst Mo looked at the camera.

'That certainly sounds like a challenge,' said Tony, 'all of that in five hours!'

'It does,' agreed Amanda, 'but you did win the golden whisk for your gingerbread church, so if anyone can do it, you can.'

*

'I'm just letting some of the heat out and then they're going back in for another five,' said Jenny, piercing each éclair to make a small chimney from which curls of heat dispersed.

She paused, running her eyes down her list of instructions and ticking things off as she went.

'Tiffin, just needs the chocolate on top. Tarts, done. Éclairs, need to go back in the oven. Gingerbread, needs assembling –'

She gasped.

'Everything all right?' said Mo, peering over her shoulder at the list.

'The tea loaf,' she said, massaging her temples, 'I made the mixture and put it to one side but I've completely forgotten to bake it.'

She pulled the bowl towards her, removing the tea towel which was draped over the top of it. The wet mixture resisted as she stirred, so that it sounded like a boot in mud.

'How long do I have left?'

Mo glanced at his watch, 'You've still got an hour.'

She dropped her head, noticing that the worktop was dotted with shiny pearls of batter and stray breadcrumbs.

'I've set myself an impossible challenge,' she said, her tone conclusive. 'The loaf needs ninety minutes in the oven . . .'

Raising the spoon, she let the mixture fall back into the bowl in thick dollops, dismayed at the thought of wasting it.

A moment later, her eyes grew bright. 'I've had an idea.'

'Go on . . .' said Mo.

'It'll be quicker if I do miniatures,' she said, suddenly invigorated. 'Coming out!'

'What is?' Mo moved his head as if navigating his way across the M25 at rush hour.

'The éclairs,' she said, removing them from the oven and transferring them on to a wire rack in twelve sharp pinches, before heading to the dresser at the back of the room in search of a tin.

'Jenny,' whispered Carys, from behind the curtain, 'left-hand drawer.'

She rummaged through the different shapes and sizes as if panning for gold, before clutching a mini-loaf tin to her chest.

'I've never actually made individual tea loaves,' she said, inspecting it for a moment before returning to her work-station, 'but it's that or nothing.'

Lining the tin in swift, origami-like movements, she divided the mixture equally between each mould.

'Going in!' she called, sliding them into the oven, her eyes blinking amidst the wall of heat, her glasses opaque. 'I have no idea how long they need.'

'I'll let you get on,' said Mo, disappearing towards Sorcha. 'Bake a leg!'

Her eyes jumped from the tiffin, to the squares of gingerbread, to the éclairs, mouthing silent sums as she did calculations in her mind. Mixing the cherry pie filling with the cream, she piped it into each éclair in an almost surgical procedure, a deep red ripple running through it.

'I'm going to kill two birds with one stone here,' she said to the camera, pulling a pan off the hob which contained a bowl of glossy chocolate. She poured half of it on top of the tiffin, spreading it into the corners with a knife, and used the other half to glaze the éclairs in a practised, dip-and-twist motion.

Remembering the loaves, she crouched by the oven,

staring in at their slightly domed tops which remained worryingly anaemic.

'I'm cutting this fine,' she muttered, growing conscious of the camera which was getting a mortifying close-up of them through the oven door.

In a sprint finish, she laid the pieces of gingerbread out in front of her on a large green cake board, running her fingers over their uneven surface which was imprinted with basket-weave. Her eyes narrowed in concentration as she painted the edges with caramel glue, layering it in generous strokes before holding the pieces in place and counting to twenty, the way Bernard did when he was fixing things with his glue gun. Using a delicate trail of white icing, she attempted to give definition to the edges, holding her breath as she wrote '*A Picnic Through Time*' on the lid in her best handwriting.

'You have five minutes left, bakers! That's five minutes,' Mo called.

It was bittersweet, the feeling that rushed through her in those final moments, every emotion arriving hand-in-hand with its opposite: relief and fear, pride and deflation, energy and exhaustion. Cutting the tiffin into neat cubes, she stacked it on to the board, his recipe book flashing through her mind as she did so. Next to it she lined up the éclairs, plump and indulgent, the cherry cream filling bursting from their seams. On the other side she placed the treacle and cardamom tarts with their neat lattice tops, the filling within like the surface of a fruit pastille. In the final minute, she swept the miniature tea loaves from the oven, preceded by rich wafts of tea-soaked fruit.

'I'm listening to see if they're baked inside,' she said to

the camera, hovering her left ear above them but hearing only the clatter of utensils. 'Although it's too late to do anything about it now.'

Easing them out of the tin one by one, she passed them between her hands before putting them on the board, steam rising from them.

'You'd think five hours would be plenty of time,' she said, as she placed three of each bake inside the hamper, neatly positioning the remainder around the outside, 'but it just never is.'

'Bakers, your time is up!' called Mo and Katie in unison.

She balanced the lid on the hamper and stepped back, relinquishing control of her fate in one long, deep sigh.

It wasn't until twenty minutes later, after the workstations had been cleared and a table had been placed at the front of the room, that Amanda and Tony joined them, poised in anticipation of their final verdict.

Up first was *Sorcha's Christmas Picnic*: brie, cranberry and bacon tarts, red and green 'bauble' macarons displayed in the shape of a Christmas tree, brandy snap cones filled with white chocolate mousse and winter berries, and a neatly plaited fig and walnut loaf. It was a pristine display of treats, presented amongst sprigs of holly, cinnamon sticks and dried orange slices.

Next was Azeez's highly ambitious *Picnic Surprise*, the surprise being that each bake contained an element of the unexpected: choux buns filled with smoked salmon and horseradish mousse, a feta and sundried tomato upside down cake, raspberry ice-cream doughnuts and a spiced apple and sultana quiche.

'And last but not least, Jenny!' called Katie.

She picked up her board which was laden with delicately balanced treats, and moved towards the judges as if on a tightrope, her hands trembling under its weight.

It was the collective gasp that she heard first, her entire being focused on the journey from her workstation to the table. As she placed it down in front of the judges, she saw that the gingerbread hamper had collapsed, her painstaking spectacle reduced to just squares lying flat against a board. For a moment she hoped that it might somehow look as if it were part of the plan, an underwhelming and slightly misjudged reveal of the hamper's contents. Instead, all that followed was a horrifying silence.

Jenny was the only person in the waiting room. It was on the second floor of a Victorian house which was cold and tired, furnished only with necessities so that it felt purely functional and barely resembled a house at all. She took a seat in the corner furthest away from the door and attempted to make herself comfortable on the hard wooden chair, smoothing her hand over the soft flesh where her bump had been. She felt a pounding sensation deep in her pelvis and squeezed her thighs together, desperate for the toilet but conscious of waking him. In front of her was a low table displaying a selection of out-of-date magazines, the corners thick and frayed. Who, she wondered, would spend these last precious moments looking at them?

James was nestled in the fold of her elbow, warm and solid. She studied the shadowed groove between his upper lip and his nose, his crescent of dark lashes, the swirl of his hair. Careful not to wake him, she threaded her thumb underneath his hand, uncurling his tiny, wrinkled fingers so that they rested lightly against hers, each nail unfathomably perfect.

'Jennifer Eaton,' said a voice, cutting through the silence. She

looked up to see a young woman, gliding towards her from across the room.

'This must be James,' she said, tilting her head as she smiled. 'He's beautiful, I love his outfit.'

'Thank you,' Jenny replied, holding him a little closer.

'I'm Miss Clarke, the adoption officer,' she said with the assurance of a school teacher. 'I'm going to show him to the couple.'

Without hesitation she cradled her arms underneath Jenny's and eased him on to her chest, 'I'll just be a moment.'

'Do you have a lavatory, please?' she said, unable to hold on any longer.

'It's just down the corridor, on the left by the stairs.'

As she walked to the toilet she felt nothing, focusing only on her immediate need. The seat was icy against the back of her legs and she rested her head in her hands as she relieved herself with a shudder, a draught pinching at her bare skin. Rolling up her stockings and rinsing her hands, she noticed the sound of muffled voices. Switching off the tap, she paused to listen. There was a female voice, undulating and giddy, joined occasionally by a deeper one which spoke softly, a measured whisper. She couldn't make out words or sentences, as if they were voices on a distant radio, but she knew it was them. They broke into joyous laughter which quickly tempered, their conversation returning to a low hum. She unlocked the door, walking and then running back down the corridor to the waiting room, where she searched the empty seats, paralysed by panic.

'Hello,' said the lady, appearing in the doorway, her arms empty. 'They think he's lovely — he even gave them a smile. You've made a couple very happy.'

Jenny stared back at her in disbelief, entirely lost, her centre of orbit ripped from her so it felt as if she were falling.

'Are these his things?' Miss Clarke added, her tone transactional *as she picked up the pale blue patterned box next to where Jenny had been sitting.*

'But I didn't see him wake up,' said Jenny.

The adoption officer appeared not to have heard her as she continued, 'I'm going to give them this; you can stay here for as long as you need to. Take your time.'

With that, she picked up the box and swept through the door, closing it firmly behind her.

'I didn't see him wake up,' Jenny repeated, falling on to a chair, a force inside of her rising up, pushing to escape.

'I didn't see him wake up!'

She smacked her hand against the chair next to her, shaking it so that its legs scraped against the hard floor. A visceral pain twisted inside her chest, as if all that was beautiful in the world was slowly draining from it, and she stood in its midst entirely powerless. James had become the purpose of her entire being, and without him all that was left was an empty chasm. Her heart was shattered.

She stepped out on to the street clutching her suitcase in her left hand, her right gripping the photograph in the pocket of her coat. He had gone, and yet he was everywhere; in passing prams, in the trees that he loved to look at, in the missing teddy bear that had been perched on the wall. A sea of faces passed her as they went about their business, men and women, young and old. You have no idea what I've just had to do, *she thought,* you have no idea.

Jenny stood in the middle between Sorcha and Azeez, their breathing amplified by the silence. Azeez took her hand, damp with nerves, squeezing it tight.

'The winner of *Britain Bakes* . . .' Mo paused, a collective inhale swooping the crowd. 'Is . . .'

She looked out at the sea of faces, men and women,

young and old, skimming the horizon of heads in search of her biggest supporter. Her eyes settled near the front on the right-hand side. He had been given a chair to sit on and was wearing a pink bow tie, neatly perched under his chin, his eyes brimming with pride as he pressed his lips into a stiff line so that it looked as if they were the only thing holding him together. Behind him stood Rose, her hand on his shoulder, and Poppy was balanced on the arm of his chair as she waved frantically, pushing her tongue between a gap in her front teeth.

'. . . Azeez!'

The crowd roared and she turned to her left, squeezing him with every last ounce of energy.

'You clever boy!' she said. 'You did it!'

He drew back, wiping his eyes on the sleeve of his shirt, smiling and sobbing all at once. Amanda and Tony walked towards them, their arms piled high with the most beautiful flowers she had ever seen, frilly delphiniums, white hydrangeas, palest pink peonies with deep raspberry flecks.

'Well done, Jenny. It was so close,' said Amanda, shaking her hand before laying the bouquet in her arms. 'You've been a brilliant contestant.'

There was so much that she wanted to say, but in the moment, the words stalled in the back of her throat. People were everywhere, darting in all directions so that she felt as if she were in the middle of a very civilized rugby tackle. She could barely see above the blooms in her arms as she held them tight, rooted to the spot, small and spent.

'Well done, darling,' said Bernard, hugging her so tightly that her feet left the ground. She buried her face deep into the soothing smell of his wax jacket, flooded with the comfort of home, tears spilling down her cheeks: tears for James, for Bernard, for the secret she would never be able to share with him. Sixty years later and the pain of that day was just as sharp, his absence a void that could never be filled.

'Aunty Jenny,' said Poppy, tugging at her apron, 'I hope I'm like you when I grow up.'

Jenny bent down and took Poppy's hand in hers, looking straight into her eyes.

'You, my darling, can be whatever you want to be. Remember that.'

As she stood up, Rose planted a kiss on her cheek. 'Thank goodness you went back,' she said. 'We are so proud, and your Baker's Delight was spectacular. It must be your most beautiful creation to date.'

Jenny thanked her, knowing well that it wasn't.

'I liked the tiffin best,' said Poppy, with a decisive nod. 'I had three bits.'

'Did you?!' said Rose. 'I can hardly blame you.'

'That's very kind of you both,' said Jenny, as Bernard blotted her cheeks with a crumpled handkerchief from the sleeve of his jacket. 'It was a bit of a disaster when the hamper collapsed, but everyone seemed to enjoy the contents.'

'Jenny!' called Carys, her arms outstretched as she emerged through the crowd. 'Flipping well done!'

'Rose, Poppy, this is Carys,' she said. 'She's, well, she's the reason I'm here.'

'Hello,' said Carys, 'lovely to meet you all . . . I just need to steal Jenny for a quick interview.'

Jenny nodded, pulling her lipstick case from the pocket

313

of her apron and contorting her mouth into strange shapes as she applied a fresh coat, navigating her reflection in a small rectangular mirror.

'I'll be just a moment,' she said, clicking the lid back on and disappearing into the crowd. She followed Carys to a quieter patch, slightly outside the epicentre of the celebrations, so that the chorus of excitement dimmed.

'I'm overwhelmed,' she said, fanning her face with her hands, her cheeks salty.

'Take your time,' said Carys, positioning herself next to the camera, 'it's a lot to take in.'

She took a deep breath, the past so vivid in her mind that she felt as if it had happened yesterday.

'Okay,' she said, forcing herself into the present, nodding to signify that she was ready.

'How does it feel to have made it to the end, as a *Britain Bakes* finalist?' Carys asked.

Jenny hesitated, shaking her head as if she were realizing it for the first time.

'I thought that I was too old to do this, that it was silly of me to even apply,' her voice caught at the back of her throat, 'but here I am, I made it, and no one can ever take that away from me.'

She dabbed her eyes with the corner of her apron.

'For anyone that feels the same, I implore you to do the things you want to do, because *you can*, and *you will*.'

Carys tilted her head back as if she were blinking away tears.

'And you've used a lot of family recipes in your journey on the show. Why are they so important to you?'

'Recipes are very precious things. They contain little

pieces of history, of nostalgia, and of people – exactly as they were at the time when they wrote them. In reading their words and following their methods, they were by my side. I thought I was alone when I headed into the barn, but I never really was.' She paused, thinking of her recipe book, of him. 'I suppose what I mean to say is: keep writing them down, keep making them, and keep passing them on.'

'Beautifully put,' said Carys, looking down at her notes. 'And you've got your family here with you today – how proud are they?'

She looked over to where Bernard was standing, chatting to Azeez in his pink bow tie, the moment tainted by a sad stone in the pit of her stomach.

You have no idea what I did, she thought, *you have no idea.*

28

Raspberry and Blackcurrant Pavlova

Bright sunlight poured in through the fabric of the curtains so that it woke Jenny from sleep, her bedroom bright, stifling. For the first few seconds she didn't know where she was and then she heard Bernard's whistle, the rumble of the kettle, the post clattering through the letterbox before hitting the mat with a thud. Since filming had finished, she had returned to the same life and yet it felt entirely different, everything that had once brought her comfort now steeped in guilt. *Britain Bakes* had prised open parts of her that she had buried away, so that the past infiltrated the present and her secret was everywhere she looked.

'Darling?' she called, noticing that Bernard's footsteps had stopped halfway up the stairs, contravening the usual rhythm of things.

The silence continued.

'Bernard?'

He sped up, his slippers pounding against the carpet.

'It's been announced,' he said, bursting through the

door and placing the tea tray down with a clatter. 'You're in the *Kittlesham Herald*!'

She felt a fizzing inside, as if someone had dropped a soluble aspirin directly into her stomach.

Joining her in bed, he unfolded the newspaper as if it were a kite, stretching his arms wide to reveal the double page spread. She leant into him, inhaling the smell of fresh newsprint, her cheek propped against the cotton sleeve of his pyjamas.

KITTLESHAM PENSIONER IN *BRITAIN BAKES* LINE-UP

Beneath the headline was a large picture of them all at the front of the barn, bunched together in a semicircle, arms folded over their aprons so that they looked as if they were rivals in a local election.

'Look at you!' he said, his face bright with excitement. 'Not bad for a pensioner.'

She studied herself in her skirt and blouse, nestled between Angela and Azeez. She had expected to see an old lady, but instead she saw a *Britain Bakes* contestant.

'"Jennifer Quinn, seventy-seven, lives in Kittlesham with her husband Bernard, who has been enjoying her baking for sixty years,"' read Bernard, clearing his throat and glancing towards her as he folded the page. 'Well, almost.

'"Having grown up in a family who loved to bake, they are at the heart of her recipes – many of which have been passed down through the generations."'

He took a slurp of steaming tea. '"Starts fifth September, eight p.m."'

'It suddenly feels very real, doesn't it?' he said, his eyes scanning the article through his glasses.

'I've got that feeling back again, the same one I used to get the night before filming.'

'The difference is,' he said, passing her a cup of tea from the tray, hovering it carefully towards her over the duvet, 'is this time you don't have to do a thing. You can just sit back and enjoy it.'

She nodded, taking a sip of Earl Grey.

'Perhaps we should have a party for the first episode, invite Rose, Jeremy, Max and Poppy . . . maybe Ann and Fred would like to come along too?'

Her fingers knitted around the cup, steam evaporating on to the underside of her chin.

'I don't know,' she said, 'I might feel a bit embarrassed with everyone watching.'

'Embarrassed?!' Tea slopped to the brim of his cup so that she steadied his arm. 'Everyone will just be so proud of you; it's not often you get to celebrate something like this.'

She considered his words, unsure. Celebrating was the last thing she felt like doing.

'All right,' she said, 'but I can't promise I won't watch through my fingers.'

He chuckled, 'Watching through your fingers is allowed.'

They finished the remainder of their tea and Bernard swung his legs out from under the duvet and disappeared into the bathroom. She listened to the familiar click of the radio as the pipes squealed into life, water splashing against the side of the basin.

Pulling the newspaper towards her, she read the article again, stunned by how real it suddenly felt. Eventually she turned the page, skimming over a story about a local MP who had used the expenses system to buy his daughter a designer handbag, and on to another about where to buy houses in the area in order to make a profit over the next five years. She licked her fingertips, giving her a little more grip as she flicked through the sheets in pursuit of something that piqued her interest. She paused. Pushed into the peripheries of page 11 was an article titled:

MOTHER AND DAUGHTER: REUNITED THROUGH FACEBOOK

Pauline Thompson, 54, from Willerby by Stow, was recently reunited with her birth mother after her son searched for relatives on Facebook. 'My son found my mother's maiden name on my birth certificate and searched for relatives with the same name. By a stroke of luck he ended up finding her brother, my uncle, and sent him a message. Fortunately, he knew about me and put us in touch.'

Her chest grew tight as she read on.

Mrs Thompson described the experience of being reunited with her birth mother as 'an emotional rollercoaster' and says that she will be forever grateful to her son for finding her before it was too late. 'I've been wondering all my life who my mother was, but I was scared of what I might find out. I'm overjoyed.'

She wound her hair around her finger, her heart thudding against her ribs so that she was sure she could hear it.

Social media is changing the way that people trace their relatives, bypassing the official channels. There are also several Facebook groups which enable both adoptees and birth parents to make contact.

Her nightie felt suddenly claustrophobic against her skin. Folding the paper into a neat rectangle, she placed it on the tea tray, her fingertips blackened by an inky film.

Heading downstairs to the kitchen, she lathered soap between her palms as she let the tap run, looking out across the garden. It was a hive of quiet activity, the fruit of Bernard's labour out in full bloom as bees floated between the flower beds and the roses threw open their petals as if surrendering their hearts to the sun. Dropping three slices of bread into the toaster, she placed butter and a jar of marmalade on the kitchen table, filling two glasses with orange juice without any direction from her brain. Bernard joined her, his face flushed from the shower.

'You know what,' he said, lowering himself into a dining chair, the legs scraping against the floor as he tucked himself in, 'we should get it framed, keep it forever.'

'Keep what forever?' she said, as the toast leapt from the toaster.

'The article.' He glanced at her as if she had forgotten her own name. 'It's one to treasure, don't you think?'

She agreed, joining him with the toast rack, the article in question eclipsed by an entirely different one.

The first episode was broadcast on a balmy late summer evening and Jenny had spent most of the day distracting herself from the inevitability that tonight she would appear on national television the only way she knew how: in the kitchen.

She rinsed the blackcurrants and raspberries in handfuls under the tap, shaking them in sharp movements before piling them into the colander so that they looked like a mound of jewels, staining the lines in her hands a deep shade of red. The warm breeze carried with it smells of burnt sugar and the hum of conversation: Ann quizzing Rose about what the judges were like in person, whilst Jeremy and Fred discovered a common interest in cars, dissecting the models they had driven over the years. There was safety in taking refuge in the kitchen at a party, cocooned by the distant chorus of muffled chatter and the heat of the oven, free to enjoy stolen mouthfuls of whichever dish took her fancy. She squashed a raspberry against the roof of her mouth, sucking the flesh away from the indestructible seeds.

'Aunty Jenny,' said Poppy, using the doorway to prop herself up as she tapped her toe against the floor.

She jumped.

'Uncle Bernard said to tell you that it's twenty minutes until it starts –' she paused. 'What are you eating?'

'A raspberry,' she held out the colander, 'would you like one?'

Poppy scanned the mound, plucking herself a particularly juicy one.

'Why is the oven off but there's a cake in there?'

'It's a pavlova – you leave them in there so that they cool slowly.'

'Why?'

'Because if the temperature changes suddenly, then they collapse.'

Poppy nodded slowly, seemingly satisfied with this explanation.

'Would you like to help me finish it?'

She nodded, her eyes brightening.

Jenny pulled a stool up to the worktop, tipped two tubs of double cream into a mixing bowl and plugged the beaters into the electric whisk.

'We are aiming for a smooth texture like thick yoghurt, rather than cottage cheese,' she said, raising her voice as she competed with the lowest setting, her hand navigating Poppy's as the power juddered up their arms. 'Make sure you keep the whisks in the cream. If you lift them up it will spray everywhere.'

Poppy nodded and Jenny let go, watching as she used both hands to maintain control as if it were a pneumatic drill.

Reaching into the oven, she retrieved the pavlova, carefully peeling off the greaseproof paper and sliding it on to the biggest plate she could find. It was a ginormous nest, the colour of palest plaster and matt like a pumice, quite the opposite of the glossy white peaks she had put into the oven. Together they crowned it with thick lashings of cream and piled it high with the berries, showering it with icing sugar and a dash of blackcurrant coulis.

'One each?' said Poppy, offering her a beater. She had taught her well.

'Absolutely.'

At first it was easy, and then they had to tilt their heads, sucking the metal to get into the trickier nooks, entirely focused on finding every trace of cream as if it were the only joy left in all the world. Somehow it tasted even better this way.

'What are you two up to?' said Bernard.

'Pavlova,' replied Poppy, between licks.

'So I see – we could smell it from all the way out in the garden.' He peered into the empty bowl. 'None left for me?'

Poppy giggled at his emphatic disappointment, as the distant chatter moved towards the kitchen until it was no longer a quiet sanctuary away from the party, but the party itself.

'Ten minutes to go, we need to sit down,' said Ann with an air of authority, ushering everyone towards the living room in an excitable flock.

'The true work of a *Britain Bakes* finalist,' said Rose, interrupted by the bright thud of a champagne cork which tore through the air, skimmed past Fred and planted itself into a cushion, closely followed by an apologetic Bernard.

They congregated around the screen, their voices hushed as if for a government announcement or the royal Christmas message, whilst Bernard filled the flutes with champagne and passed them around the room.

'I'd like to propose a toast,' he said, 'to my dear wife, who surprised me completely with the news that she had entered *Britain Bakes*, and didn't surprise me at all by making it all the way to the final. She is truly dedicated, not only to her baking but also to our friends and family, and I don't know where I'd be without her.' He paused, the corner of his mouth quivering for a fraction of a second. 'To Jenny.'

'To Jenny,' replied the room, raising their glasses.

She watched as the bubbles gathered at the sides of her glass, his praise tarnished by all that she concealed.

As the television came to life, nerves gripped her stomach like cold hands.

She plunged the cake slice through the pavlova, dividing it into eight deep triangles with a muted crunch, the crisp outer edge splintering into a sweet dust, the centre snow-white and chewy with the occasional bead of molten sugar.

'It's a sweet treat coming up next, as eight of Britain's best amateur bakers go head-to-head in a brand-new series of *Britain Bakes*.'

Everyone sat up a little straighter, grew a little quieter and exchanged knowing glances, except for Fred who was consumed by the generous slice of pavlova that had just landed in his lap.

As the familiar music struck up and Mo and Katie welcomed viewers, she felt a sense of the surreal, as if any moment now she might wake up. The barn looked slick and professional on television, the inner workings so well masked. There was no waiting around in the green room or washing up, but instead just seamless transitions between the rolling green fields and the barn, as the bakers walked over to their kitchens.

'Aunty Jenny!' said Poppy, when she appeared on the screen looking just as nervous as she had felt, looping her apron over her head as she glanced towards Azeez.

They all looked towards her, clapping their hands with glee as she sank further into the cushion, sipping from her glass for somewhere to hide. She thought about the article, her mind taking her back to the mother and baby home, to dear Mary. She wondered if she had ever found her Sarah, if she had had any other children, if she still carried the pain of her loss. Had Mary, like her, buried the secret for all these years?

'This is mad,' said Max, scrolling through his phone as he flicked his hair out of his eyes.

Her attention snapped back to the screen.

'It's already trending on Twitter and we're only ten minutes in.'

Unsure of exactly what that meant, she watched as the other bakers explained their Baker's Dozen challenges to the judges. It was interesting to see what had been going on elsewhere in the barn, little snippets of her friends' lives woven into the show: Azeez on the floor of his bedroom doing architectural drawings and Paul the fireman, sliding down a pole before presenting his colleagues with a lunch box of homemade brownies.

'You funny thing, you brought your old scales!' said Ann, as they flashed up on the screen so that she immediately wished she'd given them a good polish.

'In a twist on her niece's traditional lemon drizzle recipe, Jenny is making twelve custard sponges soaked in a tangy rhubarb drizzle,' announced the voice-over as she appeared on screen.

She took a forkful of pavlova for somewhere to look.

'Mine?!' said Rose.

Jenny nodded.

'I'm flattered,' she laughed.

'You're so eloquent,' said Jeremy, his speech distorted by a mouthful of meringue.

'Well, they cut it down, you're only seeing the best lines.'

'It's Uncle Bernard!' said Poppy, now bouncing up and down on her hands. 'They're in your house?!'

She watched as they appeared, perched on the very sofa that they were sitting on now, sharing a pot of tea as they did the crossword.

'Good heavens,' said Bernard, 'that thirty seconds took about three hours! Also, when did I get so old?'

'Oh, stop it,' she said, stroking the soft leg of his bottle-green trousers.

As the episode unfolded, they gasped as cakes came out of the oven, recoiled in horror when Amanda said she wasn't sure about rhubarb in a drizzle cake, and cheered when Angus described her Baker's Dozen as 'a great bake'. Bernard wore an expression of delight throughout, asserting at regular intervals that Jenny's was *by far the best*, his bias clouding all reasonable judgement.

The Baker's Delight ensued, and everyone moved an inch closer to the television.

'This looks so complicated,' said Rose, a close-up appearing of her hands as she arranged the different coloured sponges into a chequerboard pattern.

'That rainbow one's nice,' said Poppy, watching as Angela arranged her garish sponges like Lego bricks.

Eventually came the moment of truth, as one-by-one they brought their Battenburg offerings up to the front, placing them at the mercy of the judges.

'Twitter loves you and Azeez,' said Max, flashing his screen to the room. 'There's a Jazeez hashtag.'

'A what?' said Ann, her face twisted in confusion.

'It's a thing which –' he paused, 'it's hard to explain.'

'Who eats all these leftovers?' said Fred. 'The judges seem to only have one forkful; it seems a terrible waste.'

'Are you volunteering?' Ann asked.

'The team, mostly,' Jenny said. 'I should think they're sick of the sight of cake by the end of filming.'

'Please can we make one of these next time?' whispered Poppy, patting Jenny's knee and then squeezing it tight, as she watched her walk towards the judges clutching her Battenburg, a ruffle of candied orange peel adorning its centre.

The room grew silent as they anticipated Jenny's feedback.

'I don't like this,' said Amanda, '. . . I love it.'

They broke into a round of applause and Rose jumped to her feet, the others following suit at staggered intervals as if cheering for an encore at the theatre.

'That was a mean way to say she loved it,' said Poppy, a point with which Bernard strongly concurred.

'Epic!' said Max, when Jenny and Paul were chosen to compete for the golden whisk. The room roared in celebration, quickly growing silent as the challenge unfolded.

'I can't watch,' said Rose, hiding behind a cushion whilst the pineapple upside down cakes were flipped.

'Mum, it's just a cake,' said Max, with a slight lisp from his tightened braces, 'and we know Aunty Jenny didn't leave in week one.'

'I know, but it's just so –'

There was a collective gasp as Jenny realized that she hadn't lined the tin.

'I bet it's still the tastiest,' said Bernard, refusing to acknowledge that she could possibly have done a bad job.

'So how much do they actually tell you, then?' said Jeremy, interrupting the silence which had overtaken the room. 'In the Blind Bake?'

'Nothing at all,' she said in a whisper. 'All you have is the ingredients and the example under the cloche.'

'Blimey,' he said, stroking his chin as he thought about it.

'And so could you not even taste just a tiny bi –'

'Dad, shh!' said Max, protecting the crucial moment where the judges awarded the golden whisk.

'No!' said Bernard, throwing his hands in the air as Paul was crowned the winner of cake week. 'What?!'

'Oh, Bernie,' she said, shaking her head at his rose-tinted view of her, 'it's a miracle I didn't get sent home after that disaster.'

'I've always enjoyed this show,' said Rose, raising her voice above the clapping, 'but it's ten times more exciting when you know someone that's on it.'

'I quite agree,' said Ann, who was wearing such a broad beam that she didn't look like herself. 'I still can't quite believe my eyes.'

'Aunty Jenny,' said Max, his face illuminated by the tablet on his lap, 'people are asking questions in the comments on your Facebook page, there's loads of them.'

'What sort of questions?' Jenny asked, her shoulders raised, tense.

He joined her on the sofa and as he sat down, she was overwhelmed by the strength of his aftershave, especially for someone with little to no facial hair.

'Baking stuff,' he said, clearly impressed, 'look.'

She stared at the confusion of words and pictures.

'Read them out to me,' she said.

'Here's one. What can I make with leftover egg whites? I hate waste, from Miriam Birtwistle.'

'Okay,' she said, putting on her reading glasses, 'well, she could make almond macaroons; they're simple and they last well in a tin. You only need egg whites, ground almonds and caster sugar.'

Max's long fingers tapped away at the screen.

'If I wanted to reply to these . . .' she said, 'how would I do it?'

'I'll log you in on the computer upstairs if you like?' he said, his eyes fixed on the screen. 'Then you can just go on the Facebook website and it will all be there.'

She wasn't sure if it was the champagne, the late summer heat or the article, but as she lay in bed that night she felt as if she were navigating a rough sea, trapped in the space between sleep and consciousness, distorted thoughts flashing through her mind.

Slipping her feet into her slippers, she tiptoed downstairs to get a glass of water. The kitchen was a sleepy shadow of yesterday, glasses balanced upside down on the draining board and the *Britain Bakes* article pinned proudly to the fridge. As she leant against the worktop, serenaded by the hum of appliances, she couldn't ignore the feeling any longer. Making her way back upstairs, she pressed her ear against the bedroom door to check that Bernard was asleep. Through the silence came something that resembled both a snort and a snore, providing her with the reassurance that she needed to head into the study.

She settled her hand over the smooth dome of the mouse, moving it so that the screen crackled into life, the bright light prickling through the darkness. As she waited for the homepage to load, she thought back to her first glimpse of the application form. It seemed strange to think of all that had happened since then, of how she had changed. She recognized the same overwhelming impulse now, this unrelenting seed that was stealing her sleep so that she couldn't ignore it.

She typed 'Facebook' into the search engine and was met with a page that looked remarkably unfriendly for a website that was about friends, a confusion of white and blue with little red dots along the top of the screen. Dropping her arrow into the search box, she typed his name, the letters piercing the armour of time so that when she looked at them she felt a visceral longing. She pictured him learning to write it for the first time, little hands gripping the pencil as he steered it into the correct shapes; she could see it on the front of his school books and in the corner of the precious drawings that he gave to the woman he called his mother.

Bernard's footsteps were moving down the corridor, the floorboards groaning beneath him as they drew closer. She held her breath, straining to listen as she tried to work out where he was heading. The bathroom door clicked shut. She exhaled, pressing enter.

Within seconds a list of faces appeared, and her eyes narrowed as she scrolled through the sea of James Eatons, desperately searching for anyone familiar as if she were finding her way home using only her hands, feeling around in the darkness for something, anything. With each stranger that she studied, the hope drained from her like sand through an hourglass. She had no idea where in the world he lived or what he looked like and the chances were he would have a different name anyway, but she only had this one. In her mind he was still the James she had handed over all those years ago, fast asleep, a soft swirl of hair on his crown. Disappointment hulled her heart as she felt the weight of all that she had missed crushing down on her so that she could barely breathe: his first word, his first time riding a bike. Not only had she lost a baby; she had lost a toddler, a child, a young man. His life had passed by and she had missed it all.

She sat in the darkness, becoming a part of it as she listened to the flush of the toilet and the squeal of the tap. With nothing more to lose, she decided to give it one last hopeless try, casting her mind back to the article and typing into the search box various iterations of *adoption reunion, find adopted relatives, adoption tracing support*. Haphazardly clicking her way from group to group, she found herself on a noticeboard of messages: siblings, adoptees, aunts and cousins, all searching for lost loved ones, torn apart by circumstance. She clicked into the blank box, watching as the cursor blinked at her expectantly.

Dear Adoption Reunion Support. My beloved son was born on 11th January 1962 when I was a resident at Grant House Mother and Baby Home. I named him James Eaton and I loved him very much, but as a single mother I was given no other option but to give him up. I was told I couldn't make contact, and I have no idea who adopted him or where they were from. All I know is that I gave him away with a recipe book containing some of my family recipes. I have kept this a secret for my entire life, and so would like this message to remain anonymous. If you could offer any advice on how I might go about tracing him (if indeed this is possible), I would be most grateful. Not a day has gone by where I haven't thought of him, and whilst I've suppressed these feelings for sixty years, recently it has become unbearable.

'Darling?' said Bernard from the landing. 'Is everything all right?'

She froze, her heart thumping. 'I couldn't sleep . . . I'm just replying to an email from Azeez . . . I'll just be a minute.'

He paused, his footsteps moving closer.

She hovered over the button, pressing send.

29

Flapjack

Perhaps it was because it was live, or because it was a first, or because Jenny was usually a listener and somehow she had become a guest, but despite the fact that she had baked on national television, today's radio interview felt monumental. She looked down at her powder-blue silk suit, a gift to herself for this very occasion, and began to wonder if she had misjudged it. Was it too much? It certainly looked it against the worn seat of the train, which was a garish combination of all of the worst shades of orange. As Bernard had pointed out at five in the morning as she blow-dried her hair, no one would see her; it was radio. She ran her hand over the sleeve, silk threads snagging against her skin. That wasn't the point, she concluded. In any case, she sometimes put on lipstick to answer the phone.

'Any refreshments?' asked the lady with the trolley, operating it with notable force as she ploughed down the aisle of the train, slamming drawers and flattening handbags in her wake. 'Hot drink, bacon roll, fruit cake?'

'I'd love an Earl Grey tea,' Jenny said with a cautious wave, 'milk, no sugar, please.'

The lady assembled it in a hissing cloud of steam.

'Anything else?'

She studied the display of snacks, sensing from the tapping of the lady's fingers that her indecision was a source of irritation.

'Is that a flapjack?'

The tapping stopped. 'It is. One flapjack?'

'Yes, please,' she replied, fumbling through her purse for some loose change.

'That'll be four ninety-nine.'

Jenny counted the coins into her palm and as she did so their eyes met, the lady's expression changing as the cogs turned behind her eyes.

'Thanks,' replied the lady, dropping the money into the till whilst continuing to stare, eventually pushing onwards to the next customer.

Perhaps she wasn't used to passengers dressed up like wedding guests on the early morning train, Jenny thought, as she pulled out her lipstick case, inspecting her reflection in the sliver of mirror. Relieved to find that there was nothing untoward, she snapped it shut and unwrapped her flapjack. As she sank her teeth through the densely packed oats they broke into clumps, softening to form a sweet clay which clung to the inside of her mouth, reminding her of the homemade equivalent. She always loved the charred pieces at the edge that everyone else avoided, the bitterness of the burn almost balancing out the sweetness, gloriously chewy so that it left a satisfying ache in your jaw. Between mouthfuls, she noticed a little girl, no older than six or seven, peering at her through a gap between the seats. She returned a smile, but the little girl hid.

Taking a sip of hot tea, she turned to the window, watching green turn to grey as they sped towards the city, back yards becoming tower blocks becoming football stadiums. It had been over a week since she wrote the message and her mind returned to it in every quiet moment. The desire to check if there had been a response was compulsive, but no one had been in touch. She tried to envision telling Bernard, weaving together sentences in her mind before unpicking them and starting again. There were no words for the enormity of what she had kept from him.

Sensing that she was being watched, she looked up to see that the little girl was pressing her face between the seats again, and she worried for a moment that she had seen into her thoughts.

The train rolled into London King's Cross and her blood began to simmer, the nerves indistinguishable from the excitement. Tidying her hair and reapplying her lipstick, she tucked her handbag under her arm and stepped off the train and on to the busy platform, the air tinged with soot.

'Excuse me . . .'

She spun around patting her pockets, immediately assuming that she had left something on the train. It was the mother of the little girl who had been watching her, and she was currently doing the same thing but from behind her mother's legs.

'I hope you don't mind me asking, but are you Jenny?'

She paused, trying to place them as she stepped to one side, passengers pouring from the doors.

'From *Britain Bakes*?'

'Yes,' she said, as if the mother were a fortune teller who had struck upon a truth, 'I am.'

The mother's eyes lit up as she glanced around with a sudden self-awareness, lowering her voice.

'My daughter recognized you on the train – she's a fan of yours. We're both really enjoying watching you on the show . . . Would you mind if she got a picture with you?'

'Of course not, it would be my pleasure,' she said, turning to the little girl, 'and what's your name?'

'Tilly,' she whispered, avoiding her gaze.

'Nice to meet you, Tilly. Do you like to bake?'

'I like to make popping candy rocky roads,' she said to the floor.

'Popping candy rocky roads, I've not made those before.'

'They pop in your mouth like fireworks,' she said, as Jenny crouched next to her for the picture, feeling flattered and ridiculous in equal measure.

'Lovely,' said her mother, swiping through the images on her phone, 'Grandma will love this, she's a big fan too.' She pushed the phone back into her handbag. 'Tilly, what do you say?'

'Thank you,' Tilly answered. 'I hope you win.'

Jenny smiled, waving them goodbye.

She joined the commuters as they moved through the barriers, dividing and merging like a stream parted by rocks. The morning rush was a thousand conversations which hung like a cloud in the roof of the station, melding together to form an indecipherable hum. Occasionally she noticed that people would stare for a second too long, or nudge the arm of their friend and nod in her direction. It reminded her of when she had carried James under her duffle coat, the judging eyes of strangers feasting on her like vultures as she walked through the streets, her unborn son nestled below her heart. Here she was again, the subject of attention but for quite the opposite reason, and yet she remained the same person that she had always been.

'Jenny!' called a familiar voice.

Searching the crowds, she noticed a pair of hands waving frantically above heads and attempted to take the shortest route towards him, weaving her way between strangers until they snapped into an embrace.

'Oh Azeez,' she said, stepping back so that she could take him in, his face as joyful as his candy-striped shirt, 'I've missed you.'

'Me too,' he said, brushing the lapel of her jacket. 'I like this little number.'

'Do you? I got it especially. You don't think it's too much?'

'Not at all, not for the nation's sweetheart –'

'Excuse me,' said a man wearing a suit and trainers, his hair peppered with premature grey. 'Jenny and Azeez from *Britain Bakes*, right?'

They looked at each other as if to be sure, nodding simultaneously.

'That's awesome! I've got Jenny in the office sweepstake.'

'Ahh,' she replied with feigned enthusiasm as she attempted to respond without giving anything away.

'Saw you in the papers this morning,' he said, pushing his hands deep into his trouser pockets with a shrug.

'Yes, there's lots of press this year,' said Azeez, glancing at his watch. 'We'd better go – it was nice to meet you.'

With that, he looped his arm through hers and steered them both towards the taxi rank.

'Oh dear,' she said, 'I don't even know the man and now I feel guilty about his office sweepstake.'

'Yeah, if only he'd picked me,' said Azeez, so that she pinched his arm. 'Don't you think this is all a bit . . . mad?'

'Yes, a little girl on the train just asked for a picture with me – I couldn't believe it.'

'At least she asked. I keep noticing people taking sneaky ones on their phones. Did you see the thing about your scales last weekend?'

'My scales?'

'It was in one of the weekend supplements; there's been record sales of cast-iron scales since you appeared on *Britain Bakes*. It's virtually impossible to get hold of a pair – second-hand ones are going for a small fortune.'

'You're pulling my leg,' she said, watching as he waved down a taxi.

'I'm not, I swear. I should've brought it to show you.'

'But they've been around for years!' She shook her head in disbelief, gripping the car door as she stepped inside. 'I can't wait to tell Bernard that.'

Presence was usually a quality reserved for people and not buildings, but Broadcasting House certainly had it. As Azeez helped her out of the taxi and on to the pavement, she stretched out her aching limbs and spent a moment looking up, humbled by what she saw. It was a towering, glass-fronted palace with the letters 'BBC' worn proudly at its centre, a constant stream of official-looking people entering and exiting so that it felt alive.

'Ready?' said Azeez, one eyebrow raised.

She took a deep breath, her skin prickling as she soaked it all in.

'How on earth have I ended up here?' she said, her eyes shiny.

'Don't set me off,' said Azeez, ruffling his hair self-consciously. 'Come on.'

They walked through the revolving doors and into an atrium, joining the back of a long queue of preoccupied people wearing nice shoes, glued to their phones. The air was cool and smelt of other people's coffees, and everywhere she looked there were large screens simultaneously showing the news. It looked like the future, the walls huge panes of glass so that you could see vast rows of uniform desks beyond, journalists tapping away on their keyboards.

'Hello! I'm Dom, one of the producers,' said a wiry young man who looked endearingly unshaven, one side of his shirt untucked as he intercepted the queue.

'We're based just over the road at Wogan House,' he said, shaking their hands before issuing them each with a guest pass.

They followed him back through the revolving doors and across the street, the heat and the noise of central London hitting them with a blast.

'How was your journey?' he asked, pushing open the door into a more traditional stone building.

'Good, thank you,' she replied, pressing her pass against the barriers, half-expecting it not to work on the grounds that she was an imposter. The gate snapped open and she stepped through it, Azeez following closely behind.

'This is a bit different to the barn,' said Azeez, as they went up in a lift.

'I bet, no way near as fun,' said Dom. 'We're really enjoying watching you; you all seem to be great friends this year. It's probably the proudest my parents have ever been when I told them that we'd got you two on the show today.'

Jenny smiled, giving a modest shrug as she stepped out of the lift and followed him down a carpeted corridor.

'I was a fan of the show too for many years, and I must say, it didn't disappoint. It really brings you together because you've all experienced something.'

'Agreed,' said Azeez. 'It's all just completely surreal, even this.'

'Here we are,' said Dom, leading them into an office which smelt of cold tea and carpet, the desks dotted with empty cups and scribbled reminders. Radio, she gathered, was very different to television, with its glossy exterior and hidden inner workings. Radio *was* its inner workings.

'The studio is through there,' said Dom, pointing towards a window. It was then that she spotted Jon Rodgers, surrounded by buttons and screens, chatting away into a microphone. He looked smaller in reality and she couldn't help but stare, trying to assimilate the person in front of her with the voice on the radio.

'Tea or coffee?' said Dom, ushering them towards a tired-looking sofa which was squashed into the corner of the room.

They politely declined.

'Firstly, thank you for coming – we're so excited to have you here,' he said, clicking a pen against his thigh. 'I'll talk you through briefly how it will run . . . You will be asked about your experience on *Britain Bakes* – not going beyond week three, of course – but also about the role that baking has played in your life, how you came to apply for the show, your family background, that sort of thing.'

'Cool,' said Azeez, 'sounds good to me.'

'And just a reminder to keep it PG.' He cleared his throat, taking a sip of water. 'No swearing or offensive language.'

'I'll try not to,' said Azeez, his voice giddy as he glanced towards her. 'It's Jenny you'll need to watch out for.'

'Oh, stop it,' she said, rolling her eyes.

'It's so funny,' said Dom, his face delighted, 'you two are exactly like you are on TV.'

He scanned the document on his knee, licking his finger and turning the page.

'Jenny, you'll of course be asked about the article in this morning's papers. It's such an emotive and important subject and I know a lot of listeners will be interested to hear your story.'

A silence followed as she looked at Azeez in the hope that he understood, but he appeared none the wiser.

'I'm sorry,' she said, 'you'll have to remind me. I haven't looked at the papers this morning.'

Dom's face grew serious, his eyes flicking between them.

'Oh, well, there's an article about . . . the adoption?'

The blood drained from her face, her mouth dry. She tried to speak, to ask where he had got this from, but the words never arrived.

Azeez looked at her, his eyes wide, reading her expression.

'I don't think Jenny knows about this – she's been on the train all morning.'

'Right, sorry,' said Dom. 'I assumed you would have seen it, it's a good job I checked. Is it something you'd rather avoid?'

She nodded blankly, a rush of adrenaline making her feel distant, out of control.

'All right, let me just go and speak to the team,' he said, leaping to his feet and disappearing into the studio.

'Are you all right?' asked Azeez, searching her face. 'Do you know what he's referring to?'

'I . . .' her throat tightened. 'Have they found James?'

'Who's James?' he said, his forehead lined with concern as he pulled his phone from his pocket and typed her name into a search engine. He wiggled his knee as he waited for it to load, selecting the top article. The headline read:

A RECIPE FOR DISASTER: JENNY QUINN'S SECRET HEARTBREAK

As he scrolled down, his face slowly dropped.

'James . . . is your son?' he said.

She covered her face with her hands, leaning forward over her knees.

'They've written an article about the post that you wrote . . . on Facebook.' His eyes flicked from left to right as he skimmed through it. 'They haven't found him.'

'I . . . but . . . I didn't leave my name,' she said, the shock of it driving the air out of her lungs so that she felt as if someone were standing on her chest.

'I don't think you can be anonymous on Facebook. If you were logged in, it will have your name and photo . . .'

Her skin began to crawl with guilt, a panic rising inside

344

her so that she felt as if she were trapped in a desperate nightmare, unable to wake herself up.

'Bernard,' she said.

'What about him?'

'He doesn't . . . I haven't . . .'

'He doesn't what?' said Azeez, a realization shading his eyes like a cloud passing over the sun. 'The secret . . .'

'Hi,' said Dom, walking towards them with an uncomfortable stiffness, 'so I've just spoken to the team and –'

'I can't do it,' she said, gathering up her belongings. 'I'm sorry, but I have to go home.'

'Right,' said Dom, looking between them like a deer in the headlights. 'We go live in thirty minutes so if –'

'And I'm afraid I'm going with her,' said Azeez. 'She can't go on her own.'

'No,' she said, gripping his arm, 'you mustn't. You need to do the interview.'

Dom looked at Azeez, who looked at Jenny.

'I really don't think you should go alone,' said Azeez, shaking his head. 'I'll come.'

'I mean it,' she said, 'you *must* do the interview.'

'I'm so sorry about all of this,' said Dom. 'I didn't mean to –'

'It's not your fault, it's all just come as a bit of a shock,' said Azeez.

'I can understand that. Shall I order you a taxi to the station, Jenny?'

'Thank you,' she replied, her hands shaking. She reached into her bag and turned on her phone, greeted by a barrage of beeps.

'I think that's the *Britain Bakes* press number,' said Azeez, reading over her shoulder. 'They must've been trying to call you.'

She opened her messages, her heart skipping as she spotted an envelope with Bernard's name next to it, sent early this morning: GOOD LUCK, I'LL BE LISTENING. SO PROUD. LOVE BERNARD X

She pushed her phone back into her bag.

'I've got to go,' she said, jumping to her feet. 'I'm so sorry.'

30

It was a Saturday night and Jenny walked down the stairs in her best dress and heels, her hair in shiny curls. It was a beautiful dress with a full skirt, so that when she twirled, it grew around her like a spinning top. Not long ago she would have felt excited about tonight, she would have been talking about it all week with Sandra on their walks to college, but instead it was the last thing on this earth that she wanted to do. It was as if her existence before had been in colour, and now she lived in black and white.

'You look lovely,' said her father, as she passed him in the hallway.

'Thanks,' she said, a flatness to her voice which she could not shake.

'I'm glad you're going,' he said with a forced enthusiasm, 'it'll do you good.'

She combed her fingers through her hair, certain that it wouldn't.

'I don't want to go,' she said, dropping her head. 'I don't want to go at all.'

He looked at her as if her words hurt.

'You'll enjoy it when you're there.' He pressed his lips into a sorry

347

smile. 'And seeing Sandra will cheer you up – you haven't seen her in so long.'

Jenny nodded. There was no point in trying to explain. He would never understand; no one would. It was as if her heart had been ripped from her chest and she was walking around with a wound that nobody else could see.

There was a knock at the door.

'That must be her,' he said, 'have fun.'

She held her breath, preparing to pretend as she answered.

'Hello,' said Sandra, their time apart instantly palpable as she smiled where they would usually hug, a shyness between them that had never existed before.

'How are you feeling?'

'Much better, thank you,' she said, betrayed by her vacant eyes, her uneasy smile.

The dance hall was filled with loud music and hot bodies. They stood in a dark corner, and it was as if she were on the outside looking in as she watched groups of friends huddled together, laughing and chatting, envious of their fun, their innocence.

Sandra took a drag on her cigarette, smoke curling from her lips.

'How's college going?' said Jenny, trying to fill the shoes of the girl she used to be.

'It's all right,' said Sandra, tucking her hair behind her ear as her eyes followed something in the distance. 'I passed my shorthand exam.'

'Well done,' she said, struck by a pang of jealousy.

There was a moment's pause.

'I've missed you, Jen,' Sandra said, meeting her eyes. 'For the first few weeks after you left, I kept forgetting and waiting on the wall for you to pick me up.'

Jenny looked down at her heels, her skin prickling with guilt.

She longed to share with her friend the terrible mistake she had made and the perfect miracle that had come from it, to explain the undying love that she had felt and the grief she had carried with her since. She wanted Sandra to know why she was no longer the girl she knew before. Instead, she censored her words until there were none, their friendship and her secret like oil and water.

'Are you sure you're all right?' said Sandra, tilting her head, her face lined with concern.

'I'm fine,' she said, standing a little straighter as she grew conscious of herself. 'I'm sorry if I'm not the best company tonight, I think it's just tiredness.'

'Don't apologize,' said Sandra, 'it's understandable. You've been bed-bound for months – this must be quite a shock.'

Jenny forced her lips into an uncomfortable smile.

'Are you going to come back?'

'Perhaps,' she said, 'if I'm able to . . .'

'He's looking at you,' said Sandra, her attention diverted.

'Who?'

'The tall one, with the ears.'

She followed Sandra's eyeline towards a group of men on the other side of the room, all dressed in their best suits.

'The one with dark hair?'

'Yes, him. He keeps looking over.'

'I'm sure he's not,' she said, turning back to face Sandra as she thought of her next question. 'How are your family?'

Sandra gasped.

'What?'

'He's . . .' she lowered her voice, 'I think he's coming over here.'

'He's probably just seen someone he knows,' she said, her cheeks burning.

'Are you going to go back to Lady Jane's?' said Sandra, her eyes still fixed on the gentleman. 'Once you've fully recovered.'

Jenny shook her head a little too vigorously.

'But what about Ray? Have you heard from him?'

'No,' she said, a sour taste in her mouth, 'I couldn't think of anything worse. Please can I have one of your cigarettes?'

'You've changed your tune,' Sandra said.

She watched as Sandra reached into her bag, fumbling to find one, when a hand took hers.

'Excuse me,' interrupted the tall gentleman with the ears, attempting to compete with the music, 'can I have this dance?'

She could feel Sandra watching her.

'That's if your friend doesn't mind,' he added, his face breaking into the kindest smile.

'Of course I don't mind,' said Sandra, biting her lip to suppress her grin.

The band burst into life, a charge of energy shooting through the room as people leapt to their feet. Part of her wanted to stay with Sandra, to hide, but there was something safe about him, something familiar, so she let him lead her on to the dance floor where he twirled her around, swinging her from corner to corner in a sort of half-jive, half-twist. It was a relief to be with a stranger, someone who didn't know her before so that she didn't have to pretend, and for the first time in months she was forced to exist in the moment, focusing only on moving her body, the rhythm of the music.

The song tailed off and a slower tune struck up, the couples on the dance floor drawing closer together. He leant in, lightly placing one hand in the small of her back.

Her palms were damp from holding on so tight; she hoped he wouldn't notice.

'I'm Bernard, by the way,' he said, 'or Bernie, for short.'

As she looked up, she could see his eyes twinkling through the darkness, shaded by enviable lashes.

'Nice to meet you, Bernard,' she said, breathing in the musk of his Old Spice. 'I'm Jenny.'

His face strained so that she could tell he hadn't heard her, and as he stooped closer his shoe caught the edge of her toe so that she leapt backwards.

'Sorry,' he said, a look of horror on his face, 'I'm too tall to dance.'

There was something about his expression that tickled her so that her shoulders began to shake, a weight lifting as she giggled.

'And in spite of these ears, I can barely hear,' he said, visibly relieved to have made her laugh. 'What's your name, sorry?'

'Jenny,' she said a little louder, catching sight of Sandra in the corner of her eye. She appeared to be humouring a gentleman who was using a chair to prop himself up, his cigarette hovering half an inch from her dress.

'Jenny, I know I've only just met you,' Bernard said, his hand cupped over her ear, 'but are you free tomorrow evening? I'd very much like to take you out . . . to the pictures, perhaps?'

'Yes, I am,' she said, surprising herself as the words left her lips before she could stop them. 'I'd like that.'

'I'll pick you up. Where do you live?'

Sandra was now rolling her eyes, pushing a glass of water towards the man opposite who appeared to have lost control of his legs.

'Chestnut Road, number twenty-nine . . . I'd better go and check on my friend, I think that man is bothering her.'

He caught her hand.

'I know him, that's Larry, he's my neighbour. He was in the pub earlier . . .'

He led her through the crowd, navigating the dance floor towards Sandra and Larry, their fingers still linked, warm, electric.

'Is he your friend?' said Sandra, her arms folded as she glared up at Bernard. 'Because I think he needs to go home.'

Bernard pulled Larry's arm over his shoulder, propping him up as he bowed under his weight.

'I must apologize. I'll take him home before he causes you any more trouble,' he said. 'Jenny, I'll see you tomorrow. Twenty-nine Chestnut Road. Six o'clock?'

'Six o'clock,' she nodded, a smile flickering at the corners of her mouth.

'Good night,' he said, his brown eyes lingering until the very last moment, before he turned, disappearing into the crowd.

'You've got a date?' said Sandra, squeezing her arm.

She nodded, a crack of light finding its way into her darkness. 'I suppose I have.'

On the 112 bus from Kittlesham station to the village green, Jenny realized that once again, she stood to lose the very person she loved the most in the world. She had chosen to sit in the front seat on the top deck, her forehead pressed against the cold pane of glass so that no one could see the tears that rolled down her cheeks. Just one more stop and she would be home.

As the bus screeched to a halt, she heard the thundering of feet ascending the narrow staircase.

'Robbo, you idiot,' came a loud bellow, as a can was kicked down the aisle, rattling towards her feet so that she looked over her shoulder. It was a group of boys from the local secondary school, their ties loose and their skin pimpled, a shadow of a moustache on their top lips.

'That's that old granny from the baking show,' came a voice that was caught awkwardly between two pitches, diverting the group's attention away from the can and on to Jenny like a pack of wolves.

'Hello, lady!'

Her heart pounded against her ribcage, her body tight as she took shallow breaths. *Not now*, she thought, holding herself as still as a statue in the hope that if she didn't react they would lose interest.

'Baker lady, why are you ignoring us?'

There was a collective snigger.

'It's rude not to answer!' came a voice.

'Where's your baby?' came another.

They fell about laughing and her insides grew hot, burning with fear and anger and powerlessness. She wiped her cheeks with the sleeve of her jacket, silent tears streaming down her face, tickling as they found their way under her chin and down the neck of her blouse.

The bus started to slow down so that the can rolled forward. To her relief, the next stop was hers. She grabbed her handbag and counted to three before heading towards the stairs, her eyes glued to the flecked vinyl floor. The bus swayed and she gripped the handrail, her knuckles white as she navigated her way down the stairs, blocking out the noise. The doors snapped open and she stepped on to the pavement, pacing through the streets, desperation swelling inside her so that she could barely breathe. Her heart propelled her towards the only person who could make her feel better, the axis upon which her world revolved.

When she arrived at their gate, she could just about make out the blurred shape of the front door through her tears. Twisting her key in the lock she pushed it open, slamming it shut behind her as if she were being followed. The lights were off and the house still.

'Bernard?' she called, listening as her voice was absorbed by the silence.

She peered into the kitchen, out across the garden and into the living room, walking over to his chair, an extension of him, and stroking the worn velvet of the armrest. On the coffee table were his reading glasses and a packet of Liquorice Allsorts, but beside them a folded newspaper caught her eye. It caught her eye because on the front of it was a picture of her that was taken during a tense moment during the show, so that she looked tired, distressed. She snatched it up, skimming the accompanying article that had been written about her, disclosing to the world her deepest secret. It was too late – he knew. *A Recipe For Disaster*, indeed. How could she have been so stupid? She had jeopardized all that was precious. She had known, deep down, that somewhere misfortune lay dormant, waiting to remind her of who she was and what she deserved.

'Bernard!' she called, her feet hammering against the carpet as she dashed upstairs and across the landing, flinging wide the bedroom door, the bathroom door, the study. She rattled the key in the garden door, forcing it open with her foot. As she scanned his pristine borders, he was nowhere to be seen.

She approached the shed quietly, terrified that if he wasn't in there then she had exhausted all hope. The door resisted with a slow creak, then slowly swung open. Inside it was cool and damp, overwhelming her with smells of sawdust, wax and polish. Her heart dropped and her head began to throb; it was empty. The only place he would have gone was to Rose and Jeremy's, but the car was outside so that didn't make sense.

Heading back into the hall, she picked up the phone and dialled his number. With each ring she felt hope diminish, noticing as she listened that the coat stand looked different, sparse. It was missing the bulk of his jacket. He had gone.

She paced the streets of Kittlesham, searching the faces of strangers for his brown eyes, his tufts of white hair, the cords he would inevitably be wearing, even on a warm day. She walked up to the church and past the newsagent's and through the park. Familiar routes felt unfriendly, anonymous, when they were trodden without him by her side. There were children screaming with glee as they kicked a ball back and forth, a young couple watching them as they enjoyed a picnic on a bench, but their happiness served only to highlight her distress. She put her hand against the rough bark of a tree, catching her breath as tiny dots dashed across her vision.

She slid down the trunk until she was slumped on the thick, wooden roots, the last sixty years flashing before her eyes in the warmth of his smile, his whistle, the flutter of his heart as she pressed her ear to his chest and wrapped her arms around his waist.

'Bernie,' she said, muffling her cries with the silk of her jacket, his absence carving into her. All this time she had acted in fear of losing him, of hurting him, but in keeping her secret she had done those very things. It was more than she could bear.

Treacle Sponge Pudding

Jenny studied the rails of tiny clothes, consumed by the beautifully knitted cardigans, patterned rompers and smocked dresses. It had been fifteen years, and yet in her mind he was still six weeks old; his tiny fingers, his shell-like ears, the soft rings around his wrists. She picked up a pair of palest blue dungarees, the buttons painted with jolly yellow ducks: age two. So this, *she thought,* is how big he was at two. *Had he kept his thick head of dark hair, or had it gone blonde? Had his eyes stayed blue like her own, or did they darken over time? As she placed the dungarees back on the rail, a bottle-green duffle coat caught her eye. Age four; he would have been at school by now. She threaded the shiny wooden toggles through the string loops as if he were wearing it, the stitches in her heart, unpicked. She stroked the collar of the empty coat, just a prop from which to imagine all the things that she would never know about him.*

'Can I help you, madam?'

She flinched, as if she had been caught looking through someone else's wardrobe.

The shop assistant was an older lady with warm eyes which twinkled behind a large pair of glasses.

'I'm looking for something for my sister-in-law, she's just had a baby,' said Jenny, swallowing the sadness in her throat, 'a girl.'

'Congratulations,' the assistant said, her face creasing into a smile. 'Does she have a name?'

Jenny nodded, 'Rose.'

The woman's face lit up.

'My dear, I know exactly the thing.'

She headed with intention towards the far corner of the shop, an arthritic sway to her walk.

'This has been waiting for you to come in,' she said, as she rummaged through the rail, holding up a white smock dress, the collar embroidered with rosebuds.

'That's just perfect,' said Jenny, running her finger along the intricate needlework as if it were braille.

The lady smiled, making her way back over to the till, before folding the dress into a neat parcel and dropping it into a paper bag.

'Anything else, dear?' she said. 'I noticed you looking at the green duffle coat over there.'

'Oh no,' said Jenny, 'I was just admiring it.'

'There you are!' said Bernard, a tickle of excitement in his voice as she bustled through the front door with her shopping bags, bringing a gust of fresh air in with her.

His thick dark hair was slightly damp where he had taken to it with a wet comb in an attempt to control it, and she noticed he was wearing his best shirt for the occasion.

'Sorry, I got caught up in the children's clothes shop in town,' she said, opening the paper bag and holding up the tiny dress by the shoulders. 'I got this for Rose. Look . . . it's even got little rosebuds on it.'

'Good choice,' he said, stooping to take a closer look. 'Margot will love that.'

'How are they doing?' she asked, walking through to the kitchen.

'They're doing well.' He glanced at his watch. 'She's home and they're looking forward to seeing us. I'm itching to get there.'

'That's great news,' she said, opening her baking cupboard, her eyes scanning the shelves. 'I was just going to make them a treacle sponge pudding to keep them going; I thought we could give them that with some fresh cream.'

He leant against the kitchen worktop, tracing his newly cultivated moustache with his fingers. It was still a novelty, and neither Jenny nor Bernard had quite got used to it.

'Does it ever make you –' he paused, rearranging his words, 'with Rose coming along, the joy of it all . . .'

Jenny busied herself, folding open her Be-Ro cookbook, retrieving the ingredients, her ears tuned to his words.

'Does it ever make you wonder what it might be like to have a baby of our own?'

She rubbed the salt, flour and margarine together, adding a teaspoon of ground ginger.

'I'm thirty-two, Bernard,' she said, cracking an egg. 'I think it might all be a little too late . . .'

'I don't know about that,' he said. 'There was a boy I grew up with whose mother had him at thirty-four.'

'He was probably her last child,' she said, levering the lid off the treacle, 'not her first.'

He fell silent for a moment, the worktop creaking as he changed his stance.

'I know you've always said that you like it just the two of us, that now isn't the time, that with losing your mother at a young age you don't want the responsibility of leaving a child behind . . .' He moved towards her, wrapping his arm around her shoulders. 'I suppose what I mean, is that you can always tell me if you change your mind.'

359

She tipped the sugar into her scales to form a glistening mound, her actions concealing a void. It was as if someone had opened a trap door in her heart, so that she suddenly felt completely hollow. There was only one baby that she pined for, and that was James. How could she ever have another, and not be reminded of all that she had lost? She would never survive the pain of it.

'I shall enjoy Rose,' she said, transferring the sugar to the mixing bowl. 'I will love being her Aunty Jenny, and at the end of the day we can give her back to Margot and John, and not have any of the worry.'

She could see in the corner of her eye that Bernard was stroking his moustache again.

'That's true,' he said, but she sensed a flatness in his voice, a knot of guilt tightening inside her.

As she stirred the mixture together with a wooden spoon, she felt his arm drop from her shoulders, followed by the click of his boots as he walked away.

'Bernie,' she said, the spoon grinding to a halt. 'Is it something you want . . . a family?'

He paused, his hand on the door.

'I will love being Uncle Bernard,' he said.

Jenny sat in his armchair as the house grew dark, until she heard the click of a key in the lock. Jumping to her feet, she rushed to the front door to find Bernard standing in the hallway, except that he looked different. In fact, she hardly recognized him.

'Bernard,' she said, hugging him instinctively, but his arms hung limp by his sides. She pulled back, looking into his eyes which were glazed and vacant. The lines that usually spoke of laughter, today made him look fragile, exhausted, and he avoided her gaze with a sharp turn of his head, as if looking at her was too painful.

'I'm sorry I never told you,' she said, grief surging through her like a violent storm. 'It happened when I was seventeen . . . It was with a married man whom I thought I loved at the time, but I didn't . . . He wanted nothing to do with it . . . My father and aunt were the only people that knew . . . I was ashamed. I had failed, I had no option but to give him up . . .'

She caught her breath but she couldn't stop, as if she were looking down from a great height, compelled to jump, unravelling.

'I went to a mother and baby home to have him . . . I was away for a couple of months . . .' She swallowed, clutching her hand to her chest. 'The problem was, nobody had warned me that I would love him with all my heart, that he was mine, that I would die for him.'

Her jaw locked open and she let out a silent sob, as if someone were wringing out her heart.

'I was told that I had my whole life ahead of me, that nobody needed to know,' she gasped, 'that one day it would all make sense and that I would get over it . . . but Bernie, I never did . . .'

His head dropped.

'I couldn't bring myself to tell you . . . I knew as soon as I met you that I couldn't lose you too. I thought you might not marry me if you knew . . . and with every year that passed, I buried it deeper and deeper, until it was too late. I knew my deceit would destroy everything . . .'

Through her tears she looked at him, the curve of his

shoulders, his snowy white hair. He remained still, his head bowed; a picture of the devastation she had caused.

Unable to bear it any longer, she headed up to their bedroom. She pulled the stool from underneath her dressing table and climbed on top of it so that she could reach the top shelf of the wardrobe, where she pulled down hat boxes and shoe boxes so that they landed on the bed, as if she were throwing open the last sixty years for all to see. Inside were dusty old treasures, things she had worn for christenings, birthdays, funerals and weddings, each box a memory of herself and Bernard turning up to life as a pair. She wondered in that moment how people do it, how generation after generation choose to build a life together, knowing the only thing that's certain is they stand to lose it.

It was only after she had emptied all the memories out on to the bed, that she could reach the small wooden box at the very back. She pulled it down and placed it in her lap, making lines with her finger in the thick layer of dust which dispersed into the air and caught in her throat. Lifting the lid, she emptied its contents. The blue cot card had faded with the years – *Eaton, James. Date of birth: 11th January. Weight at birth: 8lb 3oz* – disappearing into the paper it was written on. Beneath it was the precious photo that Mary had given her of James in his cot, and she traced the shape of his newborn head with her finger, his tiny shell-like ears, his dark hair. She never wanted to forget him.

Falling on to the bed, surrounded by her life in boxes, she buried her face into the pillow, her body heaving, his absence unpicking her.

The door creaked slowly open, and Bernard's weight

sank into the mattress beside her. She turned to look up at him, her face wrung with tears.

He picked up the cot card and the photograph, studying them closely.

'Is this him?' he asked, his voice fragile, quiet.

She nodded.

'He's lovely,' he said, his words catching as his face twisted so that his eyes screwed shut, tears rolling down his cheeks. She held him in her arms, her face buried in the wool of his jumper as they cried, their fingers tight as if they were stopping each other from falling apart.

'You saved me that night at the dance, Bernard, without even realizing it . . . but you did so at such a cost . . . I said I didn't want a family of my own because I could never bring myself to have another baby after James. How could I? It would have been too painful to see his little brother or sister and know that I had given him up . . .' Her shoulders shook as she held him.

'I realize now that I've done a terrible thing, that in losing my right to choose, I robbed you of yours, and I will never forgive myself for that, Bernard . . . You would have made a wonderful father.'

They stayed like this for quite some time, until he wiped his eyes with the sleeve of his jumper. She had never seen anything quite so sad as his tear-stained cheeks.

'If my life had turned out differently, Jenny, then it wouldn't have been with you,' he said, pulling a handkerchief from his pocket, his swollen fingers shaking, 'and I couldn't have borne that.'

He blew his nose in short bursts, before pushing his handkerchief up his sleeve.

'I have loved my life,' he said, 'and the truth is, I don't dwell too much on the things I haven't had, because I know that I have had *so much*.

'I'm only hurt that I know the different cups you take your tea in at different times of the day, and how you like the curtains ajar so that you can look at the sky first thing in the morning, and how when you're worried you rub the cold side of the duvet against your top lip . . . but I didn't know this.'

His words lapped against her like icy water, so that she could barely catch her breath.

'I'm sorry that this most terrible thing happened to you, that you've carried this pain all of your life, and that you couldn't share it with me.'

'I never meant to hurt you,' she said, her stomach tightening, a pressure building within her that she couldn't contain. 'When I could no longer hide it from my father and I told him what I'd done, something between us changed . . . It was as if our love for one another bore the weight of our sadness, and I . . . I never wanted that to happen to us.'

His hand gently stroked her hair, so that in her despair she felt intensely alive, savouring his touch as if it were the last.

'Losing James is a pain that never healed . . . I'm so scared of losing you too.'

'We will always be a part of each other, Jenny,' he said, kissing the top of her head. 'I love you, and even death will never change that.'

Sticky Toffee Pudding

There was great healing in the most ordinary of things: the pegging out of the washing, the scrubbing of a sink, the baking of a sticky toffee pudding, and in the days and weeks that followed, they provided some respite amidst the moments of guilt and fear. It was the unremarkable routine of the everyday, the quiet but constant rituals, that slowly knitted them back together.

Jenny levered the lid off a tin of black treacle with the handle of a teaspoon, gouging it open as stubborn threads of sugar clung to it like cobwebs, eventually growing so fine that they cut loose, lighter than air. She couldn't resist interrupting its shiny surface with the tip of her finger, coating it in sticky, dark molasses, knowing that it would disappoint her but unable to resist tasting it, holding a tiny hope that it would be like the golden equivalent. Sure enough, it underwhelmed her with bitterness. Lesson never learnt. She plunged a tablespoon into the tin and twisted it round and round in the air before letting it fall into the pan in one long, heavy drop.

As she stirred it together with the butter and muscovado sugar, she exposed the bottom of the pan in quick, silver lines, drawing shapes which existed for a fraction of a second before disappearing beneath the surface. Adding a jug of double cream from the fridge, she swirled it together and brought it to the boil, watching as it came alive.

'Final starts in five minutes, darling!' called Bernard from the living room.

She pierced the sponge with the sharp end of a cocktail stick before dousing it in toffee sauce, dishing up two portions of the steaming pudding, Bernard's particularly generous so that it stood proud amidst a moat of cream. Just in time, she thought, as she was beckoned towards the living room by the familiar music.

'Ooh,' said Bernard, sitting up a little straighter as the warm bowl landed in his lap, his glasses reflecting the screen. 'Sticky toffee?'

She nodded, a smile twitching at the corners of her mouth.

'My favourite,' he said, pushing a napkin into the collar of his shirt. 'Thank you.'

She sank her spoon through the sponge, the inside soft and piping hot so that steam danced from it, carrying with it the smell of caramelized sugar, richly sweet as she soaked it in the puddle of cream.

'You know what,' she said, savouring each mouthful as it melted on her tongue, a welcome distraction from watching herself on the screen, 'of all the things I baked on *Britain Bakes*, I'm not sure anything was quite as delicious as this . . .'

'There's Ann!' said Bernard, his spoon clattering against the bowl as a snippet of her interview appeared.

'We are behind her all the way,' said Ann, a twinkle in her eye as she stood in front of their white hydrangeas.

'I'm pleased my hydrangeas made —'

'There's you!' she said, watching as he watched himself, frozen for the entirety of his time on screen so that it looked as if only one Bernard could exist at once.

'Strange, isn't it?' she said. 'Watching yourself?'

He nodded, speechless, then picked up his spoon and loaded it with another mouthful.

She watched as the show unfolded, the reality she remembered polished and trimmed so that it became a concentrated version of events, the big moments made even bigger, every quiet mutter amplified. It didn't matter that she knew the outcome; it was mesmerizing to watch Azeez fill his salmon and horseradish choux buns, whilst Sorcha piped her macarons on to a baking sheet in vibrant red and green dots. As the clock started to tick, her shoulders grew tense in anticipation of the dreaded moment where her hamper fell apart.

'I don't know how on earth they judge it, it's all such a high standard,' said Bernard, leaning forward to place his impressively clean bowl on the coffee table, eyes fixed to the screen. 'I appreciate Azeez has been daring in his choice of flavours and whatnot, but I don't know how much I'd like to eat a spiced apple and sultana quiche.'

She smiled, tickled by his grave expression.

'Remember when you used to watch this from behind your newspaper?' she said.

'Oh no . . .' He sat forward, his eyes following her across

the screen as she carried her hamper up to the judges, followed by a close-up of Azeez clasping his hands to his mouth when it collapsed.

She twisted her hair around her finger, pulling it tight. Reliving it was almost as traumatic as the actual experience.

'But you made one more thing than everyone else; the hamper was an extra!' he said, shaking his head as if he disagreed with the ref. 'That's just bad luck.'

They sat in silence as the judges tasted her bakes at an excruciating pace, listening to the snap of the gingerbread and the soft thud of the tiffin as they dismantled her creations, their expressions giving nothing away.

'Your flavours are spot on,' said Amanda, so that Bernard thrust his fist into the air as if he were watching a penalty shoot-out rather than someone eating an éclair.

'Go on!' he roared, so that she couldn't help but laugh.

Before they knew it, she was exactly where she had been a couple of months ago, hand in hand with Sorcha and Azeez in the middle of the manicured lawn, surrounded by an audience of friends and family. It was the moment the nation had been waiting for.

'The winner of *Britain Bakes* ... is ...' said Mo, the camera cutting between their anxious faces, the silence painful, 'Azeez!'

There was a roar amongst the crowd as they ran towards them, a flurry of tears and laughter and hugs, when all of a sudden her face took up the entire screen, eyes pink with tears.

'I thought that I was too old to do this, that it was silly of me to even apply, but here I am, I made it, and no one can ever take that away from me,' she said into the camera, so that Bernard looked across at her from his armchair, his eyes brimming.

'Oh, darling,' he said, pushing himself to his feet and walking towards her so that she felt a sudden compulsion to get up, to join him in the middle of the room. As she did so they wrapped their arms around each other in a tight embrace.

'You did it,' he said, drawing back to look at her and shaking his head, a sentimental shadow falling across his face. 'Just imagine if you'd known, this time last year, that in the next series you'd be a finalist.'

'I wouldn't have believed it,' she said. 'You just never know what's around the corner.'

He faltered for a moment as the credits began to roll, dropping his head as if he had something to say but couldn't quite bring himself to say it.

'Is everything all right?' she asked.

'I've been thinking,' he said, heading towards the table beside his armchair and flicking through the pages of the newspaper until something fell out.

'There it is,' he muttered, picking up what looked like folded letters, scribbled in his handwriting.

'I've been thinking about James.' He rotated the paper between his fingers. 'Have you ever tried to trace him, or do you want to?'

She cast her eyes down to the floor, adjusting to his name passing Bernard's lips.

'I was told I couldn't,' she said, lowering herself back on to the sofa. 'Until I wrote on Facebook, I hadn't thought it was possible in my circumstances.'

He joined her, pointing the remote at the TV to turn it off.

'I see,' he said, unfolding the sheets of paper so that they trembled like a leaf. 'Well, I think it is.'

She positioned her glasses on the end of her nose, trying to focus on the pencilled words which looked like websites and phone numbers.

'I have done a bit of research,' he said, resting his hand on her knee, 'into places that might be able to help, if that's something you want.'

'Is it something *you* want?' she said, her stomach dropping as if she were in a lift that had been cut loose.

'I just want you to know that you have my full support in finding him, if that's what you want to do.'

She studied the weave of the carpet, the rings on the coffee table, the patterns in the bowls where they had scraped them clean.

'The thing is,' he said, 'I think if this is something we do, we need to be prepared that there are several outcomes. We might not be successful in tracing him, but if we are, he would be sixty now and it could be more complicated. He might not want a relationship, or indeed even know he's adopted,' he paused, looking at her over his glasses before continuing. 'We don't know what sort of a life he might have had, or even . . .'

He caught himself, deciding to stop, but she knew what he was thinking.

'I know,' she said, taking his hand and laying it on her lap.

'But on the other hand, it could be really positive,' he added, squeezing it. 'I just want to be realistic about it.'

His use of the word *we* sounded louder than anything else, and for the first time in her life she felt as if she was not in this alone.

'Thank you,' she said, resting her head against his arm. 'So how would we go about finding him?'

'Well,' said Bernard, unfolding another piece of paper to reveal an email which he had printed off, 'I contacted an adoption charity for advice, and whilst they did say that there is very little you can do as a birth parent, there are two things . . .'

She nodded, narrowing her eyes through her glasses as she scanned the words.

'The first thing you can do is to put your name on the adoption contact register. That way, if he has done the same and he wants to be contacted, then you might be able to find him.'

Her stomach churned.

'So both of us need to have added ourselves to this register?' she said, biting the inside of her cheek.

'That's right.'

'And what's the other thing?'

'The other thing is to use an intermediary agency. Now from my understanding, it's a service you pay for and they would look into tracing James. If they found him they would speak to him on your behalf; they'd check if he is open to being contacted and having his adopted name disclosed.'

Her heart wrung at the thought of his adopted name, the idea that James was in fact a Matthew or perhaps a David, maybe even a Paul.

'And what if he says yes?' she asked, searching his face.

'Well, then they will support us, and him, in making contact and managing that relationship.'

She took a deep breath, shivering.

'How long does it take?' she asked.

He put his arm around her small shoulders, pulling her close.

'They won't know that until they start looking. He might live abroad, in which case, it could take even longer.' He folded his research back into a neat rectangle. 'I just want you to be prepared that it could go any which way . . . You'd have to hope for the best and prepare for the worst.'

She looked at the freckled backs of his hands, digesting his words.

'So there is a good chance that we could do all of this and that we might never find out what happened to him?' she said, as if in saying the words out loud, she might somehow accept them.

'Yes, darling,' said Bernard, 'but you will always know that you tried your very best.'

She thought about this for a moment.

'Then I think we have to go for it,' she said.

As she lay in bed that night she considered the infinite different ways that his life might have unfolded, something she had done a thousand times since he was taken from her, but always on his birthday, on Mother's Day, every time she passed a little boy. She wondered if he had been lucky enough to have any children of his own, if he had found love and enjoyed a career, if he had been happy. Her heart thundered in her chest as she considered the other possibilities, the ones where his life had been hard and she was entirely to blame for it. She reached for her glass of water, reminding herself of what Bernard had said, that at least she would have tried her best to find him. She sought comfort in his strength, in knowing that whatever happened now, she had Bernard to share it with. And then she thought of Bernard as a young man, and how he had always put her wants before his own. Each time he had raised the conversation of having a family, she had made an excuse, pushed it away, until one day it was too late.

'Bernard . . .' she said into the darkness, '. . . if you could do life again, knowing what you know now, would you still have chosen to do it with me?'

Her words were absorbed by the silence so that she decided he must be asleep. She rubbed the cotton of the duvet against her top lip, feeling the joy and the sorrow and the love of the last fifty-nine years.

'Yes,' he said, stretching out his foot to find the warmth of her leg, 'every single time.'

33

'A Marriage of Passions' Diamond Wedding Anniversary Cake

'It weighs a ton!' said the waitress, as she helped Jenny ease all three tiers of her anniversary cake on to the brushed steel worktop of the pub kitchen, juggling the load between them in an attempt to keep it upright.

It was a classic fruit cake, just as her wedding cake had been, and she had iced it in an ivory fondant so that each tier looked like a perfectly tucked bed sheet, not a shadow of a crease in sight. The sides she had decorated in pressed edible flowers: purples, yellows, magentas and greens, each petal as fine as a butterfly's wing so that you could see the net of thread-like veins that held it together. It was like nothing she had ever made before, so deliciously intricate that it was impossible to see it all at once but only in small, focused sections. The idea had been that it was a marriage of passions – her love of baking combined with Bernard's love of gardening – and she felt quietly thrilled with it. It was quite the spectacle and it had caught the attention of the entirety of the village pub's kitchen staff as they gathered around it.

'Please could you bring it through just before we order

dessert?' she said, the industrial kitchen reminding her of her audition.

'Of course,' said the manager, telling the others to get back to work simply by flaring her eyes. 'It really is a masterpiece, it must've taken ages.'

'It did take a while,' she said, her voice bright with the occasion, 'but I couldn't be half-hearted with my diamond wedding anniversary cake, could I?'

She headed back to the table, inhaling the hearty smell of beef gravy which drifted in warm currents from the kitchen as she weaved between the families, couples and friends enjoying their Sunday lunch together. She spotted hers and paused for a moment, watching them unnoticed as Jeremy filled up water glasses whilst Max showed Azeez and his boyfriend Ashley something hilarious on his phone. Fred reached across towards the bread basket, and Rose discussed the menu with Ann, dissecting it as if it were their last supper. At the head of the table, Poppy was perched on Bernard's left knee with her doll on his right, whom he fed dutifully with a teaspoon, much to her delight. She observed the perfect scene of chaos, able to appreciate it differently for not being in the midst of it. Family came in many different shapes and sizes, and she was proud to call them hers. The last sixty years had led her here, to this exact spot, looking on to the life that they had made together. She had been living in the pain of the past and worrying about the future, but all at the cost of the present.

'Everything all right, Mrs Quinn?' said the waitress, shuffling some menus into a neat pile on the bar. 'I think I'm going to bring over the fizz, if you're ready for it?'

'Yes, please,' she said, joining them at the table and taking a seat between Bernard and Rose.

The waitress appeared with a tray of flutes, handing the bottle to Bernard to pop so that Poppy covered her ears with such melodrama that they all laughed. She watched as the foam climbed to the brim of each glass, teetering on the edge before settling back down into a simmering pool.

'To Jenny and Bernard,' said Rose, raising her glass, 'on an incredible *sixty* years of marriage, and to many more.'

'To Jenny and Bernard!' replied the table, the joy in their voices compelling her to turn to him for a kiss; that kind, spirited twinkle as bright at eighty-two as when she had first set eyes on him.

'Thank you all for joining us today,' said Bernard, getting to his feet, 'to our wonderful family, to old friends, and to new ones. When I married Jenny, I had no idea of just how brave she was, and I speak on behalf of everyone when I say, Jenny, you are an inspiration to us all.' There was a murmur of agreement from the table as they looked towards her. 'Your ability to take life by the horns, whatever it throws your way, has now inspired a nation, and I will be forever grateful that you chose to spend your life with me.'

Jenny looked up at him, tears prickling in her eyes as she realized for the first time, that whilst she had spent sixty happy years with Bernard, it was only now that she was content within herself.

'You'll set us all off,' said Rose, fanning her face with a napkin.

'Go on then,' said Azeez, 'what's the secret?'

She looked to Bernard, the word secret making her

377

flinch inwardly. It wasn't her place to answer that after all that had happened.

'That's a very good question,' he said, pressing his lips together as if deep in thought, nine pairs of eyes focused on him, waiting for him to break his silence. 'Over the years you will both inevitably change but you will always have one thing in common, and that is that you're both only human, so try to be kind.'

He took her hand, giving it that familiar, reassuring squeeze, and she felt each one of his words settle like newly fallen snow, knowing each one to be true.

A brief moment of silence followed, so that her heart began to thud and her legs began to twitch. Perhaps, she thought, it *was* her place to answer that question, *because* of all that had happened.

She pushed back her chair and rose to her feet.

'No one teaches you how to spend a lifetime with someone,' she said, clearing her throat. 'There aren't any manuals, there isn't a recipe to follow, and at times – believe me – I've wished there was.'

There was a rumble of laughter, propelling her to continue.

'To say that I've made a few mistakes in my marriage is an understatement, but what I *have* learnt is that sometimes it is our mistakes, our greatest failings, that are the real tests – opportunities to get to know each other better, to put the word "love" into practice, to watch everything break into a thousand pieces and to glue it back together again.'

She looked at Bernard, great oceans in his eyes.

'The secret to sixty years? I'm not entirely sure . . . but one thing I do know, is that to *truly* know someone and to love them, is the greatest love of all.'

34

The Recipe Book

Jenny pressed her fingers against the surface of the desk, stretching them so that she felt a dull ache in the palm of her hand where it had been tightly coiled around her pen. Just one last push before the Christmas break, she told herself, taking a sip of water.

'Five more minutes!' said the publicist, twisting her hair into a pretzel-like roll and clipping it tightly at the back of her head. A groan of disappointment echoed down the queue. 'One book each and we'll see how many we can get through, but that means no more photos.'

What felt like the hundredth copy of *Britain Bakes: One Hundred Home Recipes* was placed in front of her and she pressed it open, inhaling the promise of fresh pages.

'Good afternoon,' she said, looking up to see a little boy, blinking at her through high-prescription spectacles. Next to him was a girl in a long puffer jacket, stroking his unruly hair which gave the impression it was rarely brushed.

'What's your name?'

'He's called Edward,' she said, as he continued to look at her as if she had jumped straight out of his television screen. 'It's for our nan, so please can you write it to Nanny Green? She's a big fan of yours and it's her Christmas present.'

'Of course,' she said, clicking her pen against the desk. *Dear Nanny Green, Keep baking! Merry Christmas, Jenny x*

'Next!' called the publicist, and the girl thanked her, picked up the book and dropped it into her tote bag.

'Have a lovely Christmas, Edward,' called Jenny, waving as he was swept away, his magnified eyes continuing to blink at her all the way across the bookshop and out of the door.

'Hello,' she said, looking up at a young gentleman wearing a fair isle jumper, his hair a brilliant red. He placed the book in front of her and she peeled a Post-it note from the cover.

'Patrick,' she said, straining to read it through her glasses, 'is that right?'

'Yes, or Pat,' he replied, punctuating his sentences with nervous laughter. 'I've actually just submitted my application for the show . . . I'm planning on using this to practise with, you know, just in case I get an audition.'

She nodded, mustering a tired smile.

'I wasn't going to apply, but then what you said on the show made me think, why not me?'

'I'm very pleased to hear that,' she said, pressing open the cover. 'Good luck.'

Patrick, she wrote, pausing as she waited for her brain to catch up. *The world is your oyster. Baking is as simple as eggs, sugar, butter and flour (most of the time), so why not you? Above all – enjoy! Happy baking, Jenny x*

He picked it up and read it back, his beam like that of a child on Christmas morning.

'Right, I'm going to have to call it a day or we'll be here all night,' called the publicist, addressing the queue whilst scrolling through emails on her phone, her manicured nails tapping against the screen. 'There are some pre-signed copies over on the table if you'd like one.'

Jenny looked at the last few people, their cheeks pinched from the cold as they exchanged discontented mumblings.

'Francesca, it's not a problem,' she said. 'I'm happy to do the last few, I don't want anyone to go home disappointed.'

Francesca looked at her watch, eyebrows raised.

'In that case, as quick as you can, please, *one* book each!'

A gentleman moved towards her. She registered only the dark green of his fleece jacket, his hand clutching something deep in his pocket.

'Have you got your book?' she asked, looking beyond him at the people behind, anxious that they didn't miss their chance.

He hesitated, placing before her the thing in his pocket. It was a book, but not the one she had been signing all day, with colourful photographs and professional fonts. The cover was a faded cassock blue, flecked with grease and chocolate, and the corners were curled with use. She studied it, overcome with a delayed sense of recognition as time fell away like sand. It was the sensation of being reacquainted with someone after a long period of time, so that all at once they appear deeply familiar and yet strangely different. She opened the cover, meeting no resistance from the well-thumbed pages. Inside it was brittle with age, the lines and margins so faint they were barely visible, but the handwriting she recognized instantly as her own. She read the words: *Jenny's Black Forest Gateau, Grandma Audrey's Chocolate Crispy Cakes* and her father's *Tiffin*. She put down her pen and looked up.

Epilogue

Two months later

It was the coldest February on record, and Jenny and Bernard had decided – against both the weather warnings and their better judgement – to make the journey.

The motorway was lined with a treacherous grey slush, quite a contrast to the thick white blanket that covered the fields either side. Jenny was just about visible in the passenger seat, behind a triple-layer coffee cake (complete with gold-dusted walnuts) and a plate of egg custards. A warm fug of coffee and nutmeg was being loudly circulated by the car heater, which was blasting hot air like its life depended on it.

They veered slightly to the left, before turning sharply right.

'Bloody hell,' said Bernard, who was positioned closer to the steering wheel than ever before. 'I've got no grip . . . it'll be a miracle if we make it in one piece.'

'You're doing a great job, darling,' she said, her knuckles

white as she clutched the plate. They had no choice, they had to get there. 'How late are we going to be?'

They eased slowly forward, her stomach doing cart-wheels.

'About forty-five minutes, I'm afraid . . .' he said, his shoulders almost touching his ears. 'I'm starting to think we should've rearranged. I don't know how on earth we'll get back in the dark.'

'I'm sorry,' she said, the reality of all that she had missed sparking an urgency in her chest. 'I've waited more than sixty years for this moment, I couldn't waste another second.'

'I know,' his eyes were fixed on the road ahead, 'I'll get us there somehow.'

She wasn't sure if it was the fact that they were late, the car heater, or the sickly smell of coffee icing, but she was beginning to feel the burn of nausea in the back of her throat. She wanted so desperately for today to go well, for him to feel even a fraction of the bond that had always existed for her, but supposing he didn't? It was like audi-tioning for a role that had already been filled; she was not the person that he knew as his mother.

'I can't believe I didn't know that egg custards were his favourite as a little boy,' she said, as they passed a car which had broken down, silently grateful it wasn't them. 'My father used to love them too . . . I feel as if somehow, I should've known.'

'Yes . . .'

She could tell Bernard was nervous because he was giving the sort of stock answers he gave when he wasn't actually listening.

'Run me through it again,' he said, peering over the

bonnet as if it were the neighbour's fence. 'His wife is called Claire and their son is called Andrew, is that right?'

'It is,' she said, her heart thundering in her chest.

'And Andrew's got two young children, a girl and a boy . . .' his eyes narrowed as if it hurt to think, 'Abigail and . . . Monty?'

'Monty's their spaniel.'

'Oh, yes,' he said, 'it's a good job I checked.'

'His grandson is called William, and his granddaughter, Abigail.'

'William,' repeated Bernard, as if he was practising lines for a play, 'wife Claire, son Andrew . . . grandchildren William and Abigail . . . Monty the spaniel.'

'It's strange to think of him as a grandparent,' she said, watching a flurry of snow float weightlessly to the ground, before vanishing into the tyre-trodden slush. 'I've missed him becoming a father, and a grandfather too.'

She looked at Bernard, whose lips were still silently mouthing their names.

They continued along the motorway in silence, a capsule of nerves, determination and cake. It was incomprehensible to her that all these years, he had lived just over an hour down the road. An hour! And she had had no idea. She imagined the times their paths might have crossed; perhaps she had queued next to him in the supermarket, or passed him in the car.

Bernard flicked up the indicator.

'Hold on to your bakes,' he said, pulling off the motorway at a truly terrifying six miles per hour.

She hugged them close.

'Right,' he said, rewarding himself with a sip of tea from

the flask which was lodged between them. 'All going well, we're about fifteen minutes away.'

Jenny sat up a little straighter, a lightness in her stomach.

'Remind me again, was it his son – Andrew – who recognized your recipes on *Britain Bakes*?' he said, his hands wrapped tightly around the steering wheel.

'Yes, apparently he was watching it with the children and he recognized the Tiffin. He knew his dad was adopted and he had used the recipe book as a child, you see, so he knew my name was Jenny . . . He rang his father straight away.'

'Oh yes,' said Bernard, his foot lightly touching the brake pedal at all times, 'and he'd been watching it too and had had the very same thought, except he'd decided he was being ridiculous and to keep it to himself.'

'Exactly,' said Jenny. 'It was only when the story came out in the papers, that he knew he was right.'

Bernard put his hand affectionately on her knee, before quickly returning it to the steering wheel.

'Just when you thought your seventy-seventh year was the most eventful of your life,' he said, 'your seventy-eighth happened.'

He made a right turn so that the coffee cake hit the side of the tin with a thump.

'I hope it's not squashed,' she said, peering under the lid to check that the brooch-like walnuts were still intact. 'It's his favourite.'

'Now . . . I think it's just down here.'

Jenny's eyes jumped between the snow-covered houses, searching for a sign, her knees trembling.

'It's number eleven,' she said, studying the gates, 'but the numbers are covered in snow.'

With each house that passed, she tried to imagine him in it, her son. Had he put a swing up for the grandchildren? Would he drive that car? Were those his boots by the door?

'There!' said Bernard, slamming his foot on the brake. 'Someone's dusted off number eleven for us, the light's on and the gate's open.'

It was the smallest things, she thought, that meant the universe.

As they pulled into the driveway, she felt almost as if it were an illusion, her body numb with adrenaline. The first thing she noticed was a snowman. He had a crooked carrot nose and two very large gloves perched on the end of his twiggy arms. The second thing she noticed was the living room curtain twitching.

'Look,' she whispered, spotting two little faces hovering just above the windowsill. She caught a two-second glimpse before they dipped back down again, just long enough to see a little girl wearing a paper crown, and a little boy with thick tufts of dark hair, his blue eyes familiar.

Bernard pulled up the handbrake and turned off the engine, leaning back into the seat.

'What a journey,' he said, taking another swig of tea as he gathered himself.

She pulled down the mirror, applying a quick coat of lipstick.

'Ready?'

'I think so,' he replied, unclicking his seatbelt. 'I can't remember the last time I felt this nervous.'

Easing herself out of the car, she picked up the tin with the plate balanced on top of it, shutting the door behind her. Gripping Bernard's arm, their feet sank through the snow in satisfying *crumps*, leaving the footprints of a journey made together.

'William and Abigail . . . and Monty the spaniel,' said Bernard under his breath, which dissipated like smoke into the cold.

She peered through the window into the porch, noticing two small pairs of wellington boots, a bobble hat, and the green fleece jacket he had worn to the book signing.

'I recognize that jacket,' she said, her heart fluttering. 'I'd know it anywhere. It's definitely the right place.'

'Go on then,' said Bernard, squeezing her arm.

One . . . two . . . she pressed the doorbell.

A dog barked, then a pitter-patter of little feet.

His figure drew closer behind the glass, and the door clicked open.

'There you are,' he said, 'and just in time for tea.'

Acknowledgements

There are a great many ingredients involved in writing a novel, more than eggs, sugar, butter and flour, but below are a few of the most important.

Thank you firstly to my family and friends, whose love and support I am eternally grateful for. To Granny and Grandpa for their steadfast companionship, which was the backdrop to my childhood, for answering my endless research questions and to Granny for spoiling me with so many delicious bakes over the years. To my parents, who have always encouraged me to pursue my dreams so that I could enable Jenny to pursue hers. Neither of us could have done it without you. To my mother, Noll, for the bedtime stories and everything since. You are the most creative and compassionate person I know, and these pages are full of your love. And to my daddy, bestower of the sweet tooth, these pages are full of your recipes.

Thank you also to my husband, James, for being the Bernard to my Jenny (but with far superior culinary skills), for your unwavering belief and encouragement at every turn and for never once complaining when I needed to write on our honeymoon. You poured your love into me whilst I poured it into this novel, and I can never thank you enough for that. Also to our cat, Colin, who sat beside me through every draft. You will never know how much comfort you brought, or how much I needed your company.

A special thanks to all those at Curtis Brown who have been a part of this journey, particularly to my wonderful agent, Lucy Morris, who was Mrs Quinn's earliest supporter and an inaugural member of the Bernard Quinn Fan Club. Your belief, guidance and exceptional mind were the key ingredients in bringing Jenny's story to the world, and there is no one I would rather have had by my side. I would also like to thank the Women's Prize Trust, whose 2021 Discoveries Prize not only gave me a much-needed boost, but also introduced me to Lucy.

Thank you to my brilliant editor, Rebecca Hilsdon, for the best letter and cake that I will ever receive – both were life-changing in their own ways. The Quinns couldn't have been in safer hands than yours. And to Pamela Dorman, whose experienced editorial eye made this story a better one. Also to all of the talented people at Penguin Random House, both in the UK and US, including Marie Michels, Jane Glaser, Lucy Beresford-Knox, Phillipa Walker, Gaby Young, Sriya Varadharajan, Jen Harlow, Jessie Beswick, Lauren Wakefield, Sarah Scarlett, Christine Choi, Molly Fessenden, Kristina Fazzalaro, Tricia Conley, Alicia Cooper, Madeline Rohlin, Claire Vaccaro, Jason Ramirez and illustrator Rebecca Hollingsworth. A big thank you to my international editors too, particularly to Dr Tim Müller and all at DTV who embraced Mrs Quinn with such enthusiasm that they published her story in Germany first.

I owe a great debt of gratitude to those who have helped with both the inspiration and research behind this novel. Thank you to Fern and Simon Bennett for so generously sharing your mother Pam's story with me, which in turn inspired Jenny's. To Jane Beedle and Andrew Smyth for taking the time to share your baking and television journeys with me. And to Rose Bell, whose extensive research on the topic of mother and baby homes was invaluable, and led me to Angela Patrick's *The Baby Laundry for Unmarried Mothers*, which informed much of Jenny's experience. Points of detail were also provided by Ann Hipkin and Sarah Jones – thank you for answering my questions.

I would also like to thank Rowan Hisayo Buchanan and the Faber writing group of 2020, who gave such helpful and heartening feedback when Mrs Quinn was just a seed of an idea.

And finally, the most important acknowledgement of all. Whilst Jennifer Quinn's story is a work of fiction, her secret was inspired by real events. It is estimated that around 185,000 babies of unmarried mothers were adopted in England and Wales between 1949 and 1976. As part of my research, I learnt a great deal about the coercion and cruelty that so many mothers faced and it has been utterly heartbreaking. Through Jenny, I hope to shine a light on this devastating injustice, which was normalized at the time and then largely forgotten. I am so sorry.

Reading Group Questions

1. Jenny keeps a lifelong secret from her beloved husband Bernard. Why do you think people keep secrets from their loved ones? Are you good at keeping secrets?

2. As a lady in her late seventies, Jenny is patronized by a shop assistant as a result of her age. How do you think society's treatment of people changes as they grow older?

3. Jenny's experience in a Mother and Baby Home in England in the 1960s was inspired by real accounts. To what extent do you think attitudes towards single mothers have changed? And to what extent do you think attitudes towards women and motherhood in general have changed?

4. *'Whilst bodies age, souls don't'* is the epigraph by Delia Smith. How far do you agree with this statement?

5. *'It's strange, she thought, how recipes outlive the people that wrote them and yet they almost bring a part of that person back to life, as if a tiny piece of their soul lives in those instructions.'* Is this true for any recipes that you have at home? If so, what are they and who do they make you think of?

6. Bernard and Jenny celebrate their diamond wedding anniversary in the novel. What do you think is key to a lasting relationship?

7. Jenny was told that she would eventually get over the trauma of giving up her son, but she never did. Do you think it is possible to overcome trauma, and to what extent?

8. Jenny says in her interview for *Britain Bakes*, *'It's sometimes easy to feel left behind at my age, as if the world has a future and you have no place in it . . . but I hope to discover that there is meaning and adventure still to be found.'* Do you think that dreams and ambitions are something generally viewed as for younger people? Do you have any quiet or unfulfilled ambitions?

9. Jenny applies to be on TV baking competition *Britain Bakes*. If you had to choose an existing TV competition to take part in, which would you pick and why?

10. What do you think happens regarding Jenny's relationship with her son after the book ends?